Mosaic & Lace Knits

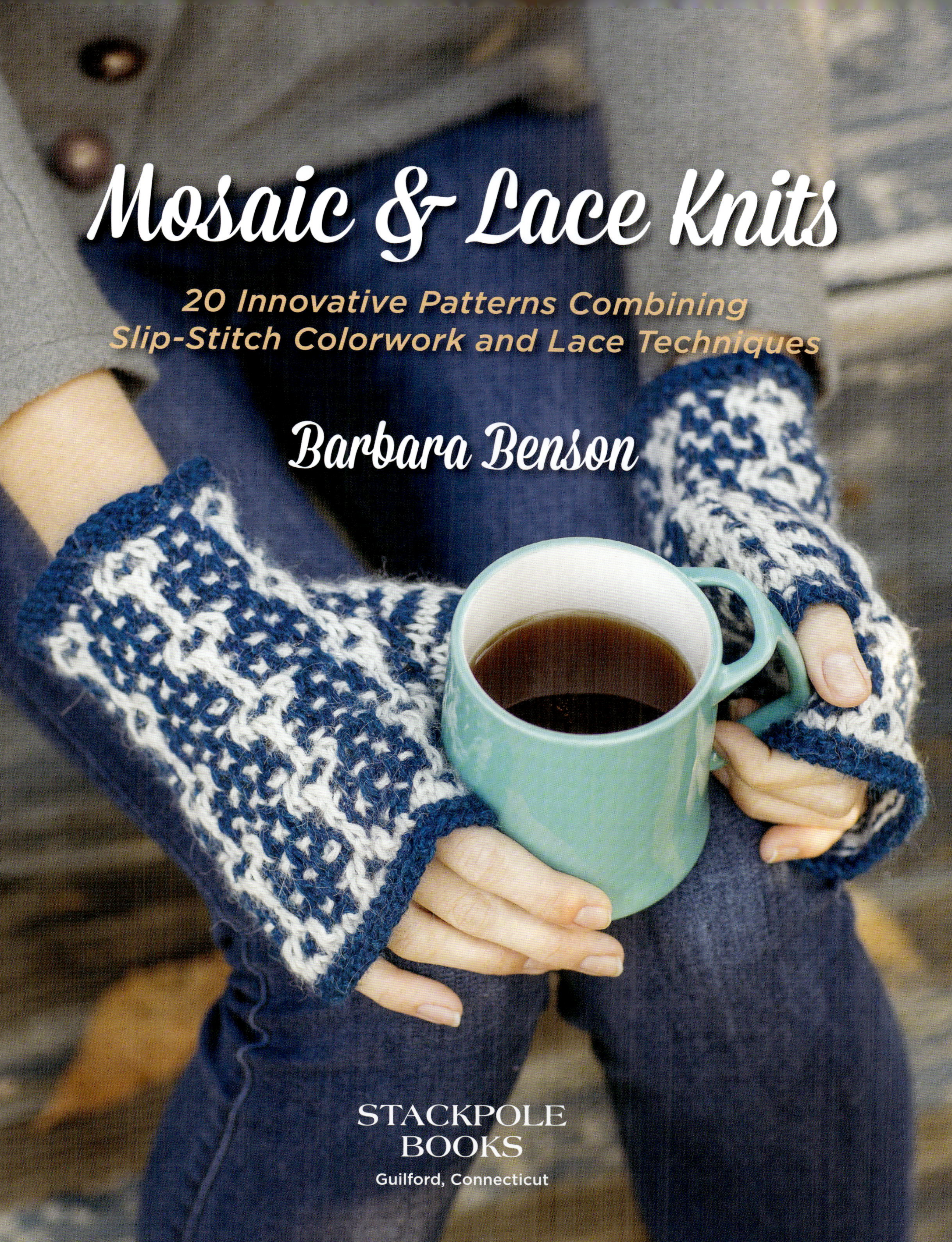

Mosaic & Lace Knits
20 Innovative Patterns Combining
Slip-Stitch Colorwork and Lace Techniques
Barbara Benson
STACKPOLE
BOOKS
Guilford, Connecticut

Published by Stackpole Books
An imprint of Globe Pequot

Distributed by NATIONAL BOOK NETWORK
800-462-6420 www.rowman.com

British Library Cataloguing in Publication Information Available

Library of Congress Cataloging-in-Publication Data

Names: Benson, Barbara, 1973- author.
Title: Mosaic and lace knits : 20 innovative patterns combining slip-stitch
    colorwork and lace techniques / Barbara Benson.
Description: First edition. | Guilford, Connecticut : Stackpole Books, 2017.
Identifiers: LCCN 2016051560 (print) | LCCN 2016058099 (ebook) | ISBN
    9780811716772 (pbk. : alk. paper) | ISBN 9780811765411 (e-book)
Subjects: LCSH: Knitting--Patterns. | Lace and lace making--Patterns.
Classification: LCC TT825 .B395 2017 (print) | LCC TT825 (ebook) | DDC
    746.43/2041--dc23
LC record available at https://lccn.loc.gov/2016051560

First edition

Printed in the United States of America

♾™ The paper used in this publication meets the minimum requirements
of American National Standard for Information Sciences—Permanence of
Paper for Printed Library Materials, ANSI/NISO Z39.48-1992.

◇◇◇ CONTENTS ◇◇◇

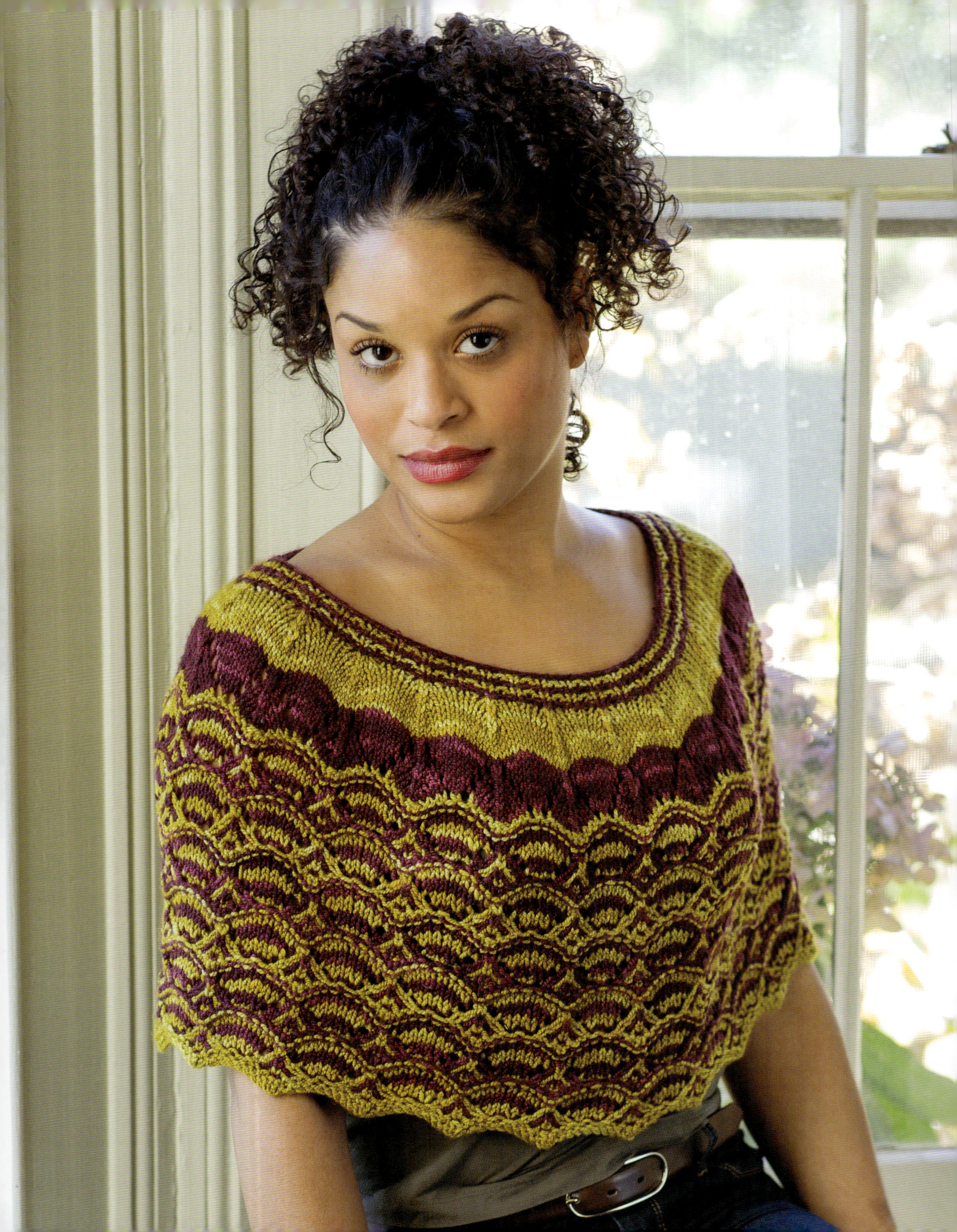

◇◇◇ INTRODUCTION ◇◇◇

Several years ago my knitting world was dominated by lace. It was all I wanted to knit. Everything about lace made (and still makes) me happy. From the intricate and visually exciting stitch patterns to the resulting fabric with its incomparable drape and flow, it has it all. But then something happened: I wanted more—specifically, more color. I had this idea of something I wanted to knit, but I couldn't figure out how to make it happen.

Combining colorwork with lace is problematic in its technical aspects. I considered intarsia, but that produced blocks of colors and my vision involved a stripy pattern. I then contemplated stranded/Fair Isle style colorwork, which presented the difficulties of the carried yarn. The floats are visible through the holes that lace creates and those additional strands confuse and obscure the lace pattern. Both techniques have the added complications of managing multiple yarns simultaneously and presenting a typically unappealing wrong side. And then there are all of those extra ends that have to be woven in . . .

It was then that I came back to Barbara Walker's book *Mosaic Knitting*. To be honest, it was probably the fifth or sixth time I had checked it out of the library (I have since purchased my own copy so that others in my area can enjoy the book), and I had already knit a scarf in mosaic. But mosaic hadn't really seized my imagination due to the fabric it tends to produce. All of the slipped stitches produce a dense fabric, which is the exact opposite of the drape and flow that draws me to lace.

However, after thought and experimentation, I came to the realization that mosaic could solve the problems I had been experiencing trying to combine lace with other colorwork techniques. Since you are working with only one strand of yarn at a time, you do not have the yarn management issues and there are no floats to be dealt with—which also makes for a relatively inoffensive wrong side. And because you are knitting stripes, the yarn is carried up the side (or inside of knitting in the round) and that seriously cuts down on the number of ends that have to be woven in. All of the give produced by the yarn overs in lace sucks some of the heaviness out of the dense mosaic fabric. It was a perfect fit.

Of course there were unanticipated challenges in getting the two techniques to play nicely with each other. It has taken time to determine what can and cannot be accomplished with the fusion, but I have had a rollicking good time figuring it all out. And by no means am I confident that I have figured out everything; it is an ongoing process and I expect to make more discoveries in the future. However, I have pieced together enough of the puzzle that I want to share it with knitters everywhere. Whether you are a fellow lace maniac or simply crazy for color (or both), I cannot wait to share all I have discovered with you.

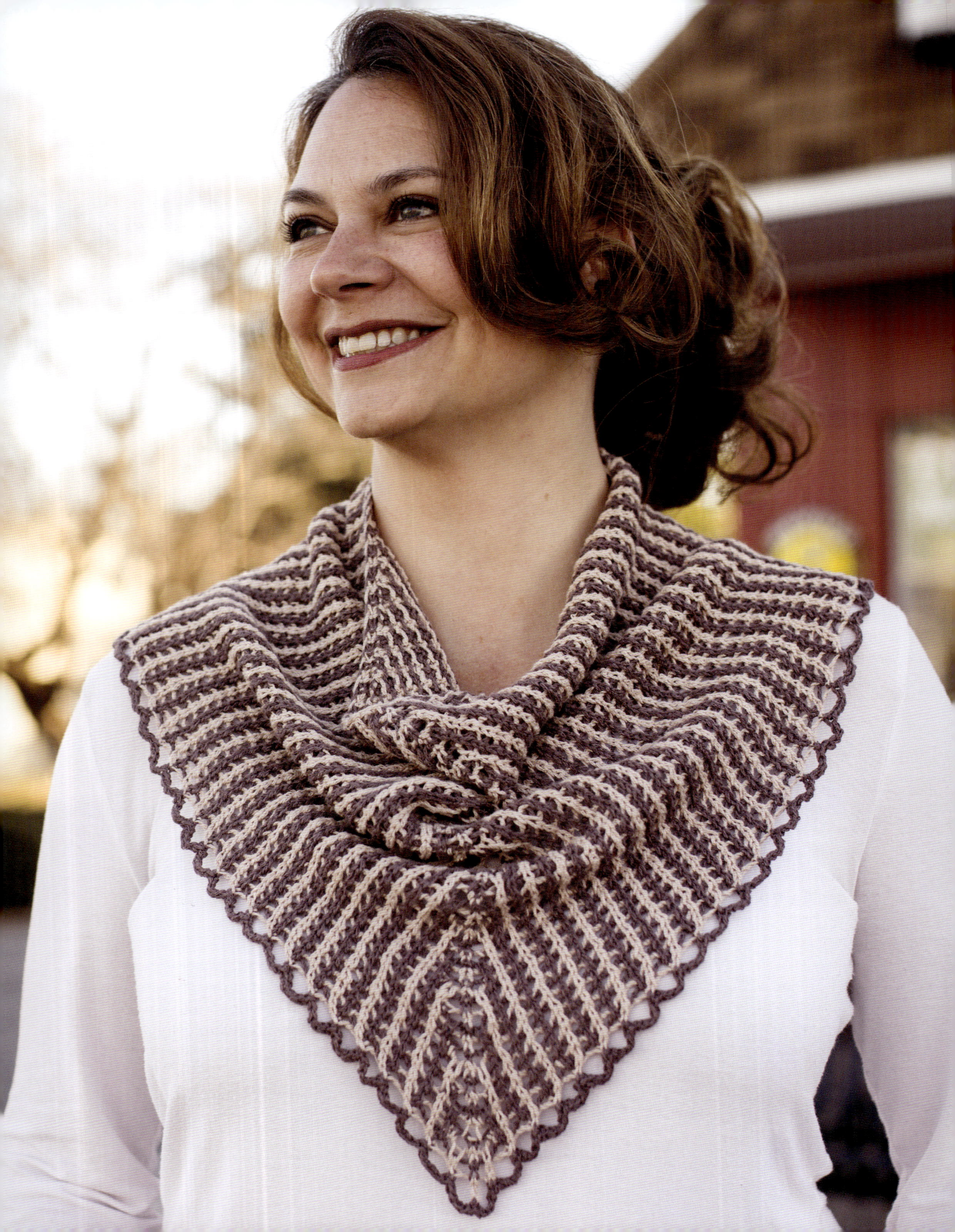

Getting Started with Mosaic and Lace

Meet the Slip Stitch

Mosaic colorwork falls under the heading of slip-stitch knitting, which is fairly self-explanatory in its title. It is easy to add the slip stitch to your knitting repertoire; to slip a stitch you simply transfer a stitch from your left needle to your right needle without actually knitting (or purling) the stitch. There are two basic ways to slip a stitch, knit-wise or purl-wise.

To slip knit-wise, insert your right hand needle as if to knit and "slip" the stitch to your right hand needle.

To slip purl-wise, insert your right hand needle as if to purl and "slip" the stitch to your right hand needle.

Slipping knit-wise changes the orientation of the stitch, creating a twisted stitch, while slipping purl-wise does not. Unless you are directed otherwise, the assumption in this book is that you are to slip a stitch purl-wise. One significant exception to this rule is when working a left-leaning decrease (ssk or skp). There are many schools of thought on how to slip the component stitches of an ssk; for the purposes of this book, you are to slip each of the two stitches that make up the ssk knit-wise.

With the slip stitch added to your knitting bag of tricks, we are ready to move on to mosaic.

Mosaic Colorwork

At its most basic, the mosaic colorwork technique is knitting stripes and slipping stitches in pattern. Mosaic patterns, as defined by Barbara Walker in her seminal work *Mosaic Knitting*, have a distinct linear and geometric appearance, frequently focusing on repeated patterns. As an introduction to mosaic, we are going to begin with understanding her original style of patterning. It is always good to know the basic rules before you set about bending them to suit your fancy.

To begin, here are a few basic rules that define Walker's mosaic:

1. You are working in either stockinette or garter stitch.
2. You are knitting two-row (or two-round) stripes.
3. You are slipping stitches of the contrasting color purl-wise while holding the yarn to the wrong side of the knitting.

The first two rules allow a Walker mosaic chart to dispose of the return row by making each row do double duty. Each row of the chart represents two rows of knitting. Using standard colorwork conventions, you read the shaded and white squares as instructions on how to work the color pattern. When reading these charts, you work a

Walker-style Mosaic Chart

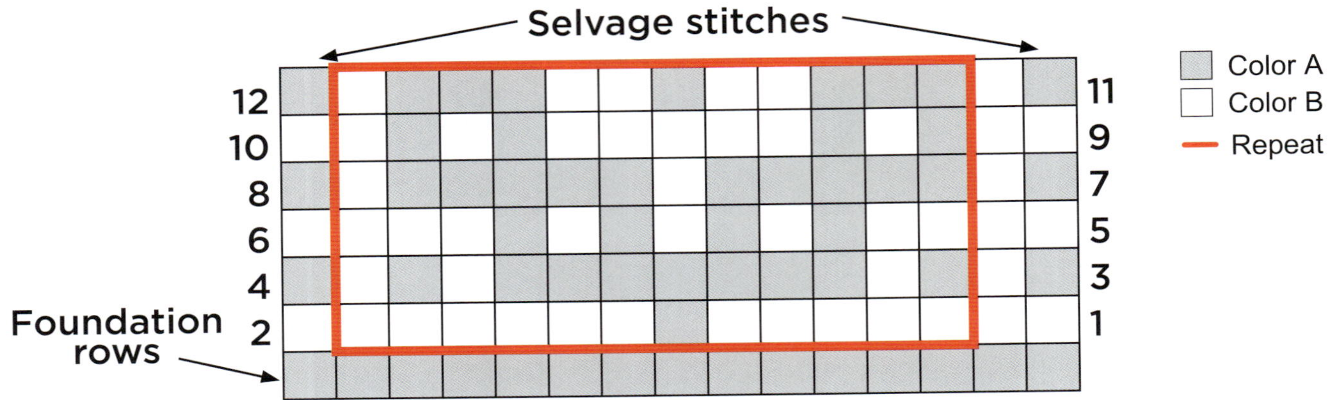

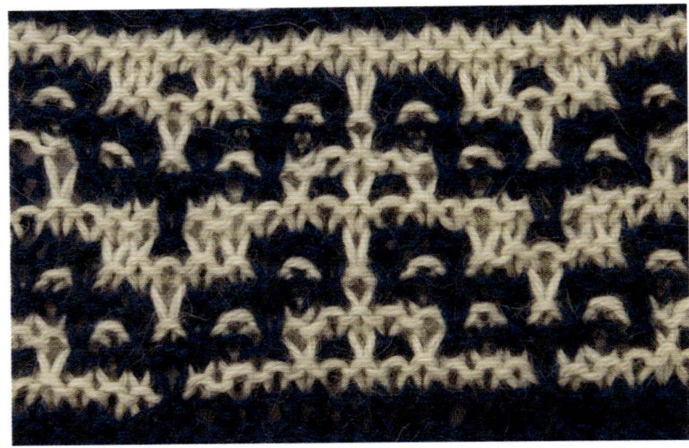

Walker mosaic chart worked in garter stitch

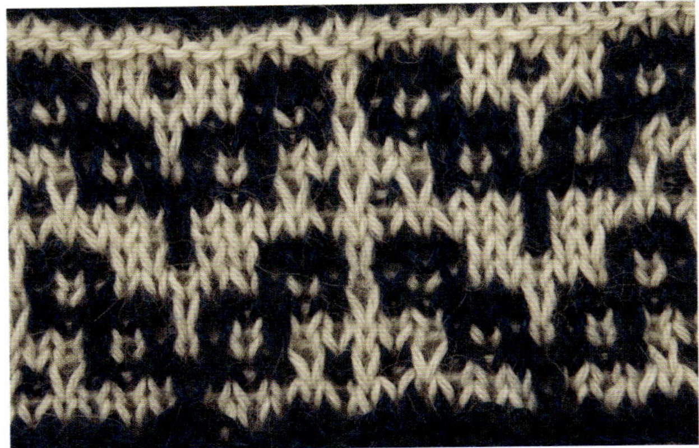

Walker mosaic chart worked in stockinette stitch

right-side row by beginning at the lower right-hand corner and reading from right to left, as is typical in all knitting charts.

The first stitch of the row lets you know the color of the active yarn (white). All white boxes indicate that you should knit that stitch. Inactive colored (shaded) boxes indicate that you are to slip that stitch (see Rule 3). You work across the row knitting white and slipping shaded, repeating any sections as indicated until you reach the end of the chart.

In a traditional chart, you would work the next row from left to right. But what? The next row begins with a shaded box. Ah ha, this is a Walker mosaic chart! Because you are always working in either stockinette or garter stitch *and* slipping the opposing color there is no need to chart the

return row. Instead, you simply work the row you just finished again, working from left to right.

Once you get the hang of it, you won't even need to look at the chart on the return row. If you are working in stockinette stitch, you simply purl the white stitches and slip the shaded stitches (this time with yarn held in front per Rule 3). In garter stitch, you knit the white stitches while slipping the shaded stitches. You will know you are doing it correctly if the yarn in your hand matches the active color of the previous row.

After working a there-and-back-again set of rows, switch your yarns and move on to the next row in the chart, which begins with a shaded box. Once again reading right to left, this row is read the same as the previous stripe, only with the yarns reversed. The shaded boxes are now active and will be knit and the white boxes will be slipped. After the entire row is completed, work the same row you just finished again from left to right to complete your stripe.

Things become slightly different if you are working in the round. The most significant change is that you read the chart from right to left on every pass through a round of the chart. Additionally, for a circular piece it is possible for the first stitch of a round to be a slipped stitch, which puts a bit of a cramp in the whole "first stitch tells you the color you are working." This is where knowing you are knitting stripes comes in handy. For any project, you will knit a few foundation rows/rounds to begin your piece. When you begin the chart, you will either switch to the contrasting color and begin the striping pattern or continue in your established pattern if you were already knitting stripes.

As long as you remember that you are knitting stripes (two rows/rounds of each color per Rule 2), then you will know when to change yarns.

While this might make working in the round seem a little fiddly, I think it is more than made up for by how it simplifies Rule 3. When you are working in the round, you are always slipping your stitches with the yarn held in back of your stitch. There are no pesky return rows where you need to remember to hold your yarn in front while slipping stitches.

Armed with this knowledge, you are now prepared to knit any pattern with a Walker-style mosaic chart.

A Little Deeper into Mosaic

Now that we have the basics down, we can move on to understanding a few more nuanced principles of mosaic. First, one of the benefits of slip-stitch colorwork in general is that you do not have to manage more than one color at a time and, as a result, you do not have to deal with carrying a second strand of yarn behind your work.

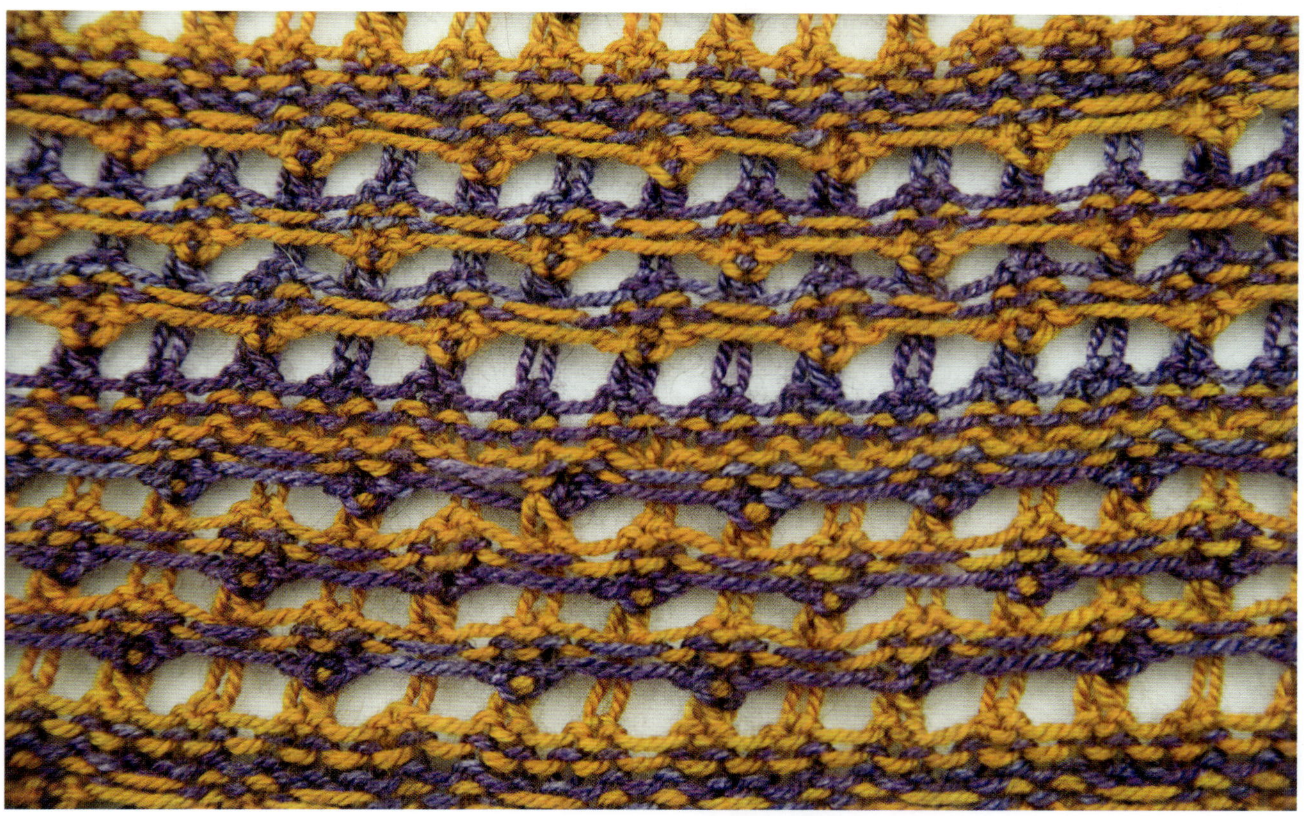

Reverse of mosaic lace showing "bars"

Due to the nature of knitting, you will have a small bar of yarn stretched across the back of every slipped stitch, but it is not a proper float akin to those found in two-color stranded knitting. When you slip a stitch, you simply need to allow the yarn to carry at normal tension across the gap between worked stitches. Special care is not needed to make sure it is loose; however, you do not want to pull it tight. A span of yarn the width of the slipped stitch is all that is needed. The overall width of your knitting will contract a bit, but I compensate for this by knitting at a looser gauge than normally called for with the yarn weight being used.

That said, as you look through the patterns in this book you will notice that you are infrequently instructed to slip more than one stitch at a time. Slipping two stitches side by side increases the horizontal compression a wee bit but not unreasonably so. Slipping *more* than two stitches sequentially begins to cause problems and is one of the limitations of mosaic-style colorwork. If you are considering playing with your own mosaic creations, keep this in mind.

Of course, the slipped stitches in mosaic knitting are also being stretched over two (or more) rows along the vertical axis and this also causes a shortening of your work. For this reason, you generally do not want to slip a stitch over more than two rows (I say generally because this is one of the principles with which one can play a little fast and loose). Again, working at a looser gauge helps mitigate this tendency.

Add these three technique guidelines to your repertoire.

1. Don't pull your yarn tight (or let it hang loose) behind slipped stitches.
2. Slip only one or two stitches side by side, usually one at a time.
3. Generally, only slip a stitch over two consecutive rows vertically.

Mosaic Lace

RETURNING THE RETURN ROW

Of Walker's original rules, the only rule that I have completely discarded to achieve mosaic lace is Rule 1. Why stick with stockinette and garter stitch when there is a whole world of stitches out there? With Rule 1 thrown out, the charted return (or rest) row is now necessary. This is not because there is a lot happening on the return/rest row, but only because I want to have fun on the right side. I like to call the rows/rounds that have all of the lace stitches on them *action rows*. I feel that asking people to work the row backwards while at the same time disregarding any action symbols would be a bit demanding.

With the return/rest row back in place, my mosaic lace charts function mostly like a standard lace chart. They are read beginning at the bottom right corner from right to left and then from left to right on the return rows. For a chart worked in the round, each chart row is read from right to left. The element that separates them from a standard lace chart is that they also convey colorwork information using the same premise as explained previously.

Because lace symbols are overlaid onto the colorwork chart, I have chosen to introduce the slip stitch symbol instead of relying on you to remember to slip the contrasting color stitches. This means that all of the lace symbols, such as a YO or k2tog, will only be found in the active color and all of the inactive color stitches will have a slip stitch symbol.

After eliminating the first rule, we are left with two remaining, slightly modified, rules:

1. You are knitting two-row/round stripes, unless instructed otherwise.
2. You are slipping stitches of the contrasting color purl-wise, always holding the yarn to the wrong side of the knitting, unless instructed otherwise.

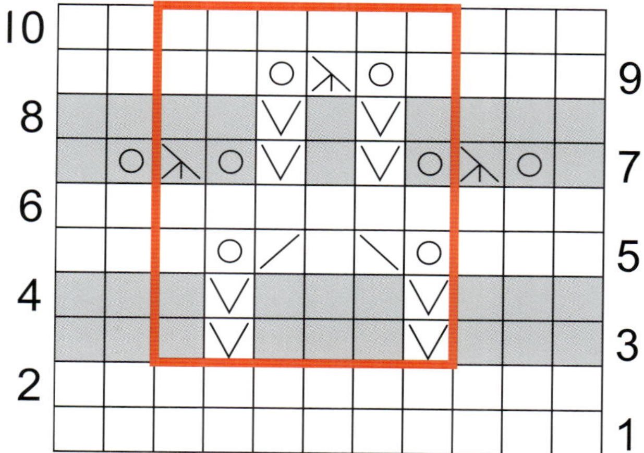

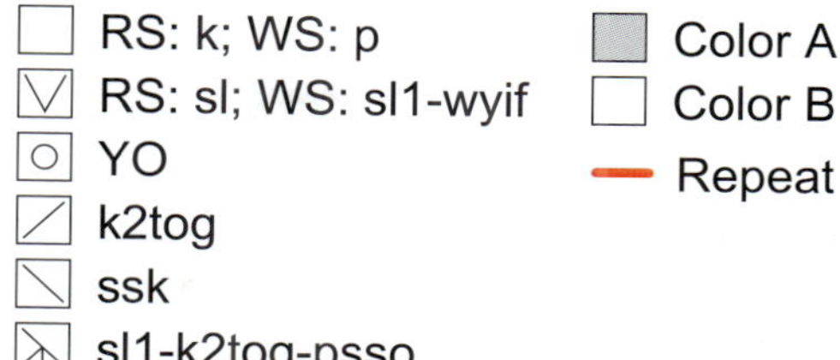

Ah, the old "unless instructed otherwise." Through the process of developing mosaic lace patterns I have found there are times where the rules can be bent a bit to achieve a desired effect. You will encounter patterns in the following pages that violate both of these rules where I've found the end result to be worth it. Don't worry! I will make the "instructed otherwise" sections very clear.

WHEN TWO TECHNIQUES COLLIDE

When trying to convince two different techniques to play nicely with each other, there are sure to be some challenges to overcome, and mosaic lace is no exception. I have found several quirks for which I have had to develop solutions, but luckily none of them were particularly difficult.

Yarn Overs on Either Side of a Slipped Stitch

When a pattern requires working a yarn over, slipping one or more stitches, and then immediately going into another yarn over, it creates a bit of a situation on the following row/round. Even though the slipped stitch(es) prevents the yarn overs from collapsing in on themselves, it works best to treat the yarn overs as one would a double yarn over. To accomplish this you have to knit one and purl the other while slipping the intervening stitches (don't worry, the

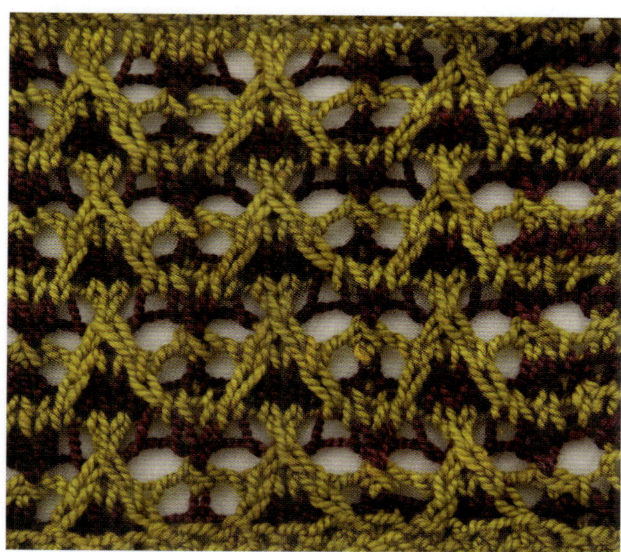

Swatch of mosaic lace chart

action symbols on the chart will tell you what to do). I have taken to calling this combination of stitches a captured double yarn over. It produces an enlarged hole similar to a double yarn over, but the slipped stitch prevents it from becoming huge and uncontrolled.

Substituting Decreases

An experienced lace knitter can often substitute one left- or right-leaning decrease for another according to their tastes without significantly changing the final look of the piece. Unfortunately, this is not the case with mosaic lace. The decreases are deliberately chosen based on how they manipulate their constituent stitches of different colors. This is especially important in the double decreases. Please review the instructions for the decreases and consider any changes carefully.

Creeping Yarn Overs

When working the row/round following an action row/round, it is necessary to pay more attention than in a normal rest row/round. Oftentimes, some of the slipped stiches decide to creep up under the yarn overs they sit beside. When you come up to a slipped stitch that is directly beside a yarn over (and there are a gracious plenty of them), make sure that you are slipping and purling in the correct order. This can be particularly tricky in the "yarn over on either side of a slip stitch" situation addressed above.

Elongated Yarn Overs
(Or Cut Yourself Some Slack)

Even with the wiggle room working at a looser gauge supplies, there are times that the slipped stitches pull in so much yarn that your lace work can get lost. At times this is desirable but at others this is not. To alleviate this tendency, I use what I think of as elongated yarn overs. To work these you yarn over twice when making the increase, then on the next row you drop one of the loops and knit (or purl) into the other one. This is not a double increase stitch and is not to be confused with a double yarn over. When you come to a pattern that uses this stitch you will see that it has its own symbol that only occupies one stitch on the chart. This can also be done with a normal knit or purl stitch but none of the patterns in this book use such a technique.

What You See Is Not What You Get

Traditional knitting charts are drawn to show you what your finished piece will look like *when viewed from the right side*. To achieve this effect, symbols are used that represent one action on the right side and a different action on the wrong side. I have stuck to this convention for my charts and the lace symbols do depict the

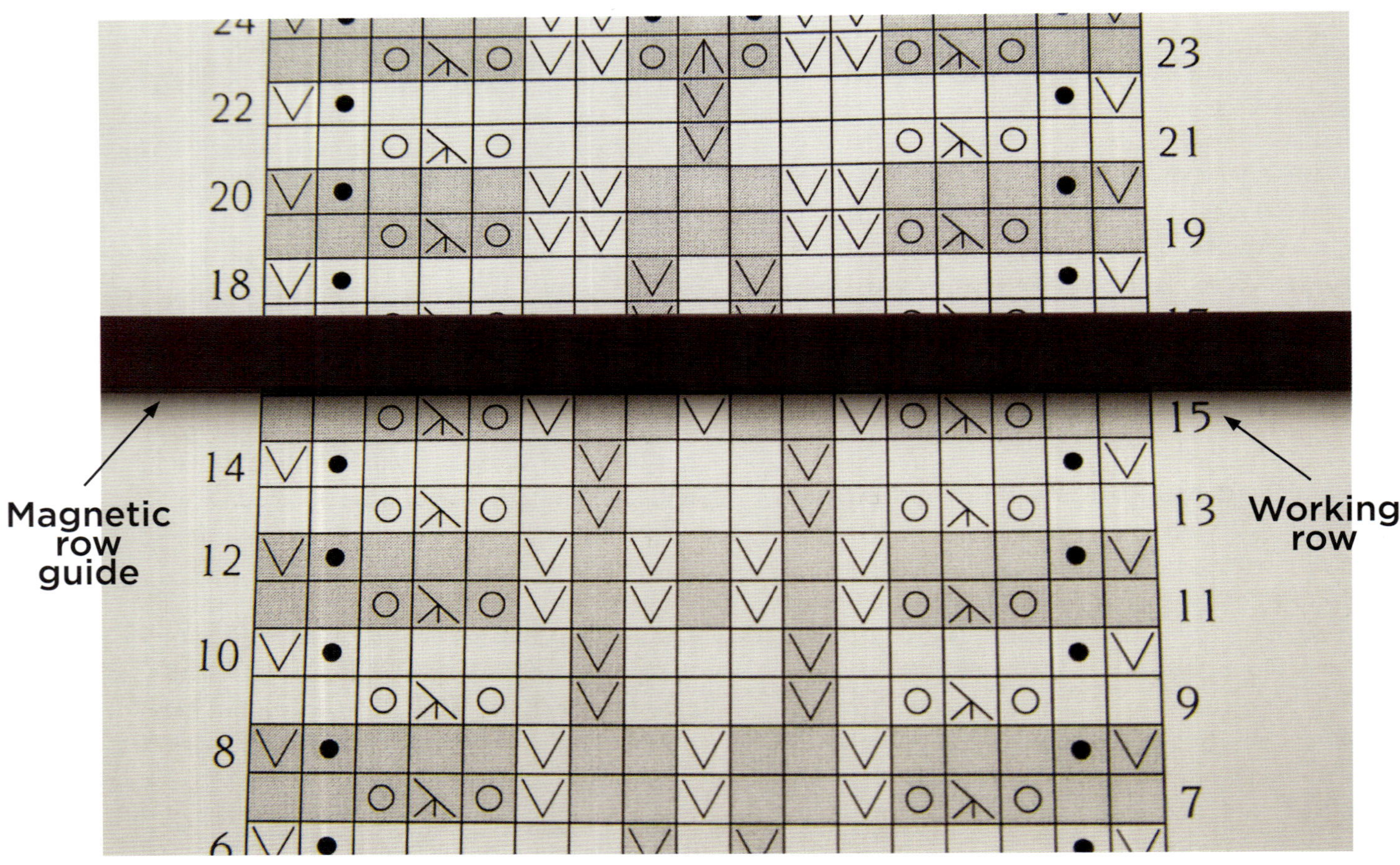

final pattern but, unfortunately, the colorwork does not follow suit.

If you are looking at a portion of the pattern where mosaic does not interact with the lace then it does indeed show you what the final colorwork will look like in that section. However, when the two techniques are used together, the visual representation becomes muddied. By using increase and decrease stitches I am able to manipulate the lines of color in fun ways, which is not accurately communicated by a grid of squares. You are simply going to have to trust me that it will work out. As you are knitting, you will see the direction the colors are moving and it should begin to make sense.

This fusion of mosaic colorwork chart and lace chart allows me to convey a large amount of instruction in a very concise way. Unfortunately, it also yields some enormous charts. Don't be afraid and take things slowly. Each chart is worked line-by-line and as you move along you will see that your knitting flows quickly.

One final chart-reading trick that I would like to leave you with is physical. Many knitters use magnets, post-it notes, or washi tape to highlight the lines of the chart they are working—all of which work great. However, if your method obscures the chart (like a magnet) make sure that you place your marker *above* the line you are working. If you place it below, then you cannot easily double check the row you just knit. In general, and especially with this style of knitting, knowing where you came from can be more useful than seeing where you are going.

ABOUT THE STRIPE

If you have ever knit stripes, the pattern probably said, "Carry your yarn up the side." But what precisely does that mean? Let's say you just finished knitting a full stripe of Color A and now you need to knit a stripe of Color B. But the yarn from your previous stripe of Color B is hanging off the edge of your work two rows below your current row. To move Color B to where you are now, you need to pull it up, or carry it up, from that previous row.

While it seems to be as simple as dropping your strand of Color A and picking up Color B,

there are a few details to consider. First, if you pull the strand of Color B too tightly then you will buckle the fabric you are creating. Next, if you do not allow the two strands to wrap around each other then you will end up with a long float of one of the colors highly visible. Finally, if you are knitting flat then you will have a "barber pole" effect running up one edge of your knitting, but not the other.

The first issue is easy to fix; simply be aware of not pulling that strand too tightly. I like to pinch the just finished stripe of knitting with my right hand and tug it down gently, to mimic the eventual blocking, while I am working the first couple of stitches of a new row. This makes sure that there is some slack in the carried yarn. But take care not to leave too much slack or you will have loops.

Second, you want to twine, or twist, the two colors around each other. You are generally instructed to lift the new color from behind or below the unused color. When worked in conjunction with the slipped stitch edge that I utilize in this book, I find it easier to remember how to lift the yarn if I visualize that I am pulling the new yarn *up* and the old yarn *down* as shown in the illustration on page 8. I prefer for the new yarn to be to the right of the old yarn, but if you simply make sure that you lift the new color in the same way each time you will be fine. Most of the time it is not necessary or even desirable to physically twist the two yarns around each other. The exception to this is if you are carrying yarn over more than two rows. When working more than two rows of one color you need to trap the unused yarn whenever you begin a right side row. To do this, pick up your unused yarn to the wrong side of your work and pass it in front of your working color, allowing it to fall again to the wrong side of your work.

Solving the third issue, non-matching sides on flat work, has occupied many of my designing hours. There are many solutions out there that purport to hide the carried yarn but none of them make me happy. After trying as many as I could find, I decided I was coming at things from the wrong direction. What I wanted was both edges of the work to match each other. Instead

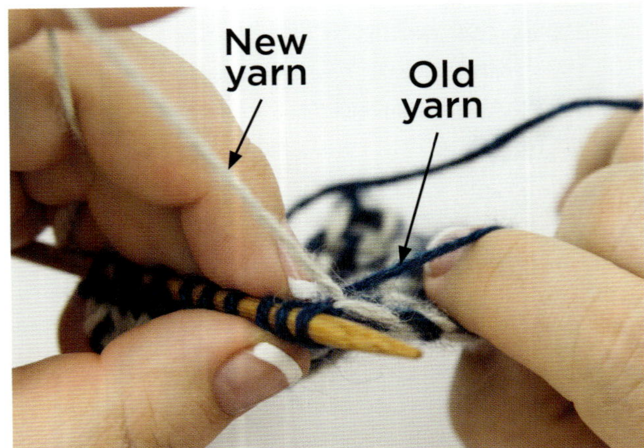

Carrying yarn up the side

of trying to camouflage the barber pole effect of the carried yarn, why not duplicate that effect with the other edge?

After a bit of experimentation I found that the way to accomplish this was with a slipped stitch edge. Of course, nothing is ever as simple as that and I had to work my way through several combinations of how to slip the edge stitches before I landed on something that I liked.

You can see in the swatch to the right my evolution of a preferred selvage. All of the selvages on my flat lace pieces have this garter eyelet edging to prevent rolling and to provide for ease of blocking. The base pattern for this swatch is as follows:

RS: K1, k2tog, YO, k5, YO, ssk, k1.

WS: K3, p5, k3.

Section A shows how it looks if you make no attempt at all to address the carried yarn. The barber pole is on the right and the left is garter stitch.

Section B illustrates that by slipping the final stitch of the RS row with the yarn held to the front, a barber pole is created on both sides but they are uneven when compared to each other.

In section C both the first and last stitch of the RS row were slipped with the yarn held to the front. While this fixed the unevenness, I found it too fiddly to manage the tension on the leading edge and the right edge was much looser than the left edge.

In section D the final stitch of both the RS and WS rows are slipped with the yarn held to

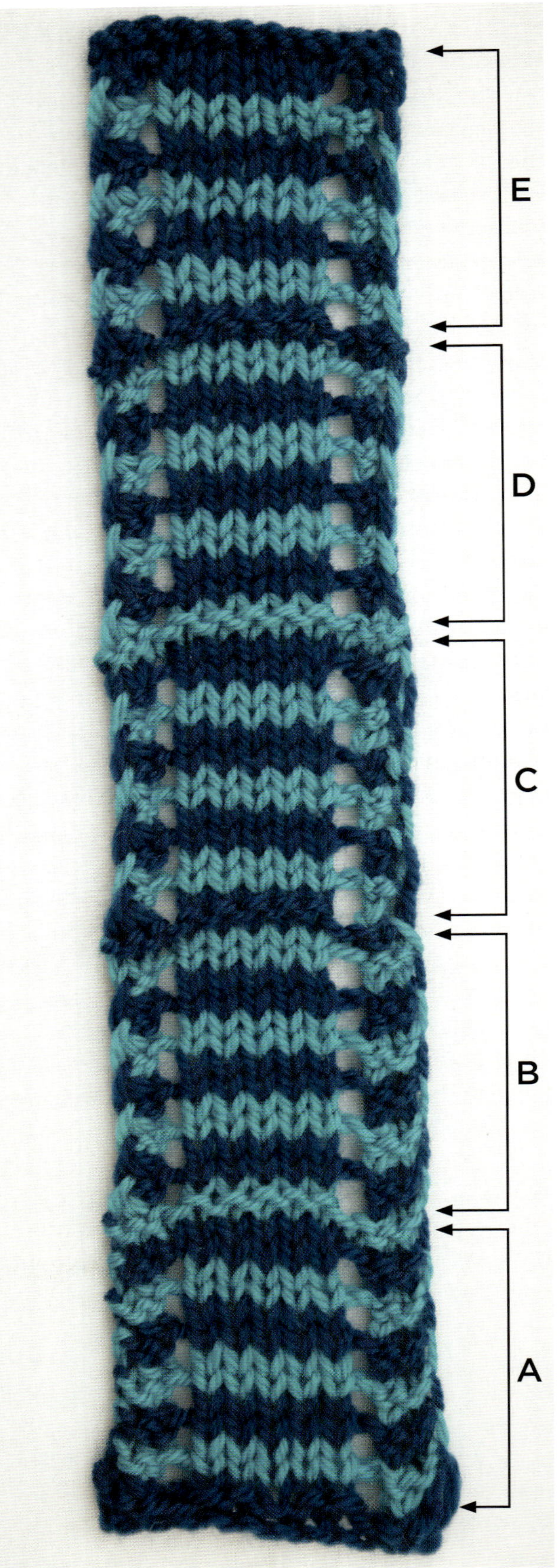

Experimenting with selvage

the front. This evened out the barber pole but I didn't like working an ssk directly before a slipped stitch.

Finally, I arrived at section E. By slipping the first and last stitch of the WS row with the yarn held to the front, I created a selvage that was easy to work and with edges that matched!

Note: If you find method D easier to work, you can substitute it on any of the flat patterns found in this book.

When knitting in the round, the carried yarn is completely hidden, so the barber pole is not an issue. But the other points still apply. You want to trap the unused yarn between the wrong side of your work and the active yarn. I find it easiest to lay the unused yarn across where the active yarn joins to your work, running the strand from right to left.

LISTEN TO YOUR YARN

The first thing that pops into your mind when planning the yarns for your mosaic and lace project is probably going to be what colors you are going to use. And of course that is a big decision, but color isn't the only thing that I would like you to think about when choosing your yarn. There are several textural elements that need to be taken into account when deciding the appropriateness of a yarn. I like to think of this as how visually "noisy" a yarn is.

What I mean by visual noise is how much the yarn has going on with regards to definition and texture. One example of a noisy yarn would be a tweed. With all of those little nubbins popping out it brings a great deal of visual interest—which is perfect for some applications, but for mosaic it can significantly obscure both the colorwork and lace patterns you will be working hard to create and, thus, would not be a great yarn choice for these projects.

What makes a yarn noisy? Texture, halo, sparkles, distinct plies, color variation, and even stitch definition can all overpower and obscure your colorwork. Which is not to say that you absolutely cannot use these noisy yarns with mosaic and lace. You simply need to understand

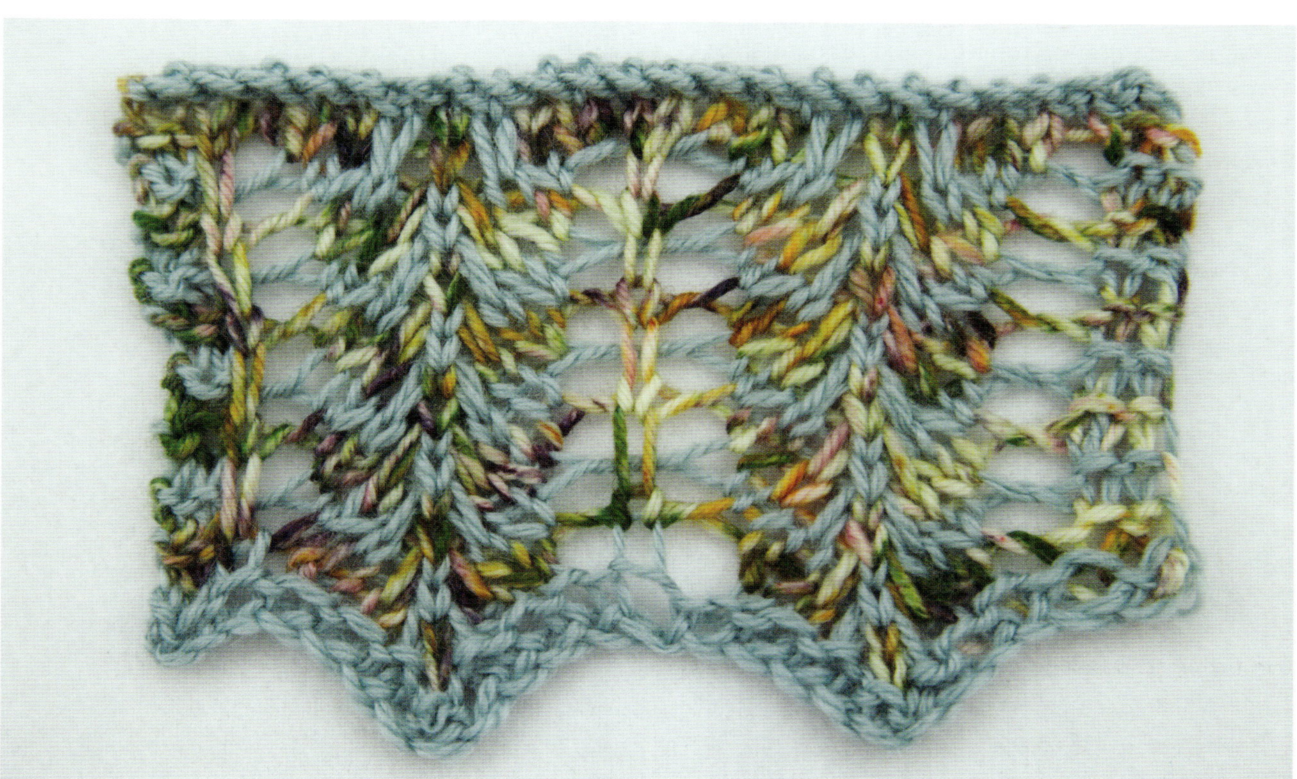

An example of a noisy yarn obscuring a pattern

how they are going to play with the stitches and plan your game accordingly. Noisier yarns need to be matched up with less visually complex stitch patterns or projects where you don't care if elements of your stitch pattern become obscured.

In the Single Flight mittens (page 15), I have chosen to pair a neutrally colored yarn with a variegated yarn to provide abundant visual interest with minimal work. The color is allowed to move through its color changes in a simple graphic mosaic pattern that highlights the yarn's assets. This pattern would also work well with two solid colors, but would perhaps be a bit less exciting.

On the other hand, the intricate work in the shawl Ves (page 77) would get lost if you used an overly noisy yarn. You might be able to get away with a long-color-change gradient yarn as one of the two colors, but if the yarns had too much texture or halo you would lose a lot of the pattern.

A good general guideline to follow is this: the more complex your colorwork pattern, the simpler your yarn needs to be. Of course, that doesn't mean boring. You can still have a world of fun mixing and matching beautiful colors in texturally simple yarns.

CONSIDERING CONTRAST

The effect attained by mosaic, and colorwork in general, is pretty much entirely dependent on using two or more contrasting colors of yarn. When considering contrast, most people jump directly to black and white or light and dark; in other words, contrast by tonal value. Tonal value is an excellent way to create contrast, but it is not the only way. Contrast can also be created with hue.

The hue of a color is simply the color. The literal definition is that it is the attribute of a color by virtue of which it is discernible as red, blue, etc.; dependent on its dominant wavelength while being independent of intensity or lightness (tonal value). Which, as definitions go, is precise but confusing. The hue is what makes blue, *blue*, regardless of it being light or dark blue—it is still blue. When selecting colors, you can create

contrast by varying the tonal value or hue, or both. Each of these pairings will have a different effect and can create very different results with the same mosaic pattern. I suggest swatching to test various color pairings.

Creating contrast with both tonal value and hue will produce the most graphic punch. It is high contrast and can result in pieces that are almost optical illusions. In this book the most striking example of this is Your Princess Is in Another Castle (page 31). By pairing black with a light, bright green I have matched a dark yarn

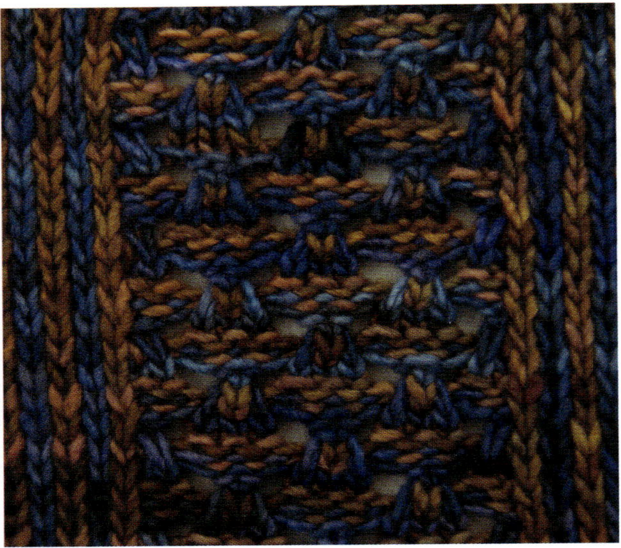

Detail of Rock City Scarf

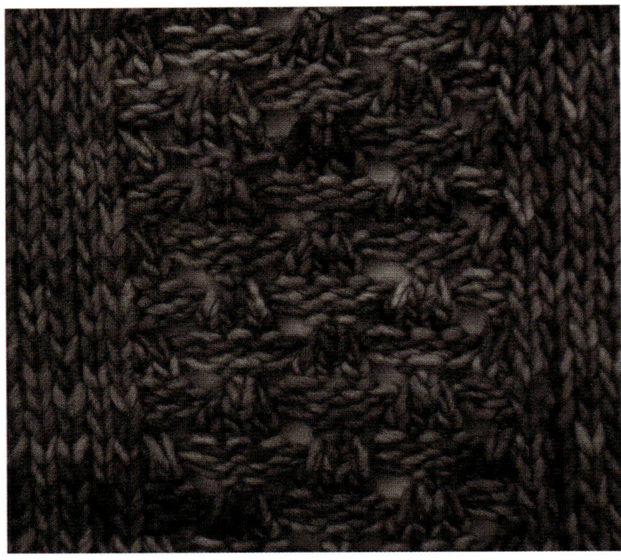

Detail of Rock City Scarf in black and white

with a light yarn as well as used two very differ-ent hues. The results are striking and bold.

For a slightly more subtle effect, you can choose two colors of the same hue but different tonal values. This is commonly referred to as monochromatic. Several patterns in this book take advantage of this kind of pairing. One example is the Sailing Diamonds hat (page 27). Two pinks, one light and one dark, provide plenty of contrast to allow the pattern to pop.

The most understated form of contrast is created by matching up the tonal value of the colors and providing contrast solely through hue. Look to the Rock City Scarf (page 39) for an example of this. When you find a color pairing just right using hue only, the colorwork will completely disappear in a black and white photo. If you are trying to downplay the complexity of a piece or make it a bit more subtle, this is an excellent choice.

In conclusion, when considering contrast, do not limit yourself to pairing a light yarn with a dark yarn. Contrast can be created in fresh ways and many differing effects can be attained with the same pattern by simply combining different colors. Have fun and mix things up.

OF COURSE COLOR

Now, I could talk about color theory and have several illustrations with a color wheel and examples of secondary and tertiary colors; but I believe that the subject has been covered extensively by other authors. It is valuable information and I highly recommend that you seek it out if you have not run across it before. For the purposes of this book, we will explore the more practical side of yarn selection.

First, look at your pattern and think about what colors you would like to wear. What would make you happy? In what context would you wear this piece? Will it be a special occasion treat or more utilitarian? These questions will heavily influence your color choices. The colors you choose for a shawl that you might wear weekly at work may need to be a bit more subdued than a winter hat that you will wear on vacation. Or not, depending on your personal situation.

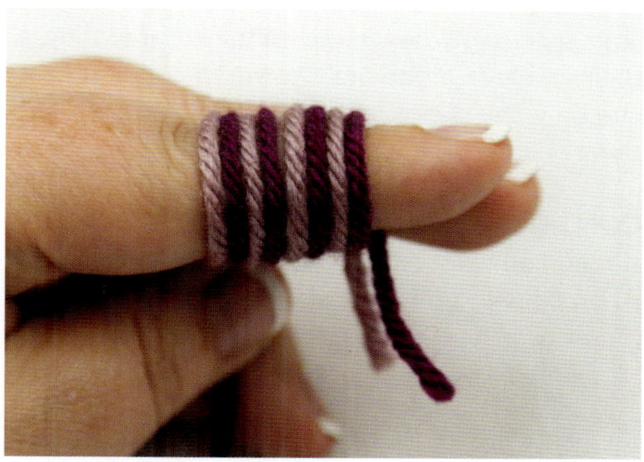

Wrap two yarns around your finger to see how they look together.

Once you have an idea of your goal, a trip to your favorite yarn purveyor is in order! Browse the offerings and pull a few skeins that might suit your purposes. Make sure to carry them to a window so you can see them in a more natural light. It is amazing how different colors can look under various lights (and it even has a name, metamerism). If the yarn is in twisted skeins I like to open them up, hold the loops side by side and then retwist the skeins together. This will give you a good idea of how the colors play with each other.

If re-skeining seems a bit overwhelming, you can accomplish the same thing in a miniature way. Take a single strand from each of the two colors you are considering and hold them side by side. Wrap them around your finger barber pole style so they make stripes. Seeing the yarn striped will give you an idea of how the stitches will look in finer detail. The re-skeining trick gives you the big picture while the single strand one is getting down to business. Both are useful techniques for picking out colors for your project.

One final way to evaluate the contrast in yarns is a gift of our modern age, the digital camera. If you have a smart device, you most likely have a digital camera. Set the candidate skeins next to each other and snap a photo. Then go into the camera application and convert the photo to black and white. If you are going for high tonal contrast, this trick will make it easier to judge your success by how dark, light, and gray the skeins appear. If you are looking to contrast by hue only, the skeins should be approximately the same shade of gray.

CONTENT MATTERS

A focus on color and texture is quite obvious when planning for colorwork, but one cannot forget to consider the fiber content of the yarn. Blocking is an essential step in allowing both colorwork and lace to fulfill their potential beauty. All of the projects in this book require blocking and you should consider this when choosing your yarn. It is easiest to achieve good blocking results with natural fibers and you will find that the yarns in this book represent a wide range of animal and plant based sources. When making your decision about the yarn to use in your chosen project, make sure to take blocking into consideration.

A NOTE ON GAUGE

All of the patterns in this book state the gauge in simple stockinette stitch as opposed to in pattern. I have done this because the interplay between the mosaic and lace makes it particularly challenging to determine gauge over pattern. This is not to say that you should not swatch. By swatching to get gauge in stockinette stitch, you will ensure that your finished piece will have the appropriate drape and that you will have enough yardage to complete your project.

PUTTING IT ALL TOGETHER

With these techniques, tricks, and color considerations under your belt, you are now ready to peruse the patterns! To begin, I have provided a pattern that is mosaic only so you can get a handle on mosaic before you tackle any combination of mosaic and lace. The rest of the patterns fall into one of the two following categories.

1. Mosaic and lace side by side but not interacting.
2. Mosaic lace where the colorwork and the lace are combined.

To keep the focus on the techniques, I have avoided any complex shaping and kept the projects relatively small. Accessories are a fun way to experiment with new concepts without the commitment in both time and yarn that a garment requires. So pick out a project, a fabulous yarn in two colors that speak to you, and have fun knitting mosaic and lace.

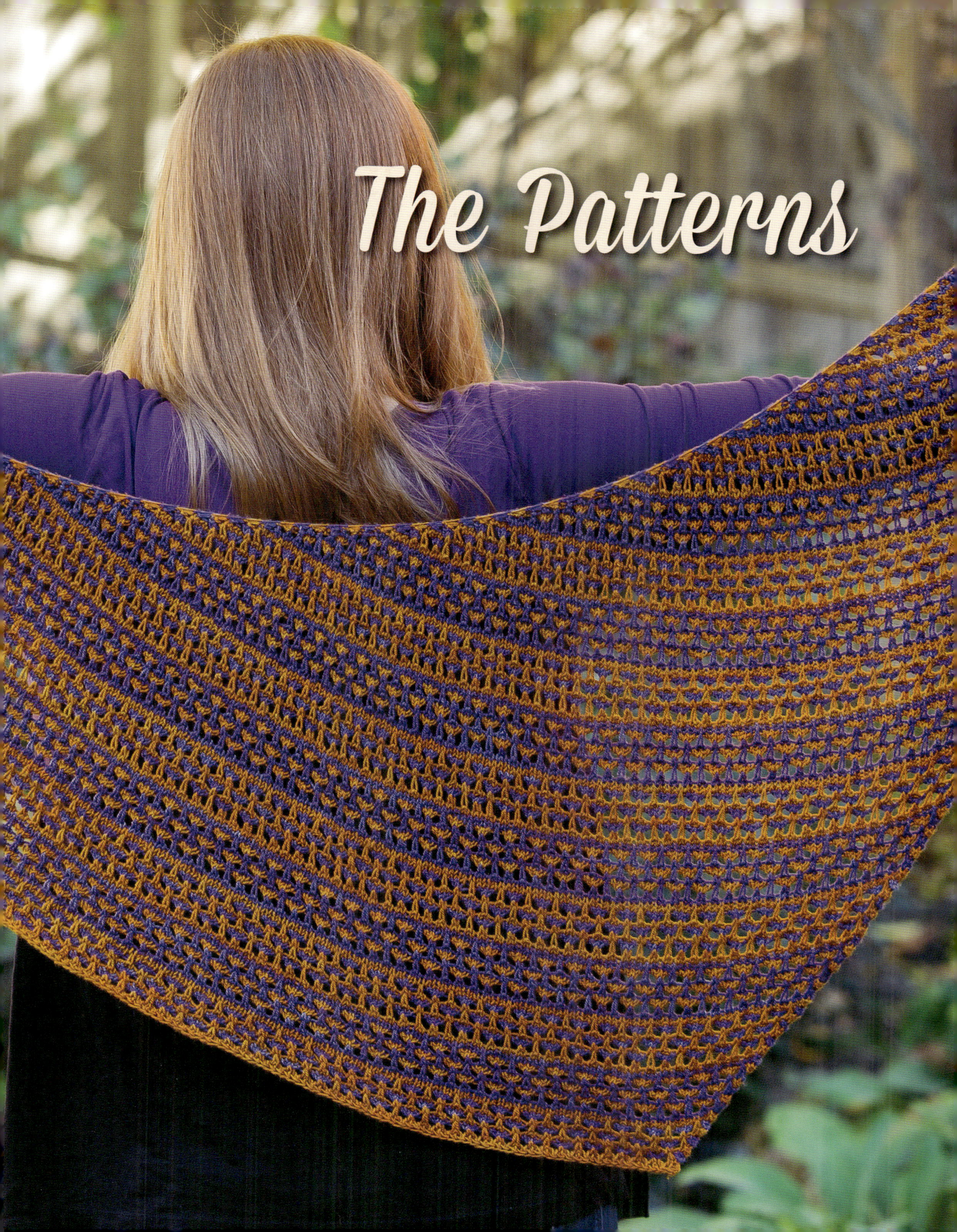

The Patterns

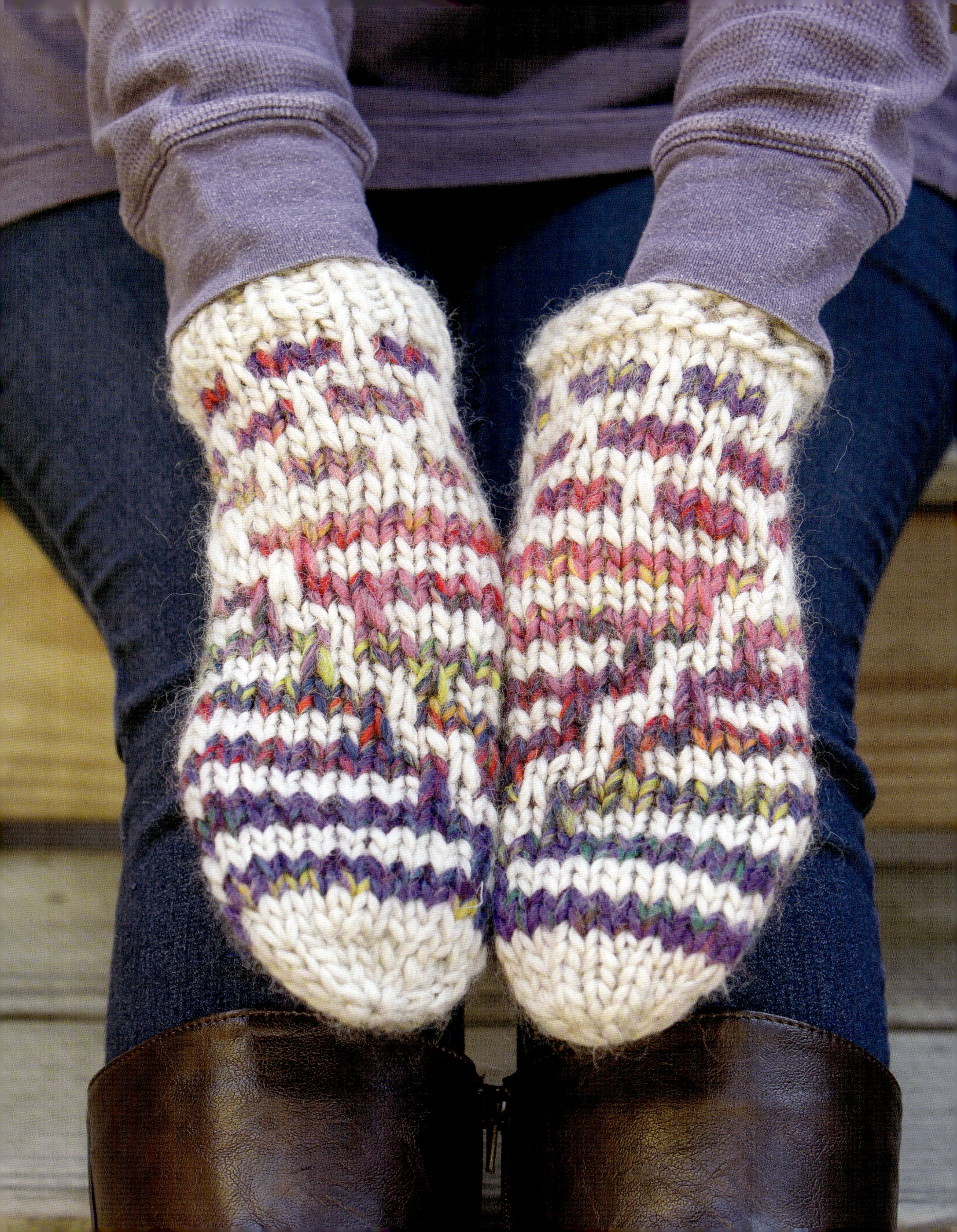

Single Flight

Here is the basic mosaic pattern so that you can give the technique a try without any lace. These mittens are designed with a small repeating colorwork pattern on the cuff and then a large motif across the back/palm. The large motif is designed so that the stair-step patterns climb in directions opposite to one another, which creates a fun flip/flop effect from the front to the back of the mitts. There are two cuff options, just in case you want a little bit of lace. The lace cuff option is good if you like to pull your mittens over the sleeve of your jacket and the ribbed cuff provides a closer fit.

Finished Measurements: 7.5"/19 cm hand
  circumference, 10.5"/26.5 cm long
Sizes: One size
Yarn
  Weight: Bulky
  Color A: Patons Colorwul in Bloom (1 skein);
    100% wool; 90 yd/82 m per 3 oz/85 g
  Color B: Patons Classic Wool Roving in Natural
    (1 skein); 100% wool; 120 yd/110 m per
    3.53 oz/100 g
Needles: US size 11/8 mm, preferred needles for
  working small circumference (see Knitting in
  the Round, page 105)
Notions: Stitch marker
Gauge in Stockinette over 4"/10 cm: 12 sts and
  18 rows (see A Note on Gauge, page 12)

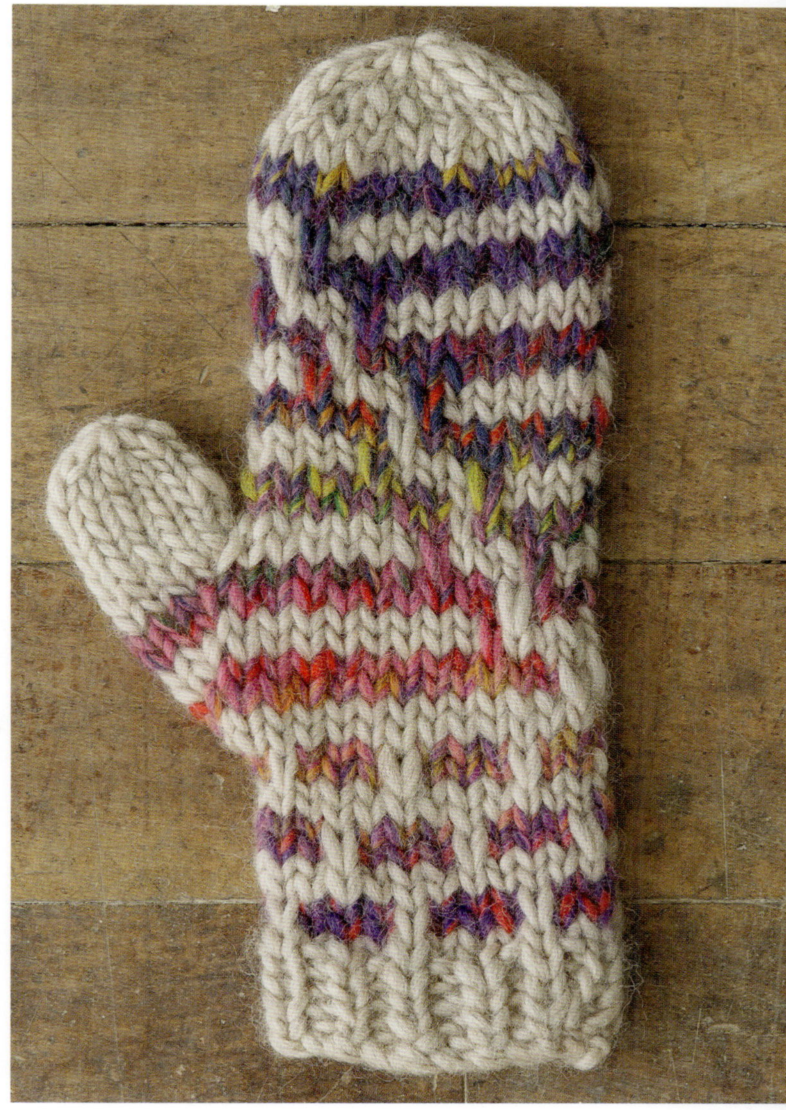

Instructions

Using Color B, knitted cast-on method (see Cast-on/Bind-off, page 107), and your preferred method of knitting in the round, CO 24 sts.

CUFF

Option 1 (Lace)

Purl 1 row.

Place marker to indicate beginning of round and join to work in the round, being careful not to twist sts.

Round 1: *K2tog, YO; rep from * to end of round.
Round 2: Purl.
Rounds 3 and 4: Knit.

Option 2 (Rib)

Row 1: *K1, p1; rep from * to end of row.

Place marker to indicate beginning of round and join to work in the round, being careful not to twist sts.

Rounds 1–3: *K1, p1; rep from * to end of round.
Round 4: Knit.

BODY (BOTH OPTIONS)

Join in Color A.

Work Chart A, repeating indicated section 6 times.

Chart A

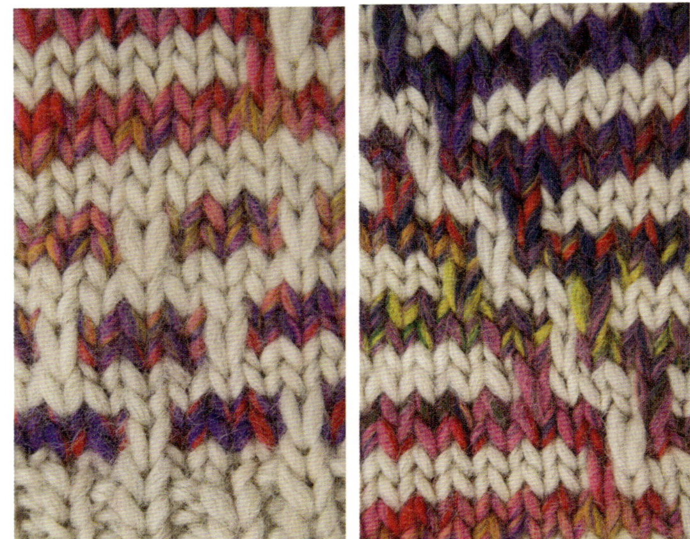

□	k	
☑	sl	
⊠	M1R	
⊠	M1L	

Color A
Color B

— Stitch Marker
— Repeat

pm = Place Marker

Repeat x 6

Gusset Chart

pm   pm

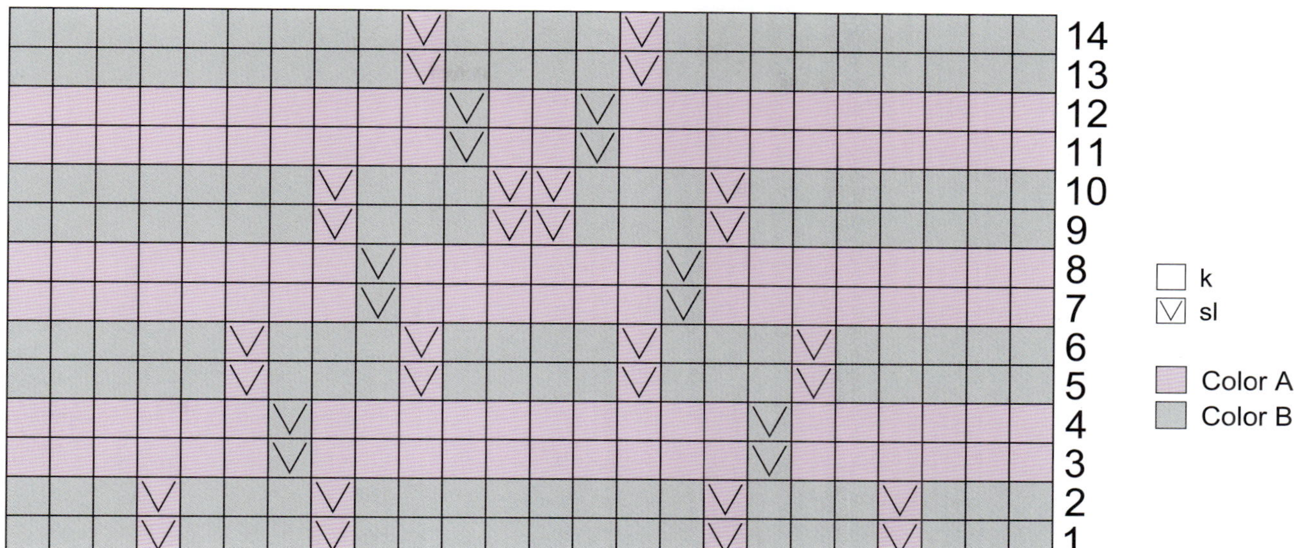

Chart B

GUSSET

Work Gusset chart. [33 sts]

HAND

Next Round: With A, k4, sl1, k7, transfer 9 gusset sts to waste yarn, k7, sl1, k4. [24 sts]
Next Round: With A, k4, sl1, k14, sl1, k4.

Work Chart B.

With Color A: Knit two rounds.
With Color B: Knit two rounds.

DECREASES

Note: Decreases will close the top of the mitten in 1 inch. If you need more length, add a few knit rounds before beginning decreases.

Round 1: With B, *k1, k2tog; rep from * to end of round. [16 sts]
Rounds 2 and 3: Knit.
Round 4: *K2tog; rep from * to end of round. [8 sts]

Cut yarn leaving a 7"/18 cm tail. Using a tapestry needle, transfer sts from needle to yarn tail and pull yarn to cinch tightly closed.

THUMB

Transfer held sts to needle. [9 sts]

With B, pick up and knit one st from each side of the thumb gap, place marker to indicate beginning of round. [11 sts]

Rounds 1–6: Knit.
Round 7: K1, (k2tog) five times. [6 sts]

Using a tapestry needle, transfer sts from needle to yarn tail and pull yarn to cinch tightly closed.

Make second mitten same as the first.

FINISHING

Weave in ends using yarn tails to neaten up any holes at the thumb joins and cuff. Block gently. If you have crease lines where piece was blocked flat, refold so that they are flattened out, steam, and pat lightly to remove creases. Trim ends.

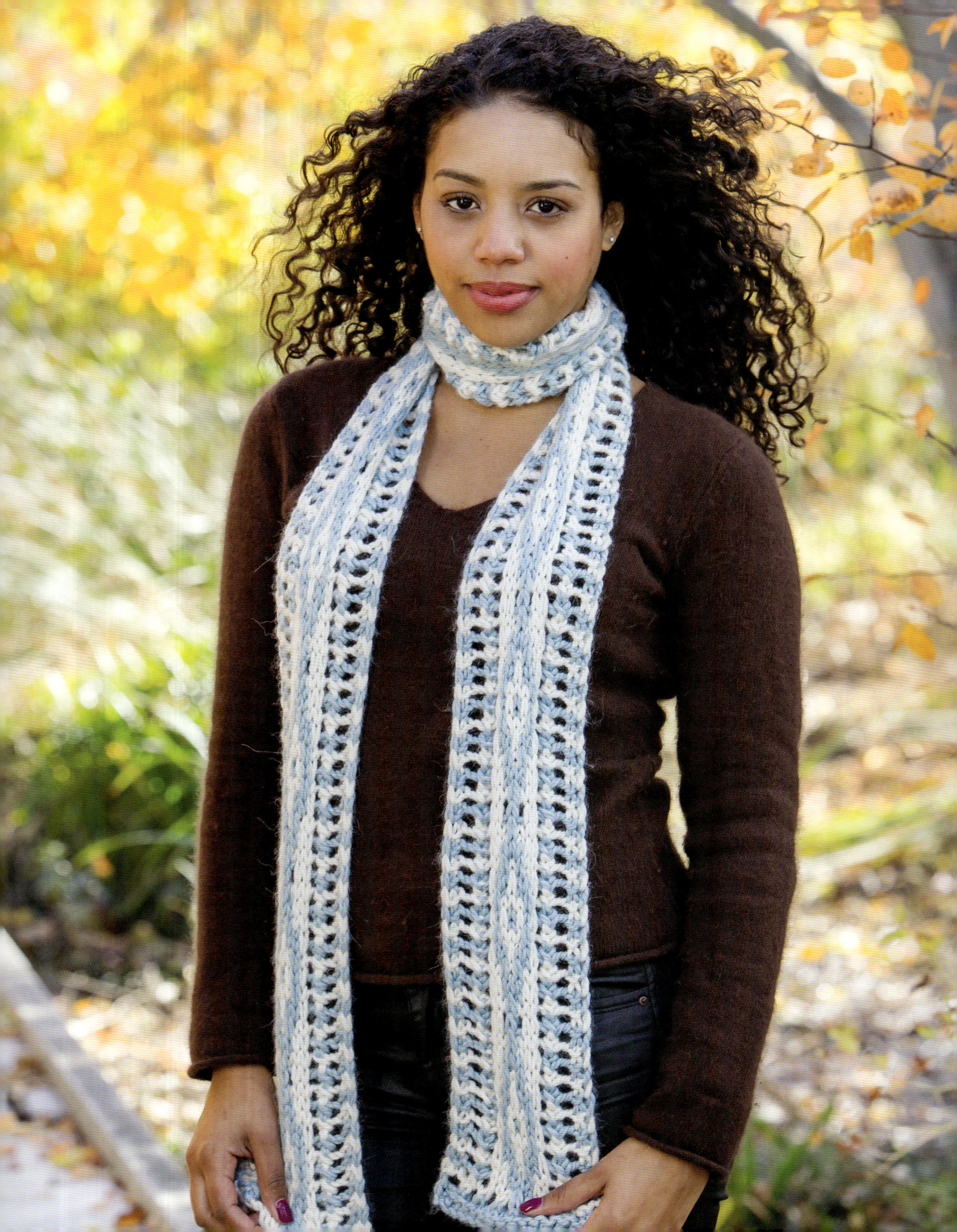

Lozengy Scarf

Using a big, soft yarn allows you to whip up this chic and graphic scarf in no time. A simple lozenge motif runs up the center between ladders of lace. Even with the holes, the alpaca will keep you nice and warm. I wanted to keep the yardage on this scarf to one skein of each color, but if you want a wider scarf you can easily use more yarn to double the central repeat to have two columns of lozenges running the length of the scarf.

Finished Measurements: 5"/13 cm wide,
   79.5"/202 cm long

Sizes: One size

Yarn

   Weight: Super bulky
   Plymouth Yarn Baby Alpaca Grande; 100%
      baby alpaca; 110 yd/101 m per 3.53 oz/100 g
   Color A: Sky #3317 (1 skein)
   Color B: Natural #100 (1 skein)

Needles: US size 11/8 mm

Gauge in Stockinette over 4"/10 cm: 12 sts and
   14 rows (see A Note on Gauge, page 12)

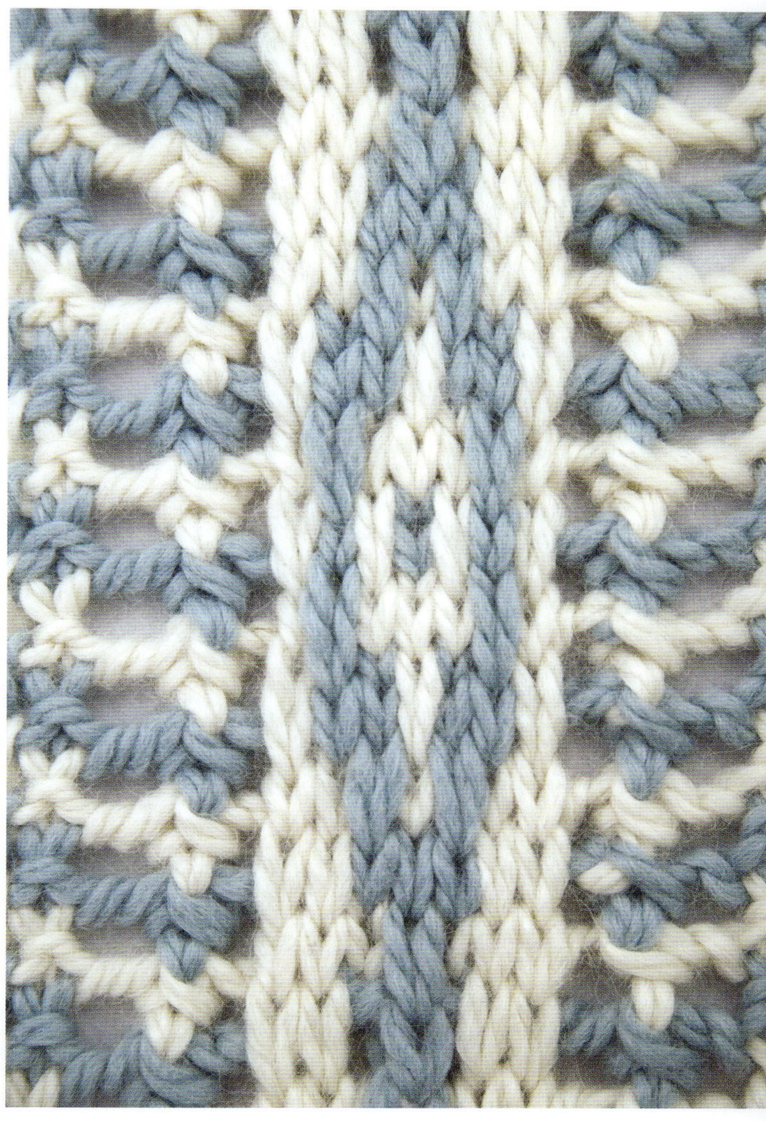

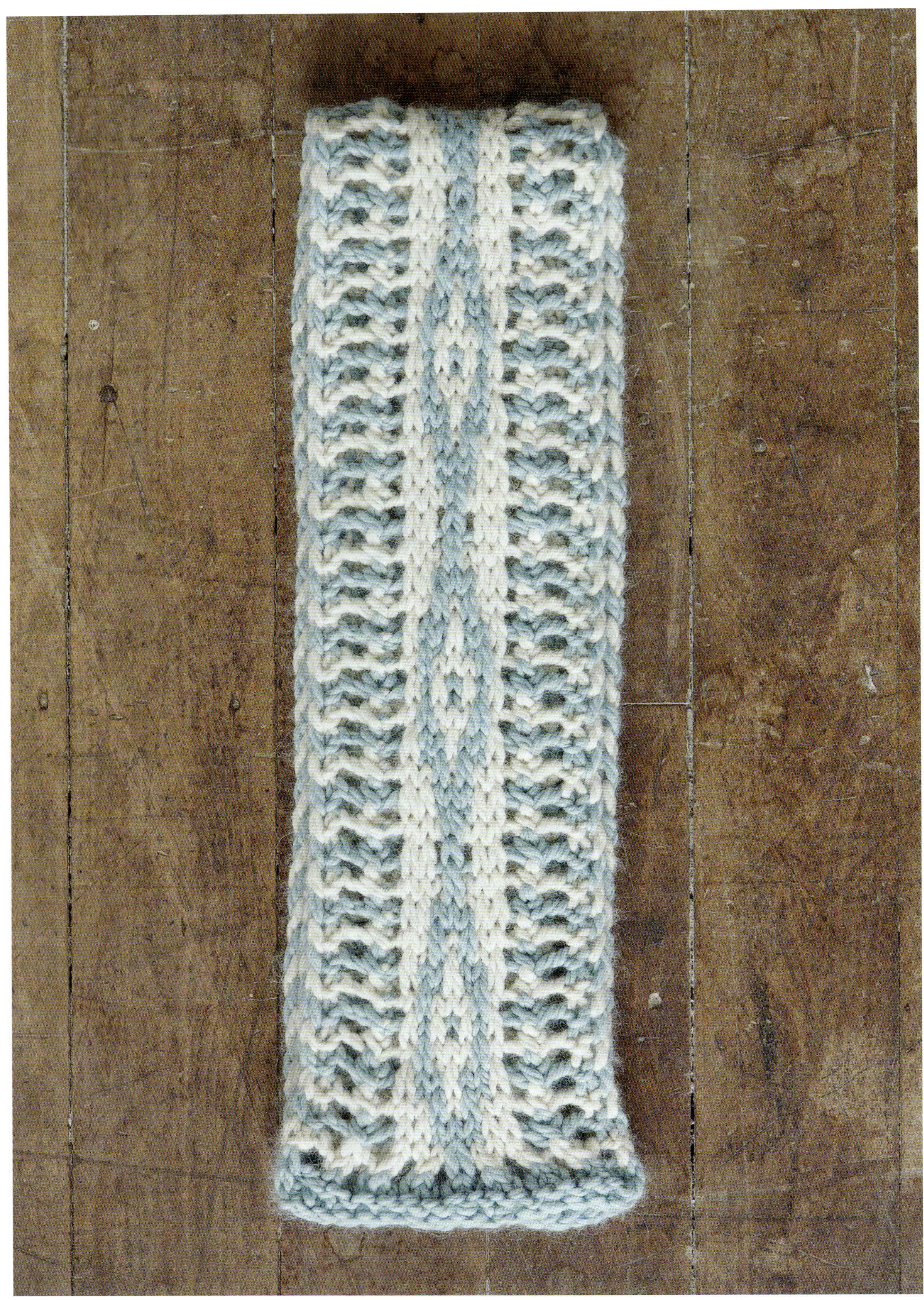

Instructions

Using Color A and knitted cast-on method (see Cast-on/Bind-off, page 107), CO 17 sts.

SET UP
Knit 2 rows.

Row 1 (RS): (K2tog, YO) four times, k1, (YO, ssk) four times.

Row 2 (WS): Sl1-wyif, k1, p5, k1, p1, k1, p5, k1, sl1-wyif.

SCARF
Work Chart A 12 times, then work Rows 1–22 of Chart A once more.

Cut Color B yarn, leaving tail to weave in later.

END
Row 1 (RS): (K2tog, YO) four times, k1, (YO, ssk) four times.

Row 2: Sl1-wyif, k1, p13, k1, sl1-wyif.

Row 3: K1, p15, k1.

With WS facing and using expandable lace bind-off method purl variant (see Cast-On/Bind-Off, page 109), BO all sts.

FINISHING
Weave in ends. Block to measurements. Trim ends.

Chart A

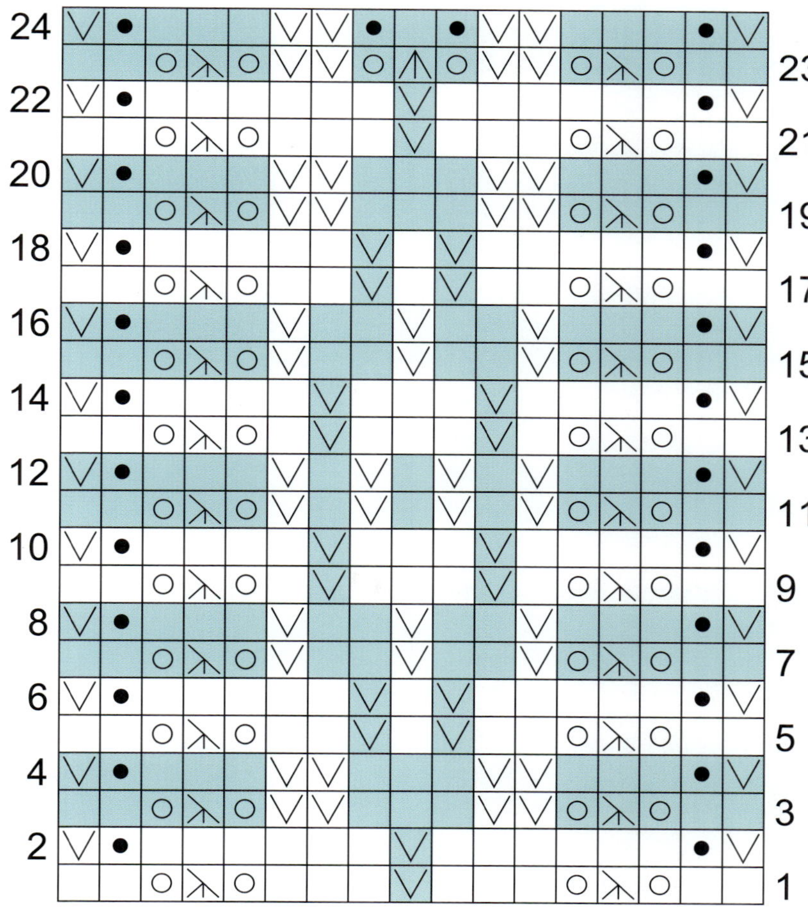

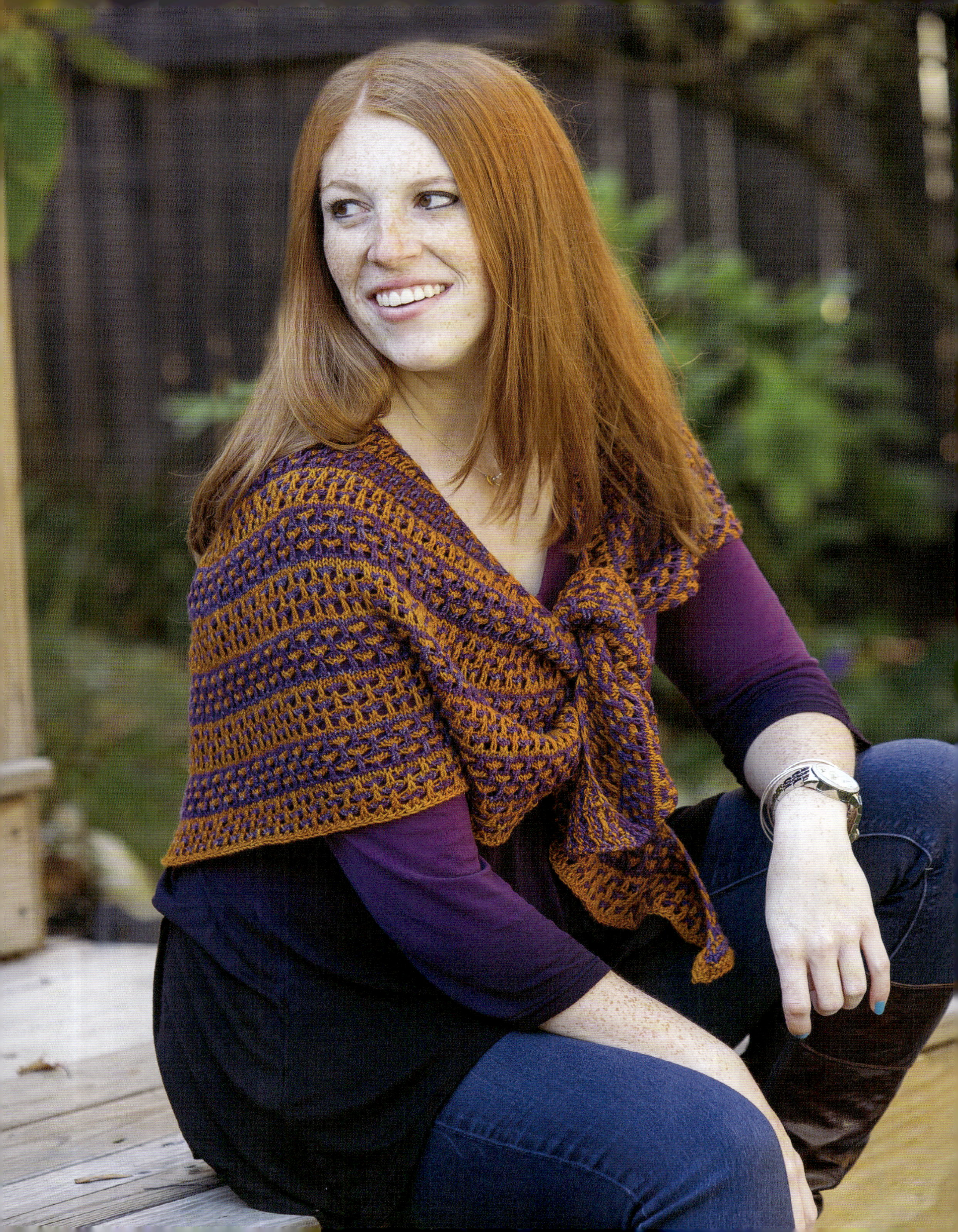

Love Child

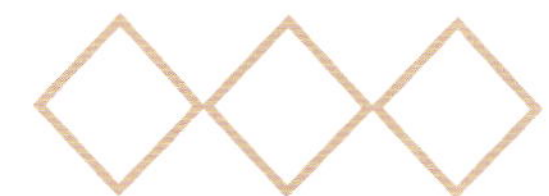

One thing I like to work into my patterns is a lot of "bang for your buck." For me that means a piece that looks like you did something quite complicated, when in fact you did not. This shawl consists of the same small motif worked repeatedly. The banded effect is created when you work an extra stockinette row between section repeats; this shifts the lace row of the motif to the opposite color. In Section One it is worked in Color A but in Section Two it is worked in Color B. This change causes a swap in color dominance, and switching back and forth creates the illusion of the wider color bands.

Finished Measurements: 20"/51 cm long x 43"/117 cm wingspan

Sizes: One size

Yarn

  Weight: Light fingering
  Gale's Art MYS 622; 60% merino wool, 20% silk, 20% yak; 400 yd/366 m per 3.53 oz/100 g
  Color A: Royal (1 skein)
  Color B: Copper (1 skein)
Needles: US size 6/4 mm
Gauge in Stockinette over 4"/10 cm: 20 sts and 24 rows (see A Note on Gauge page 12)

Special Stitch

kfYO2b: knit front, double yarn over, knit back; knit into the front leg of the next stitch but do not remove the stitch from the LH needle, wrap the working yarn around the right hand needle twice and then knit into the back loop of the same stitch. [3 stitches increased]

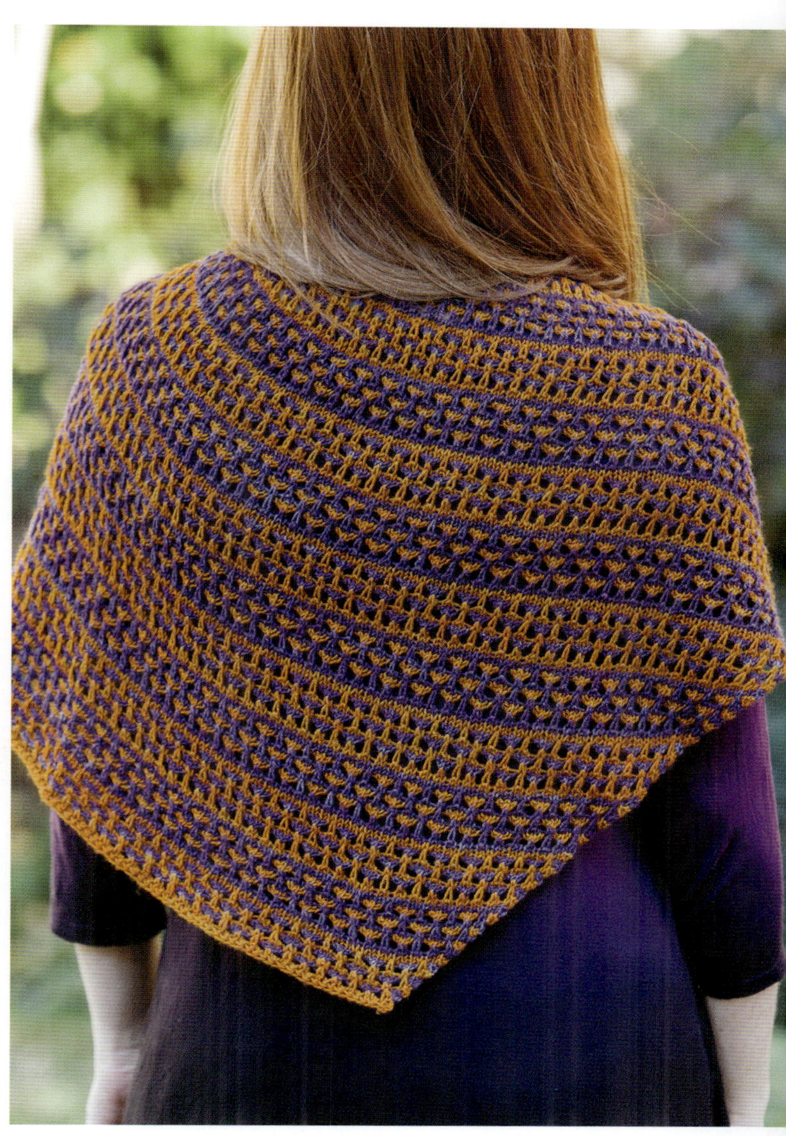

Instructions

Using Color A and long tail cast-on method (see Cast-on/Bind-off, page 107), CO 3 sts.

Knit one row.

SET UP
Row 1 (RS): K1, YO, k2. [4 sts]
Row 2 (WS): K4.
Row 3: K2, YO, k2. [5 sts]
Row 4: K2, kfb, k1, sl1. [6 sts]

Join in Color B.

Row 5 (RS): With B, k2, YO, k4. [7 sts]
Row 6 (WS): K3, p1, kfb, k1, sl1. [8 sts]
Row 7: With A, k2, YO, k2, YO, CDD, YO, k1. [9 sts]
Row 8: K1, p5, kfb, k1, sl1. [10 sts]
Row 9: With B, k2, YO, k1, sl1, k3, sl1, k2. [11 sts]
Row 10: K1, p1, sl1, p3, sl1, p1, kfb, k1, sl1. [12 sts]
Row 11: With A, k1, kfYO2b, (YO, CDD, YO, k1) twice, ssk. [14 sts]

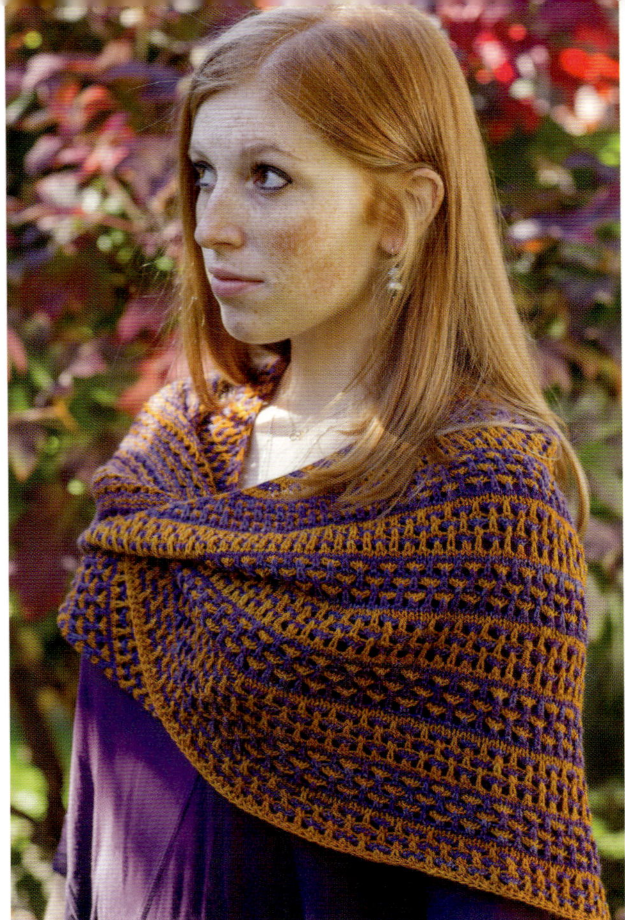

Row 12: K1, purl to double YO, knit into the front leg of the first YO and then the back leg of the second YO, k1, sl1.

SECTION ONE
Work Rows 1–4 (as follows) three times. [12 sts increased]

Row 1 (RS): With B, k1, kfYO2b, *sl1, k3; rep from * to last 4 sts, sl1, k1, ssk. [2 sts increased]
Row 2 (WS): K1, purl to double YO, slipping all Color A sts, knit into the front leg of the first YO and then the back leg of the second YO, k1, sl1.
Row 3: With A, k1, kfYO2b, *YO, CDD, YO, k1; rep from * to last 2 sts, ssk. [2 sts increased]
Row 4: K1, purl to double YO, knit into the front leg of the first YO and then the back leg of the second YO, k1, sl1.

TRANSITION ONE
Row 1 (RS): With B, K1, kfYO2b, knit to last 2 sts, ssk. [2 sts increased]
Row 2 (WS): K1, purl to double YO, knit into the front leg of the first YO and then the back leg of the second YO, k1, sl1.

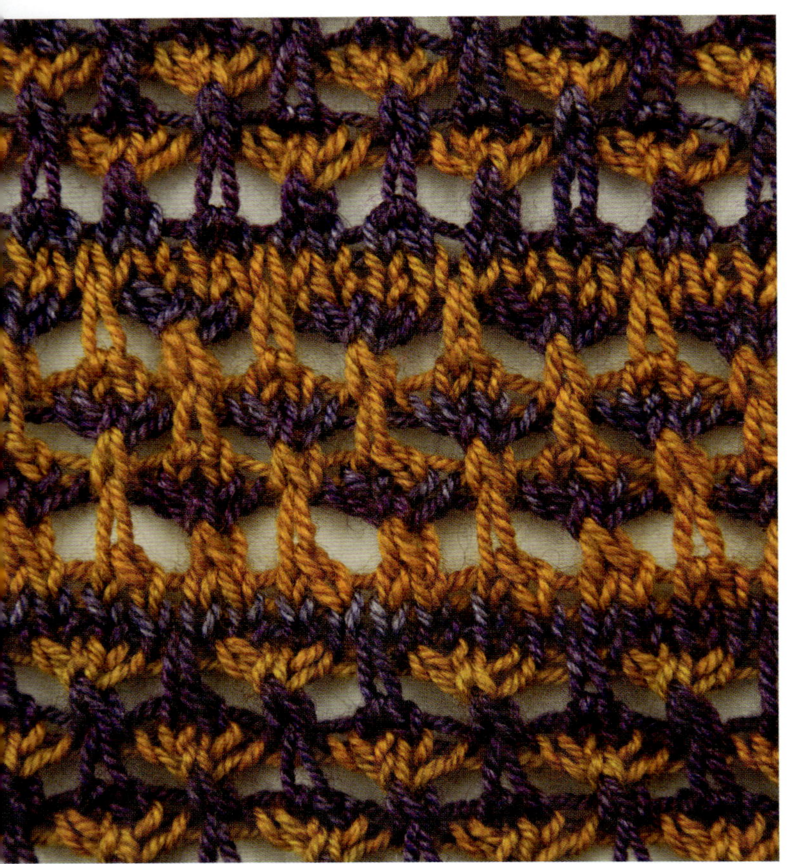

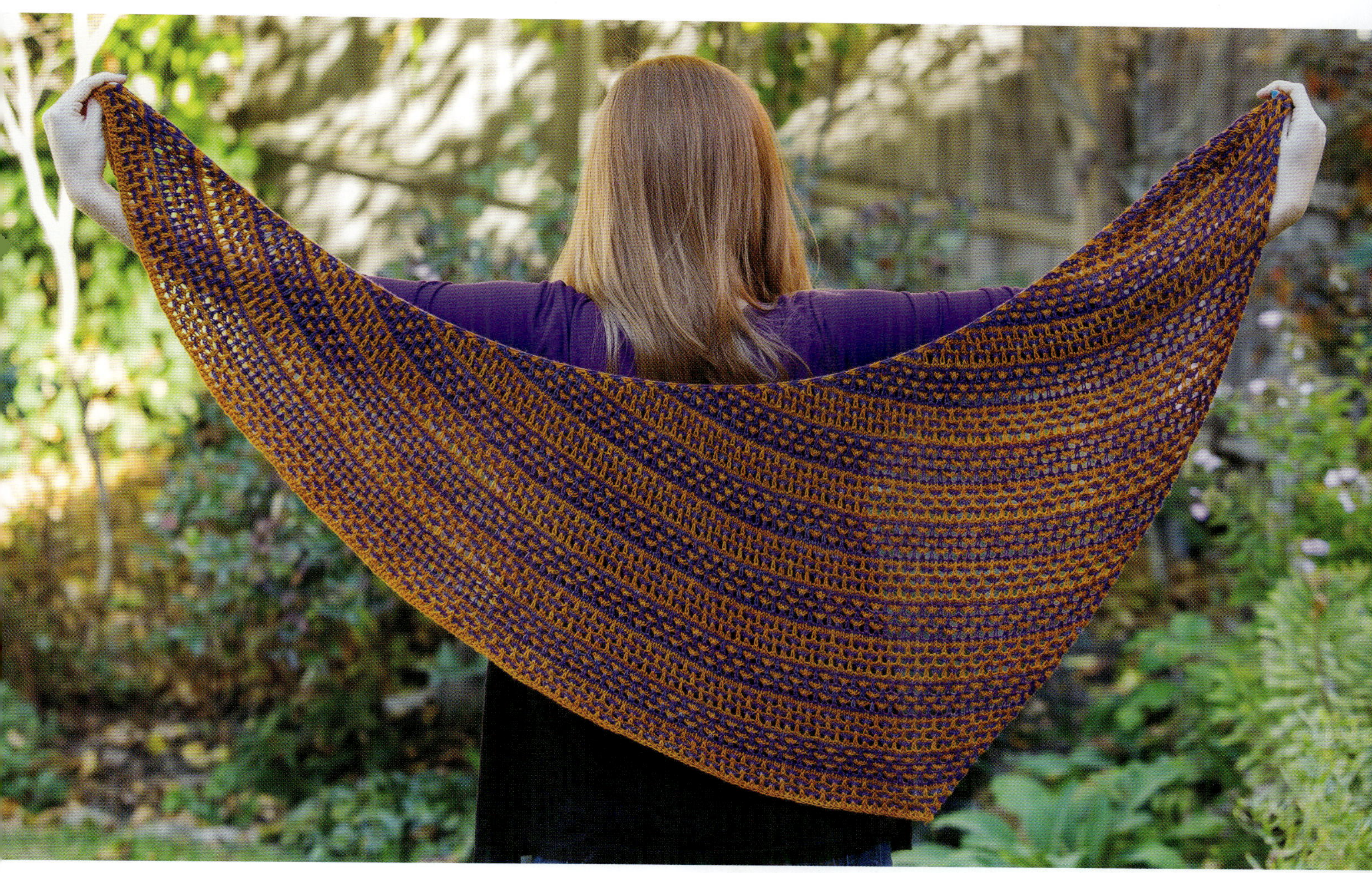

SECTION TWO

Work Rows 1–4 (as follows) three times. [12 sts increased]

Row 1 (RS): With A, k1, kfYO2b, k2, *sl1, k3; rep from * to last 4 sts, sl1, k1, ssk. [2 sts increased]

Row 2 (WS): K1, purl to double YO, slipping all Color B sts, knit into the front leg of the first YO and then the back leg of the second YO, k1, sl1.

Row 3: With B, k1, kfYO2b, k2, *YO, CDD, YO, k1; rep from * to last 2 sts, ssk. [2 sts increased]

Row 4: K1, purl to double YO, knit into the front leg of the first YO and then the back leg of the second YO, k1, sl1.

TRANSITION TWO

Row 1 (RS): With A, k1, kfYO2b, knit to last 2 sts, ssk. [2 sts increased]

Row 2 (WS): K1, purl to double YO, knit into the front leg of the first YO and then the back leg of the second YO, k1, sl1.

Work Section One through Transition Two seven more times, then work Section One through Section Two once more. [264 sts]

With RS facing, using B and the very stretchy lace bind-off method (see Cast-on/Bind-off, page 110), BO all sts.

FINISHING

Weave in ends. Block well to open up the lace. Make sure to pull the bound off edge out into a nice, swooping curve. Trim ends.

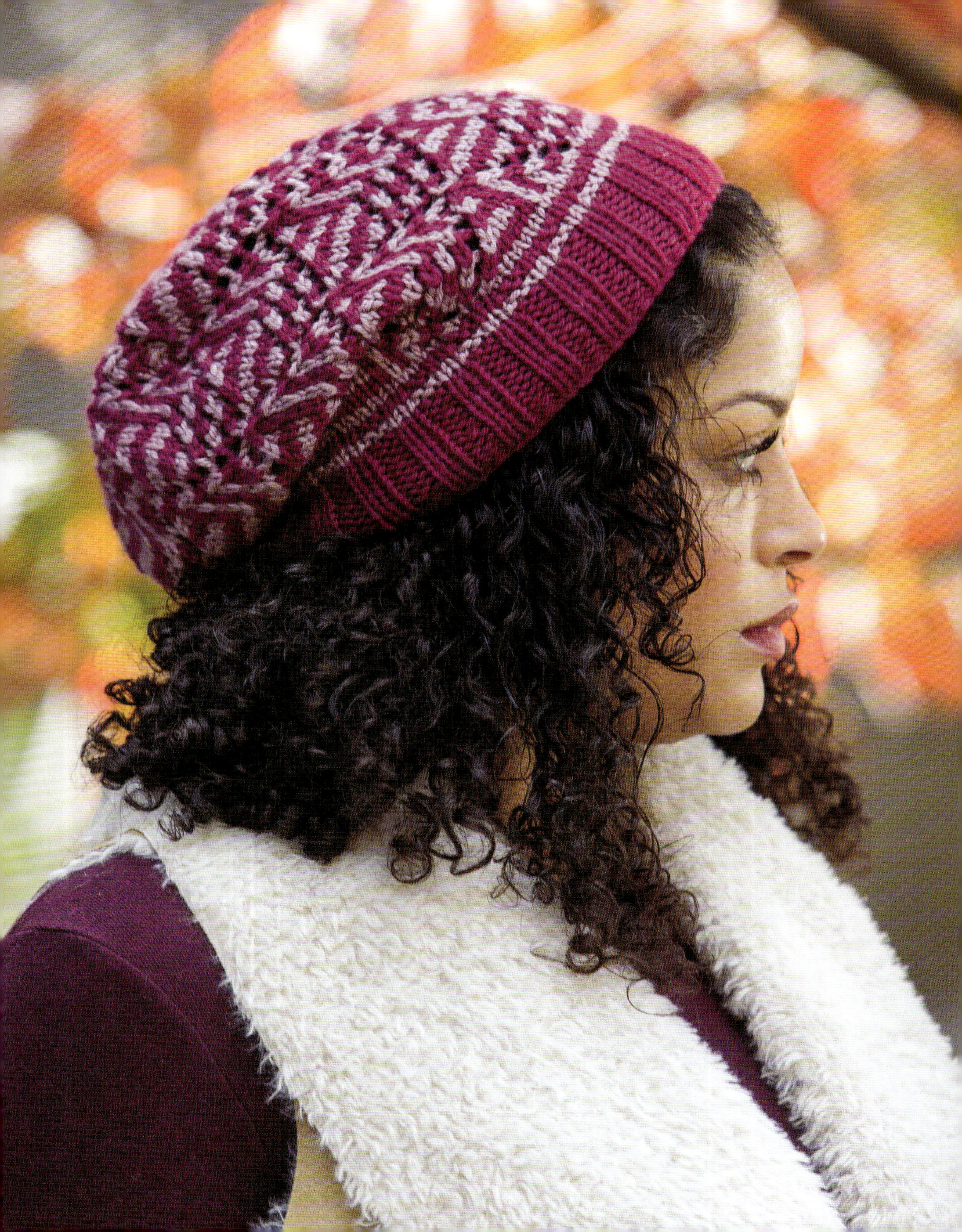

Sailing Diamonds

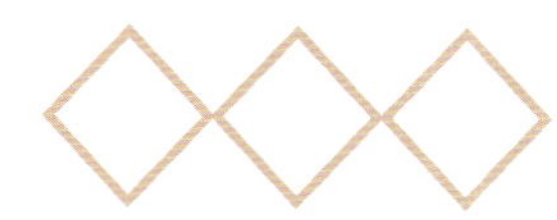

Combining mosaic and lace allows me to do something that gives me no end of joy—make my knitting do something that it isn't "supposed" to do. Causing horizontal stripes to magically become vertical stripes is one of those tricks. The horizontal stripes in this hat run directly into vertical stripes that flow up out of the lace at the base of the diamond motif. I thought it gave the diamonds the appearance of a sailboat, hence its name.

Finished Measurements: 18.5"/47 cm around brim (stretches to 24"/61 cm), 11"/28 cm tall

Sizes: One size

Yarn

  Weight: DK

  Knit Picks Gloss™ DK; 70% merino wool, 30% silk; 123 yd/112 m per 1.76 oz/50 g

  Color A: Fairy Tale (1 skein)

  Color B: Velveteen (1 skein)

Needles: US size 6/4 mm and US size 5/3.75 mm, preferred needles for knitting in the round (see Knitting in the Round, page 105)

Notions: Stitch marker

Gauge in Stockinette over 4"/10 cm: 16 sts and 24 rows (see A Note on Gauge, page 12)

Notes

- Because there are decreases that bridge the rounds there are spots where it is necessary to juggle the stitches a bit at the beginning of some rounds.

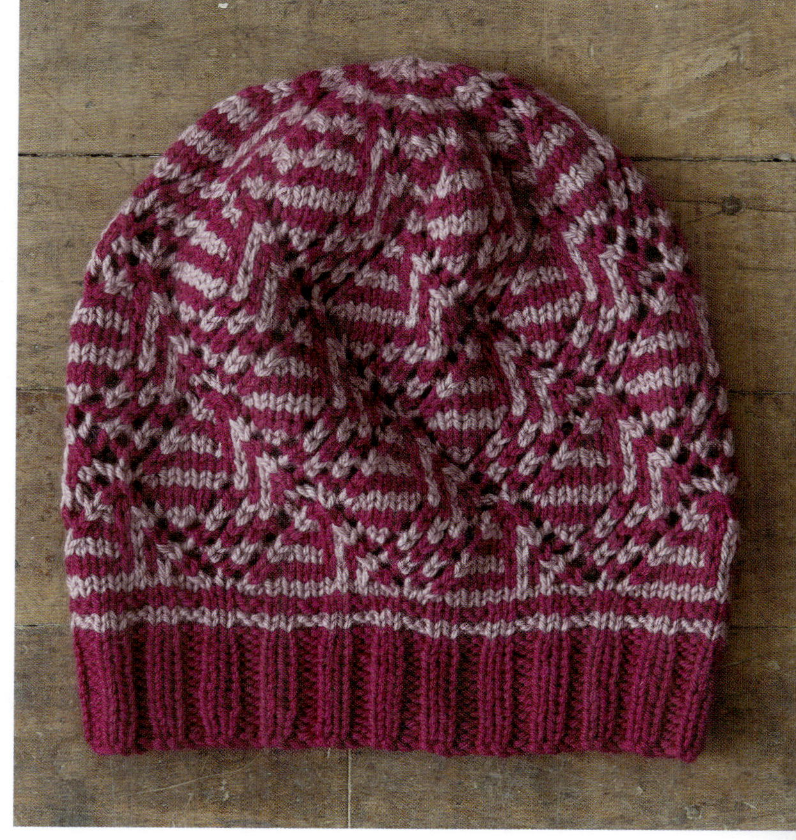

Instructions

Using Color A, cable cast-on method (see Cast-On/Bind-Off, page 105), smaller needle, and preferred method of knitting in the round, CO 96 sts. Place marker to indicate beginning of round and join to work in the round, being careful not to twist sts.

Chart A

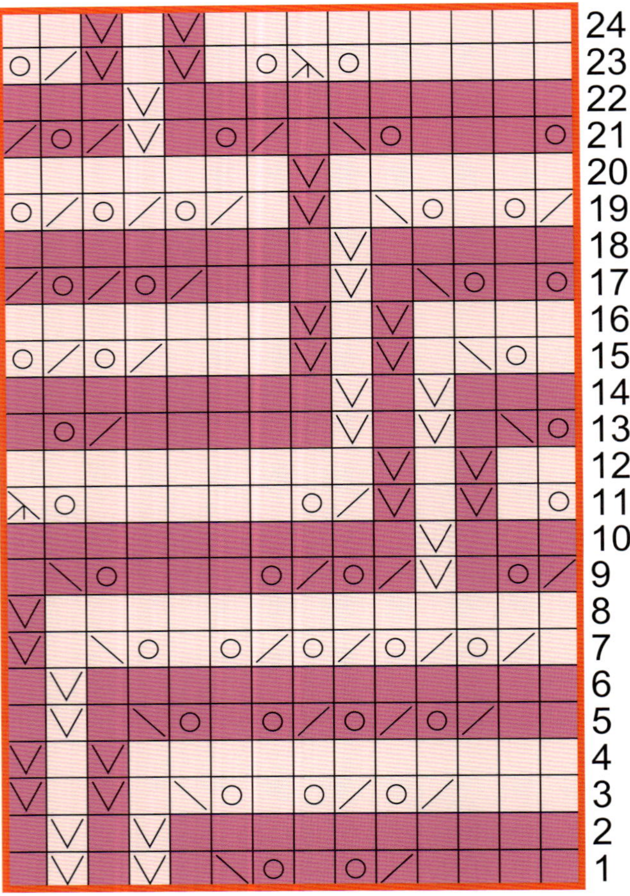

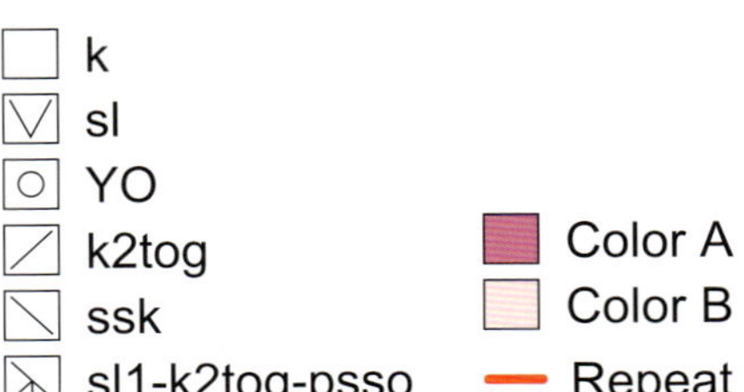

Repeat x 7

	k
∨	sl
⊙	YO
╱	k2tog
╲	ssk
⋈	sl1-k2tog-psso

Color A
Color B
— Repeat

BRIM

Rounds 1–12: *K2, p2; rep from * to end of round.

Join in Color B

Round 13: With B, knit.
Round 14: Sl1, k1, p2, *k2, p2; rep from * to end of round.
Round 15: With A, knit.
Round 16: Sl1, k1, p2, *k2, p2; rep from * to end of round.
Round 17: With B, (k1, M1, k47) twice. [98 sts]

Switch to larger needle.

Round 18: Knit.

Work Chart A twice, repeating each round 7 times around.

Note: Begin Rounds 11, 17, and 21 by removing beginning of round marker, slipping first st, replacing marker, then working chart as shown. This first stitch needs to be "borrowed" for the last decrease of the round.

Decrease Chart

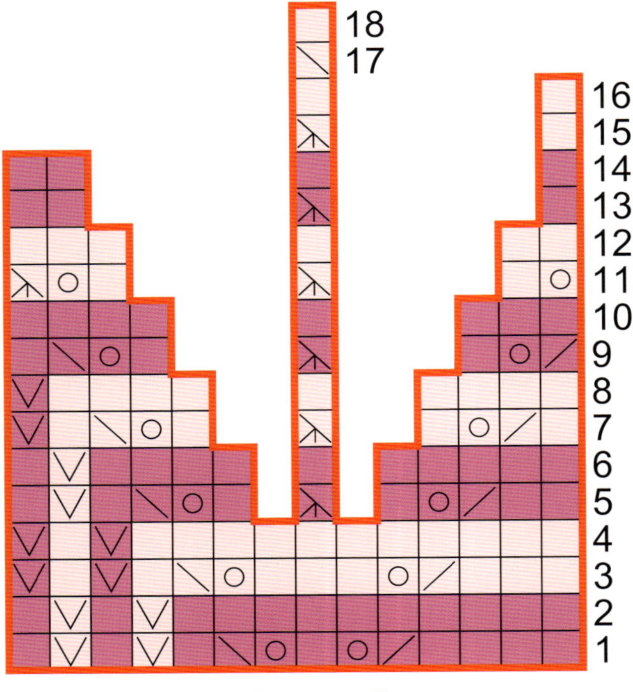

Repeat x 7

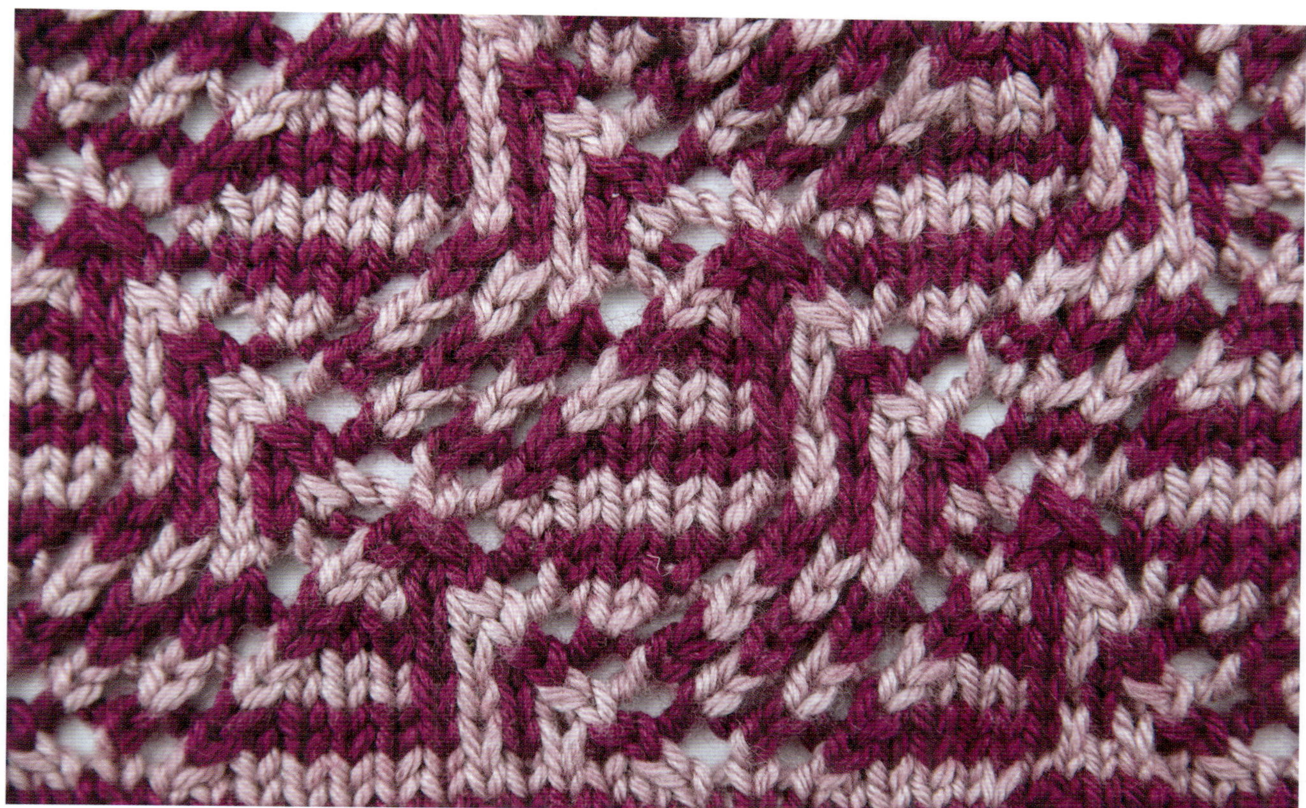

CROWN

Work Decrease Chart, repeating each round 7 times around. [7 sts]

Note: Begin Rounds 11 and 15 by removing beginning of round marker, slipping first st, replacing marker, then working chart as shown. This first stitch needs to be "borrowed" for the last decrease of the round.

Cut yarn leaving a 7"/18 cm tail.

Use a tapestry needle to transfer sts from needle to yarn tail. Pull tail to cinch tightly closed.

FINISHING

Weave in ends. Block over bowl or balloon, being careful to not stretch out ribbing. Trim ends.

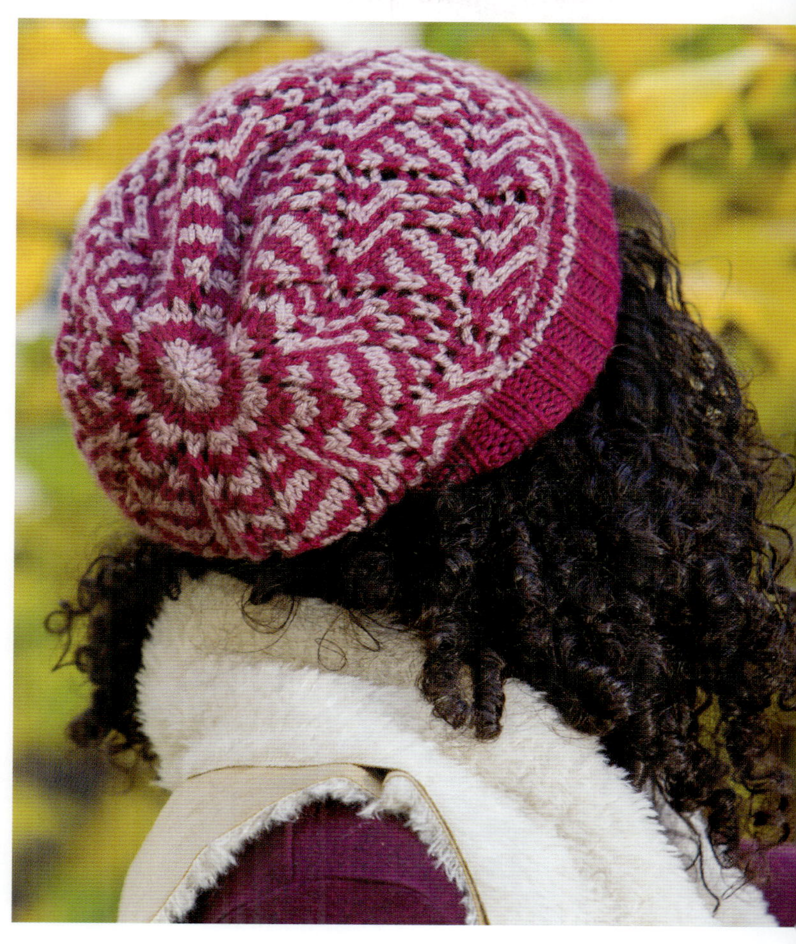

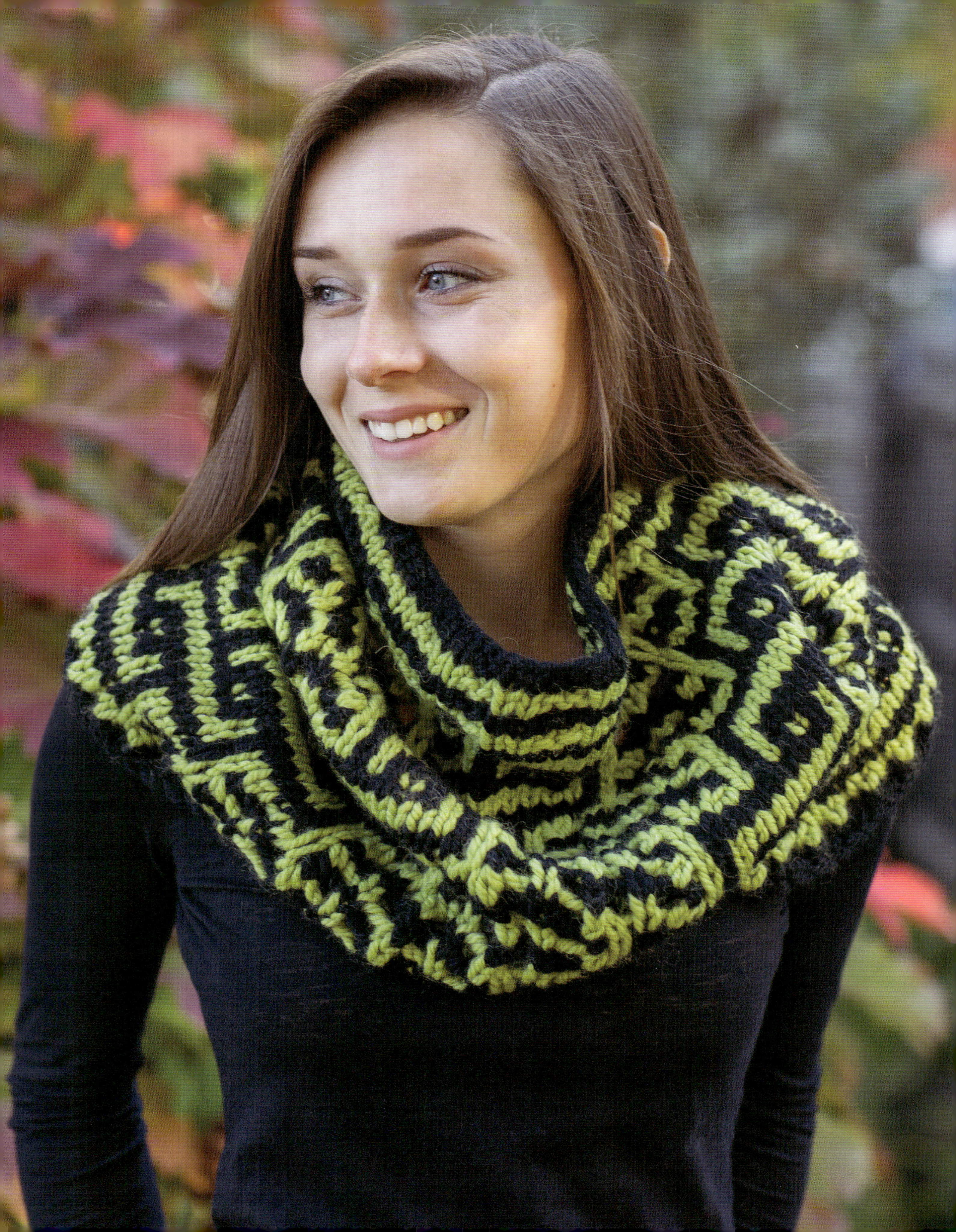

Your Princess Is in Another Castle

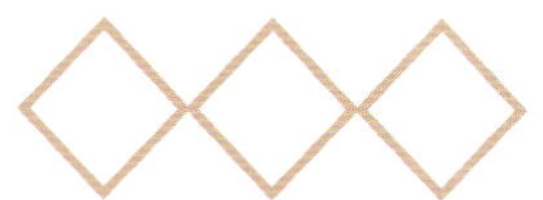

I hope you will forgive me my little joke with this name. It is a reference to a video game from my childhood where you battle your way through bad guys only to find that your objective (the princess) resides in another location. Both the graphically punchy combination of colors and the twisting, climbing motifs in this oversized cowl are intended to evoke thoughts of early 8-bit gaming graphics. If this piece were worked solely in mosaic it would be able to stand up by itself. The addition of the separating lace allows it to bunch up nicely around the neck.

Finished Measurements: 18"/46 cm long, 24.5"/62 cm circumference at neckline, 36.5"/93 cm circumference at hem

Sizes: One size

Yarn

  Weight: Bulky

  Patons Classic Wool Bulky; 100% wool; 78 yd/71 m per 3.53 oz/100 g

  Color A: Black (2 skeins)

  Color B: Spring Green (2 skeins)

Needles: US size 13/9 mm circular needle, 40"/100 cm in length (see Knitting in the Round, page 105)

Notions: Stitch marker

Gauge in Stockinette over 4"/10 cm: 10 sts and 14 rows (see A Note on Gauge, page 12)

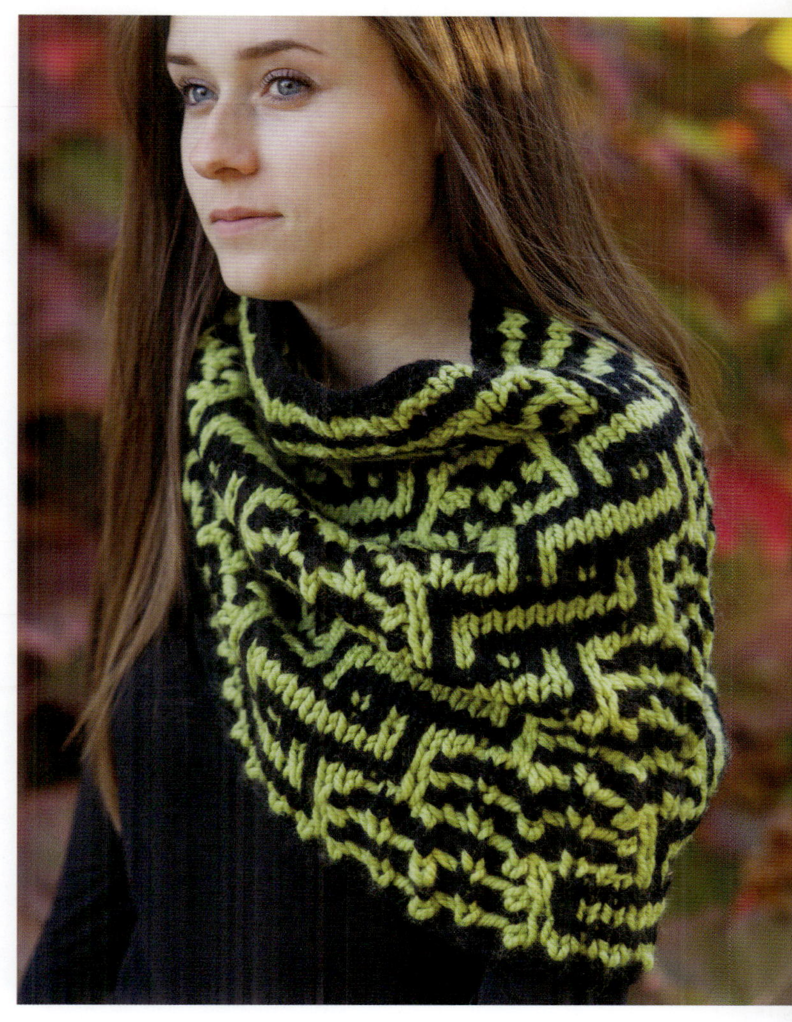

Instructions

Using the cable cast-on method (see Cast-On/ Bind-Off, page 105) and Color A, CO 88 sts, do not join.

SET UP

Foundation Row (RS): *K1, p1; rep from * to end of row.

Use the following technique to join to work in the round, being careful not to twist sts. Slip first stitch purl-wise to RH needle, place marker to indicate beginning of round.

Round 1: With B, *YO, k2tog; rep from * to end of round.
Round 2: Knit.

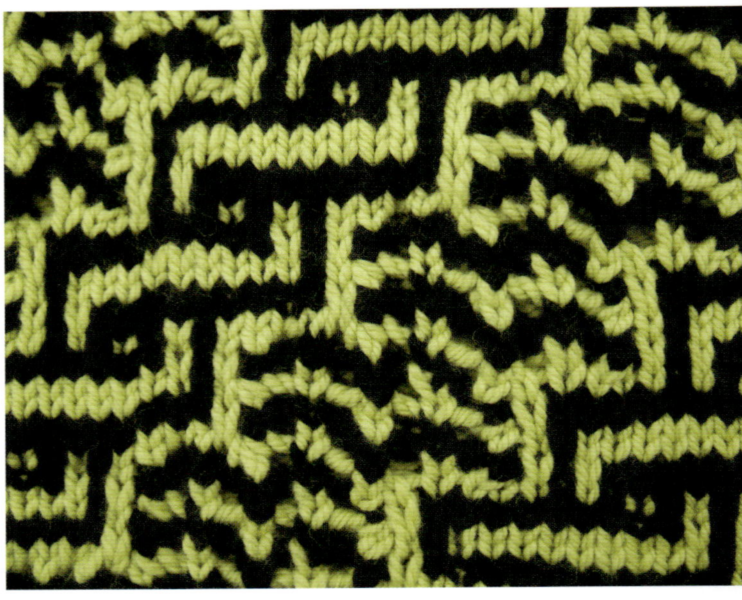

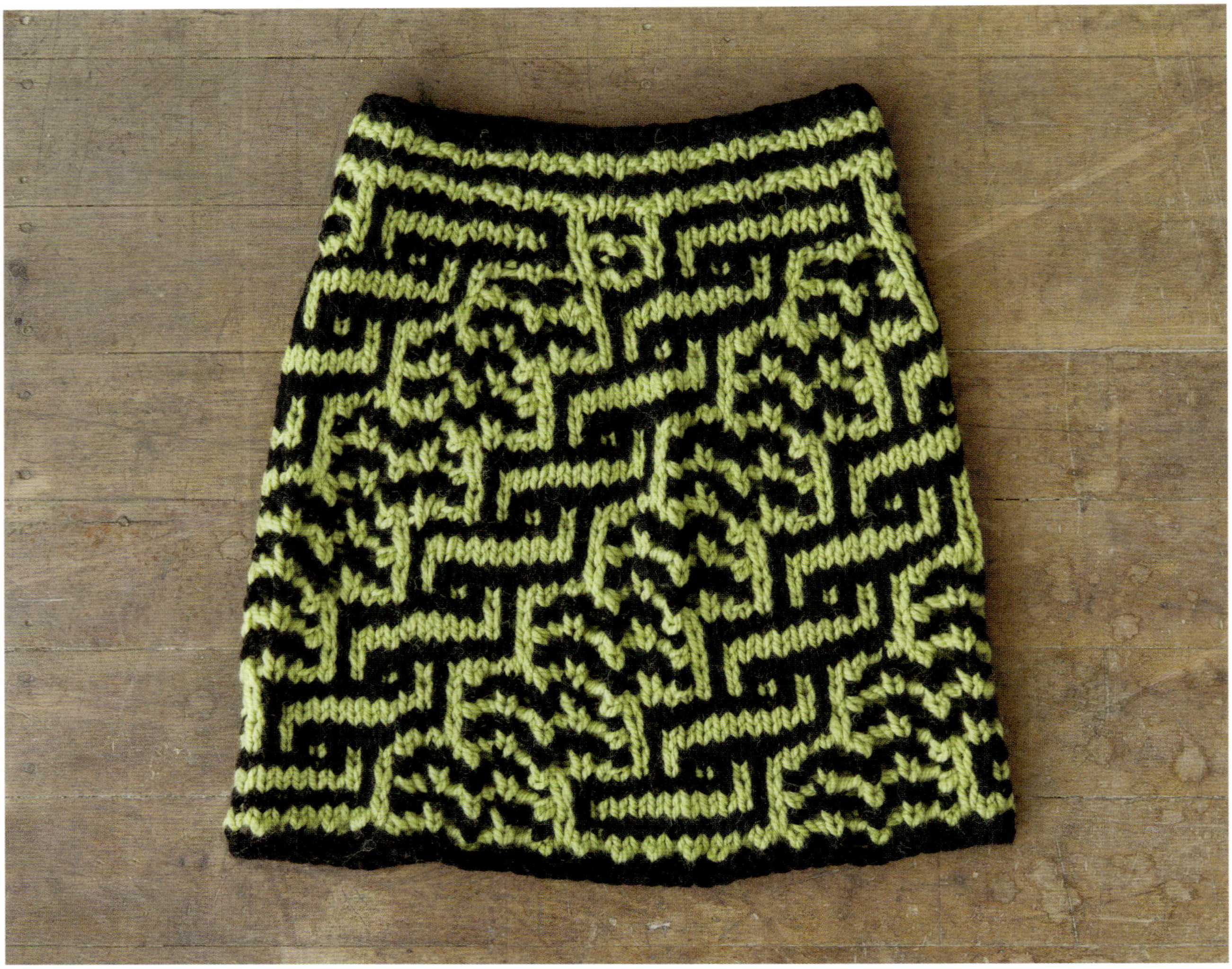

BODY

Work Charts A, B, and then C, repeating each chart 4 times around. [64 sts]

END

Round 1: With B, knit.
Round 2: *K2, p2; rep from * to end of round.
Rounds 3 and 4: With A, repeat Rounds 1 and 2.

Work Rounds 1–4 once more.

Using the 2 x 2 ribbing method (see Cast-On/Bind-Off, page 109), BO all sts.

FINISHING

Weave in ends. Block assertively to shape, tapering to match where the decrease section begins. If you have crease lines where the piece was blocked flat, refold so that they are flattened out, steam, and pat lightly to remove crease. Trim ends.

Chart A

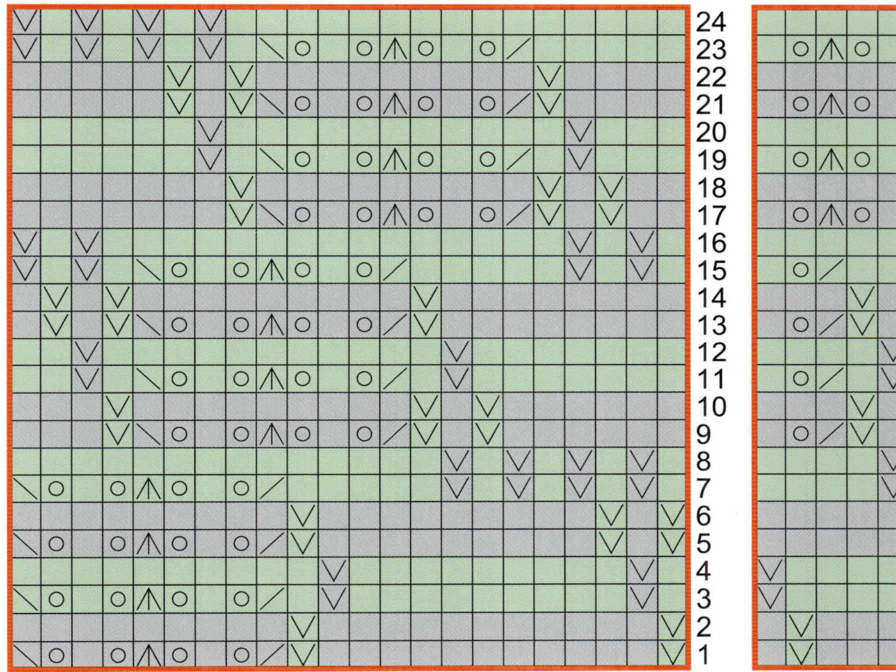

Repeat x 4

Chart B

Repeat x 4

Chart C

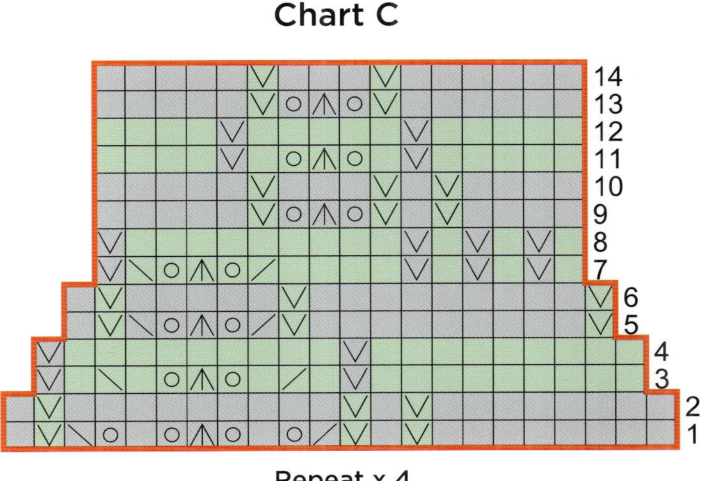

Repeat x 4

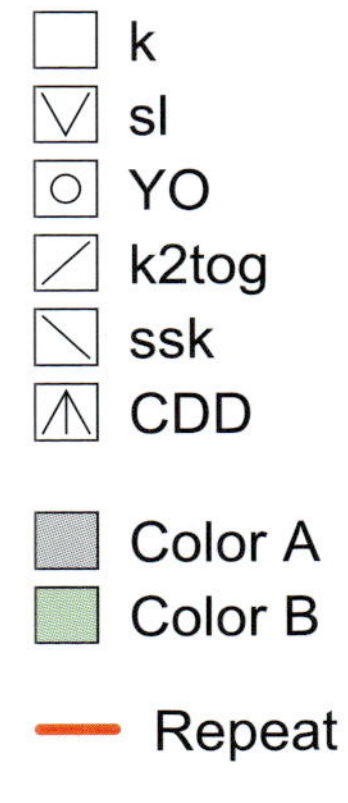

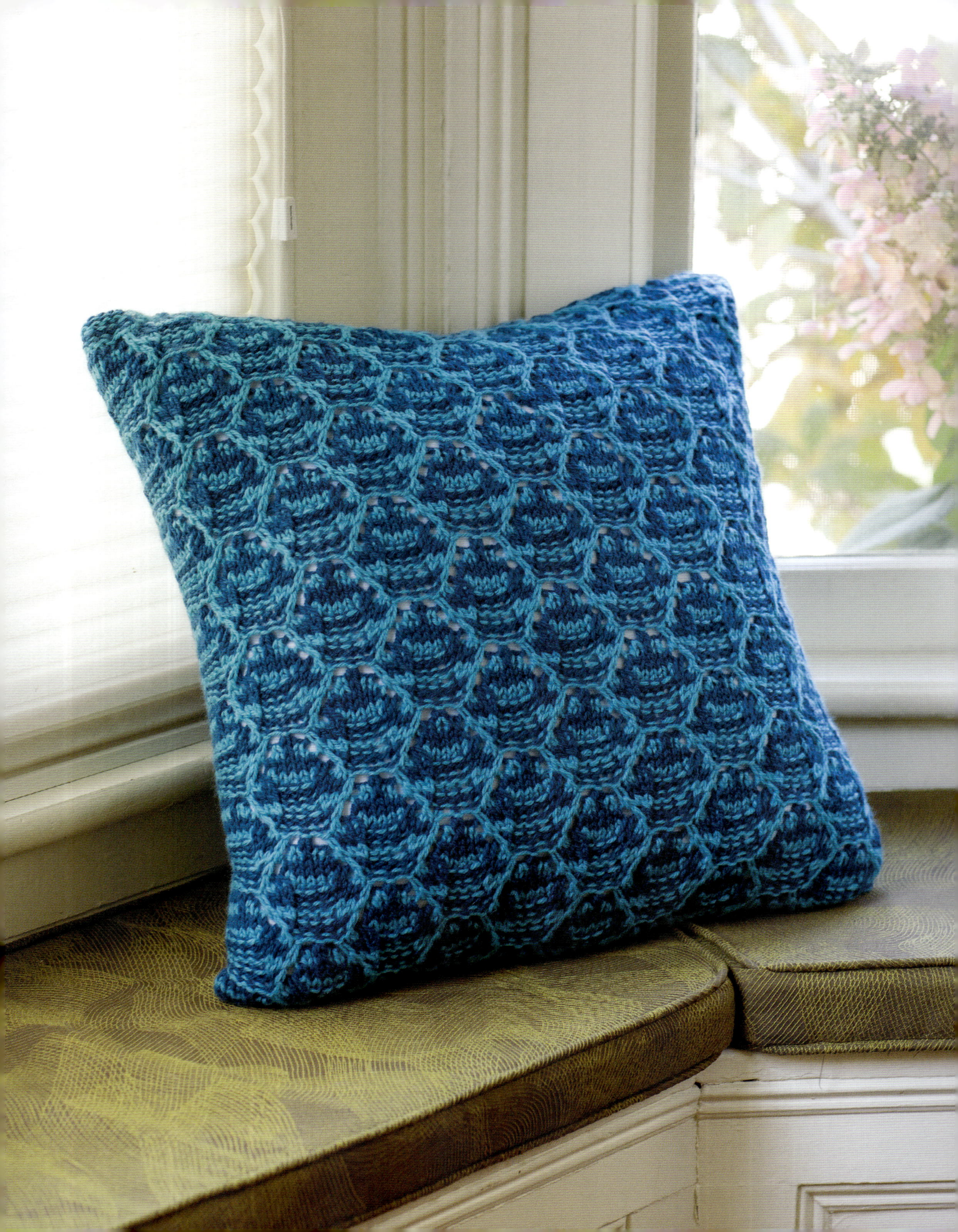

Cush Job

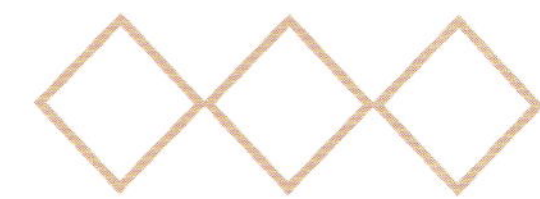

The fancy side of this pillow features a hexagonal pattern created by combining the manipulation of the slipped stitches with the distortion caused by spacing increases and their decreases apart. If you were to work this lace without the colorwork, you might not believe that the hexagons were possible. On the flip side, I chose a simple, solid mosaic pattern to provide a styling option for your home.

Finished Measurements: 20"/51 cm square
Sizes: One size
Yarn
  Weight: Worsted
  Patons Classic Wool Worsted; 100% wool;
    210 yd/192 m per 3.53 oz/100 g
  Color A: Peacock (2 skeins)
  Color B: Aquarium (2 skeins)
Needles: US size 8/5 mm circular needle,
  32"/80 cm long (see Knitting in the Round,
  page 105)
Notions: Stitch marker, 20"/51 cm square
  pillow form
Gauge in Stockinette over 4"/10 cm: 16 sts and
  24 rows (see A Note on Gauge, page 12)

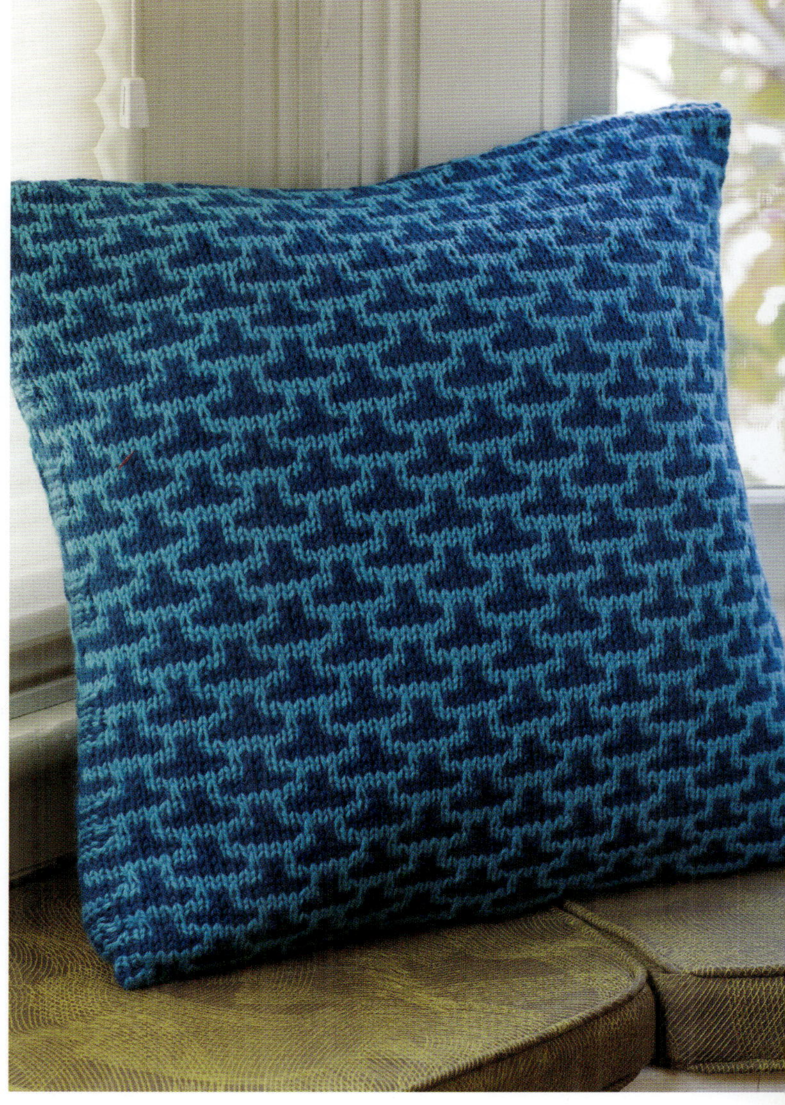

Instructions

Using Color B, cable cast-on method (see Cast-On/Bind-Off, page 105), and your preferred method of knitting in the round, CO 154 sts. Place marker to indicate beginning of round and join to work in the round, being careful not to twist sts.

Knit 2 rounds.

BODY

Note: YO2 are not increases—on the following round drop one of the loops and knit into the other.

Work Chart A across first 77 sts, repeating indicated sts 5 times, place marker, work Chart B across final 77 sts, repeating indicated sts 7 times.

Repeat Rounds 1–16 of both charts 7 more times for a total of 8 repeats.

With A, knit 2 rounds.

Using the expandable lace bind-off, knit variant method (see Cast-On/Bind-Off, page 109), BO all sts.

FINISHING

Block to finished measurements, or slightly smaller. Do not over block.

Use mattress stitch (see Joining Techniques, page 112) to join the cast-on edges, insert pillow, and then use mattress stitch to close bound-off edges.

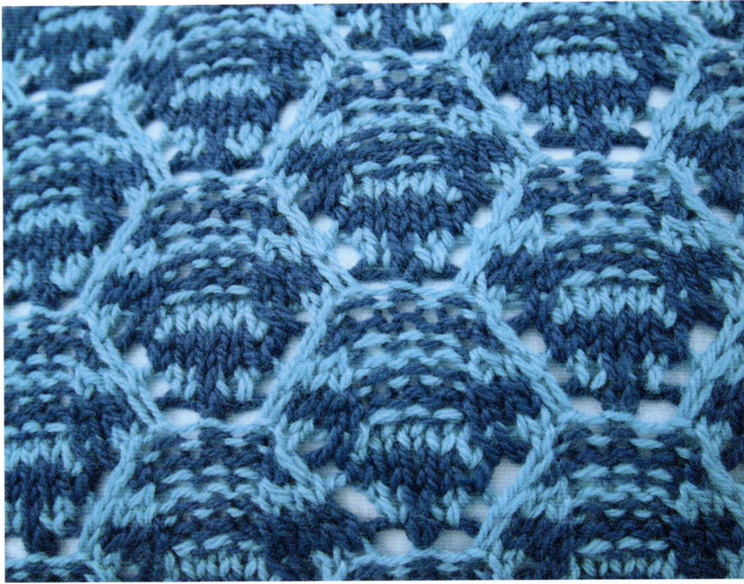

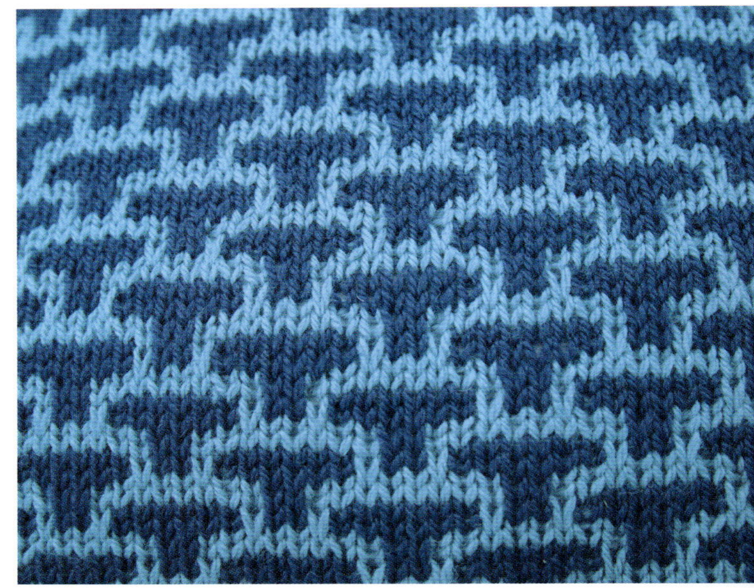

Chart A

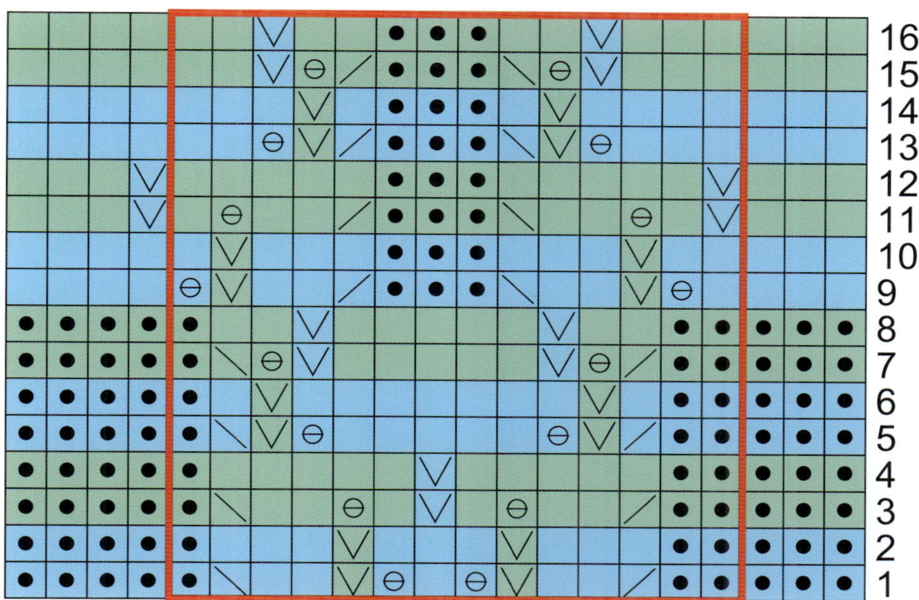

Chart B

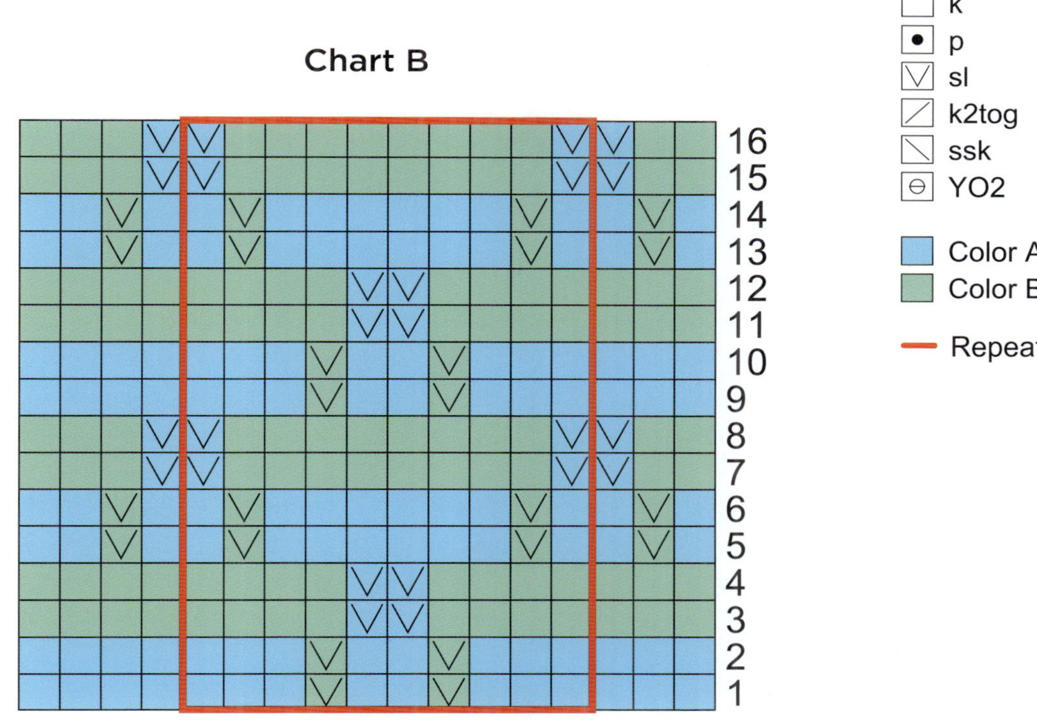

k
p
sl
k2tog
ssk
YO2

Color A
Color B
Repeat

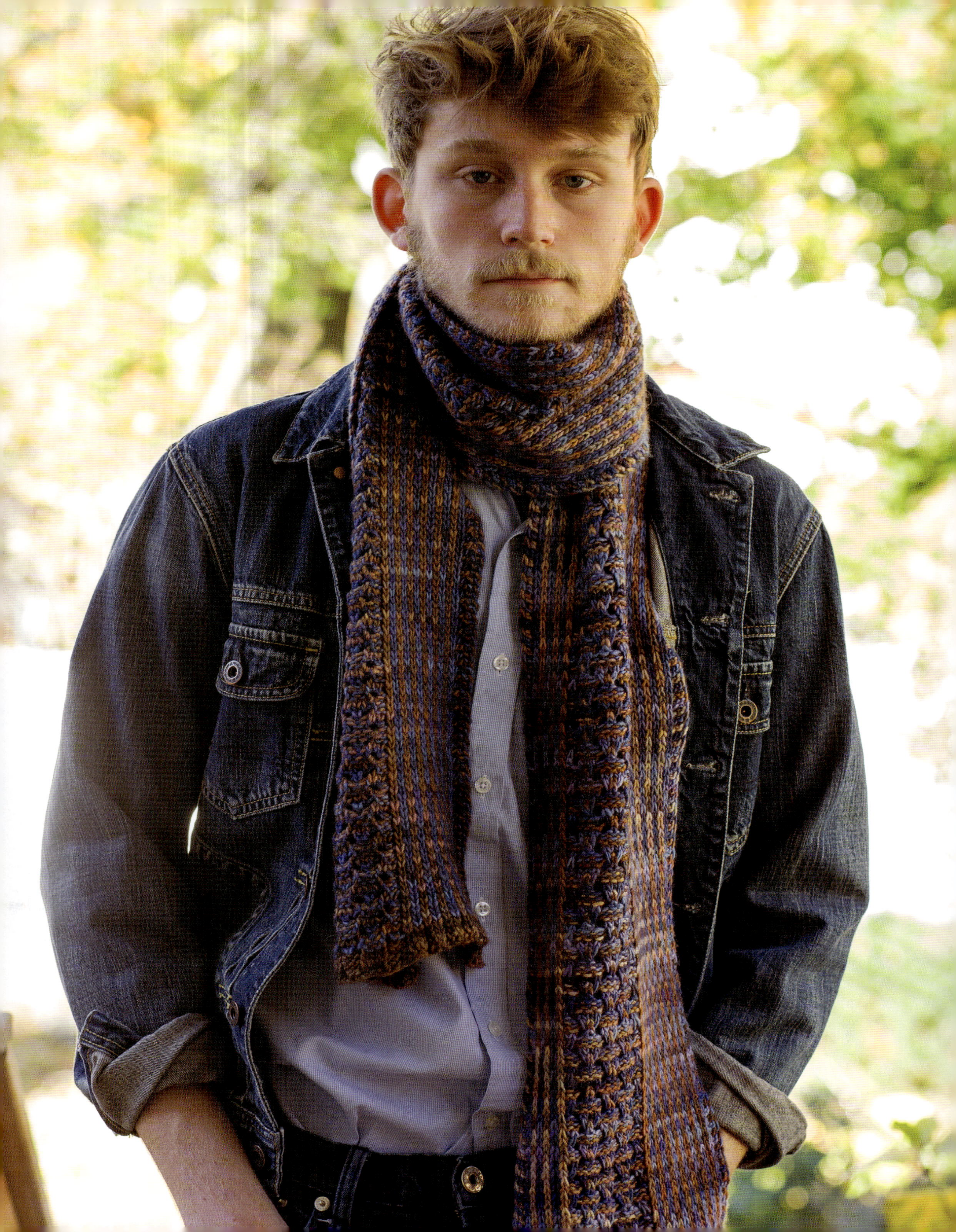

Rock City Scarf

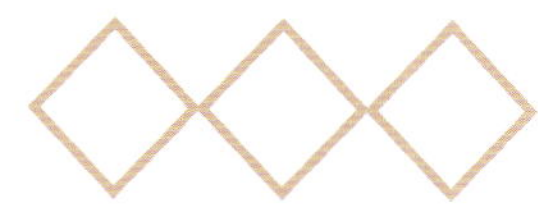

Creating a design that incorporates lace and yet is still unisex enough to look good on a man is quite a challenge. The subtle mosaic lace offset into the body of vertical striping manages to fit the bill. Of course, color choice is a big part of swaying the finished piece towards either masculine or feminine and fortunately there are many colors to choose from! Another fun element of this scarf is that it is fully reversible. The particular combination of slipping with the yarn in front and back depending on what color you are using creates a fabric that is essentially double knit.

Finished Measurements: 7.25"/18.5 cm wide, 75"/109.5 cm long

Sizes: One size

Yarn

  Weight: DK

  Malabrigo Rastita; 100% merino wool; 310 yd/283 m per 3.53 oz/100 g

  Color A: Peacock (1 skein)

  Color B: Piedras (1 skein)

Needles: US size 7/4.5 mm

Gauge in Stockinette over 4"/10 cm: 16 sts and 26 rows (see A Note on Gauge, page 12)

Notes

• This project falls into the "unless directed otherwise" category. Please note that there are many stitches where you slip a stitch with the yarn held to the right side of the work. This is deliberate to create the reversible vertical stripes.

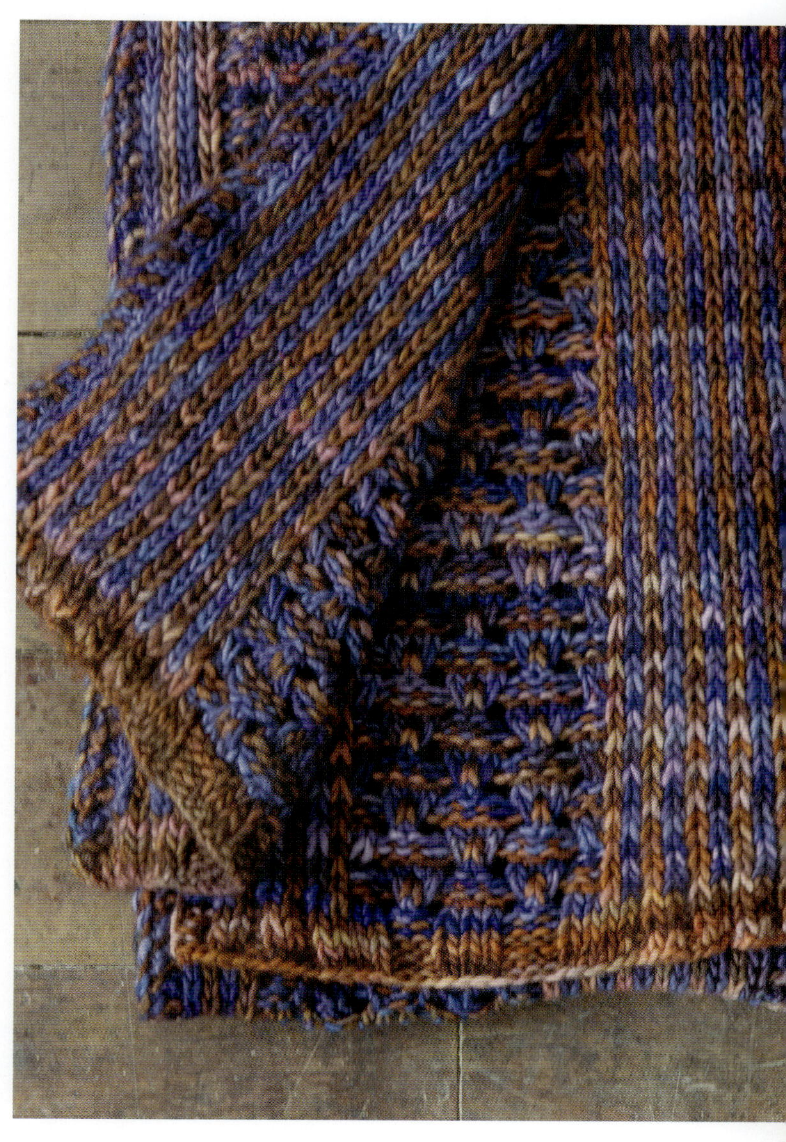

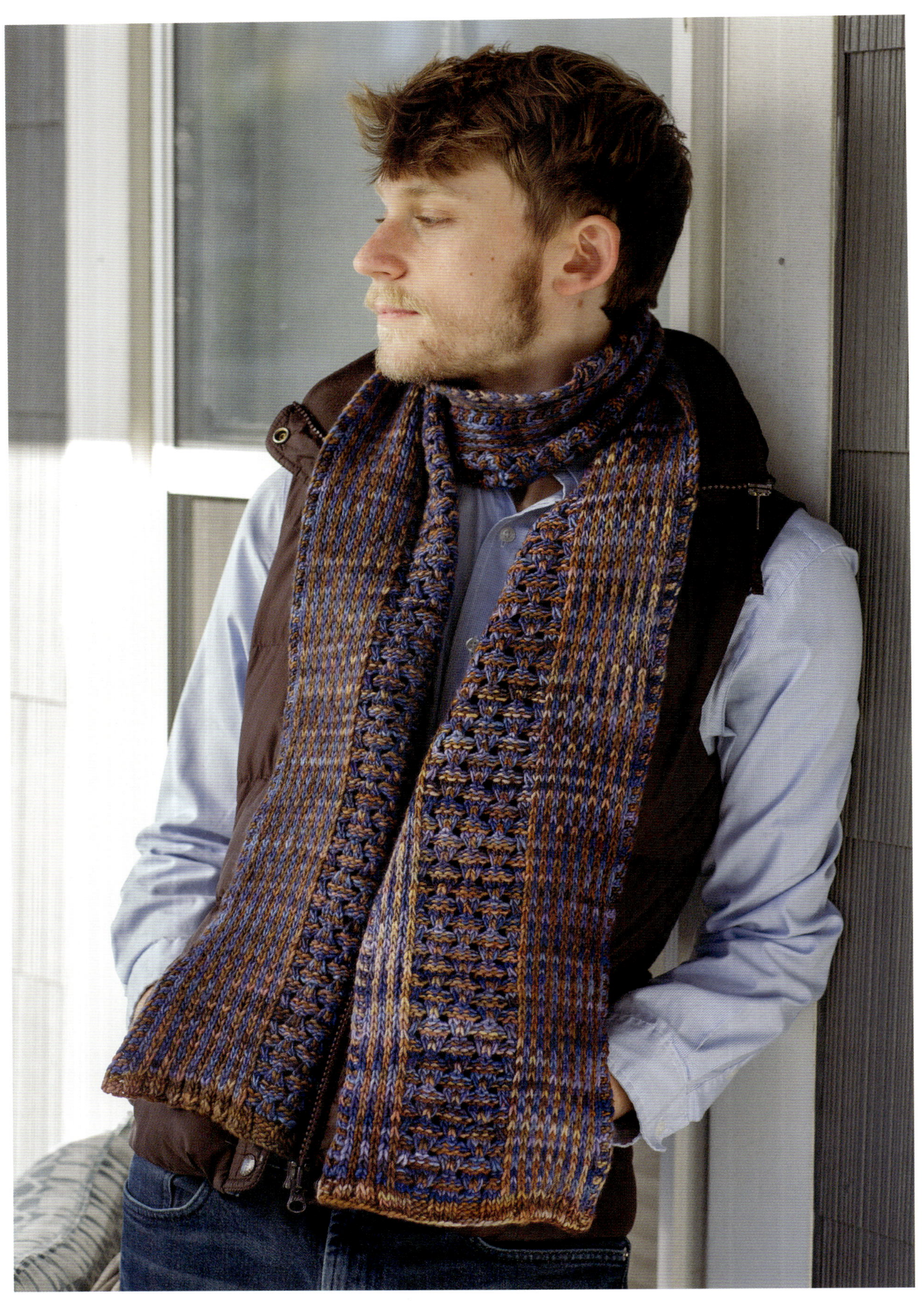

Instructions

Using Color B and cable cast-on method (see Cast-On/Bind-Off, page 105), CO 55 sts.

RIBBED EDGING

Row 1 (RS): K1, k2tog, YO, (k2, p2) twice, k4, p3, k3, p3, k4, (p2, k2) six times, YO, ssk, k1.

Row 2 (WS): Sl1-wyif, (k2, p2) six times, k2, p4, k3, p3, k3, p4, (k2, p2) twice, k2, sl1-wyif.

Repeat Rows 1 and 2 once for a total of 4 rows of ribbing.

BODY

Join in Color A.

Work Chart A, repeating indicated sections as written, until you have used up most of your yarn (approximately 84 repeats), ending with Row 6.

RIBBED EDGING

Switch to Color B and work Ribbed Edging as before. On final stitch, knit instead of slip.

Using knit/purl stretchy bind-off method, in pattern variant (see Cast-On/Bind-Off, page 110), BO all sts.

FINISHING

Weave in ends. Block assertively. Trim ends.

Chart A

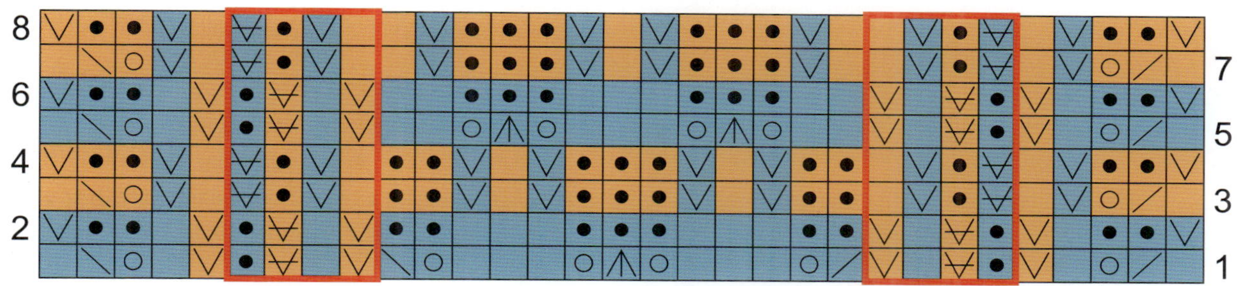

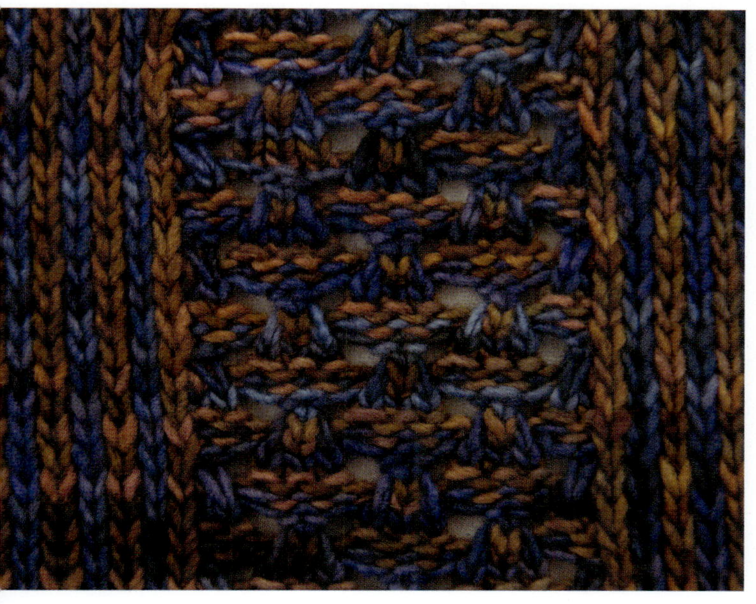

	RS: k; WS: p
•	RS: p; WS: k
V	RS: sl; WS: sl-wyif
ⱴ	RS: sl-wyif; WS: sl
O	YO
/	k2tog
\	ssk
⋀	CDD

Color A
Color B
— Repeat

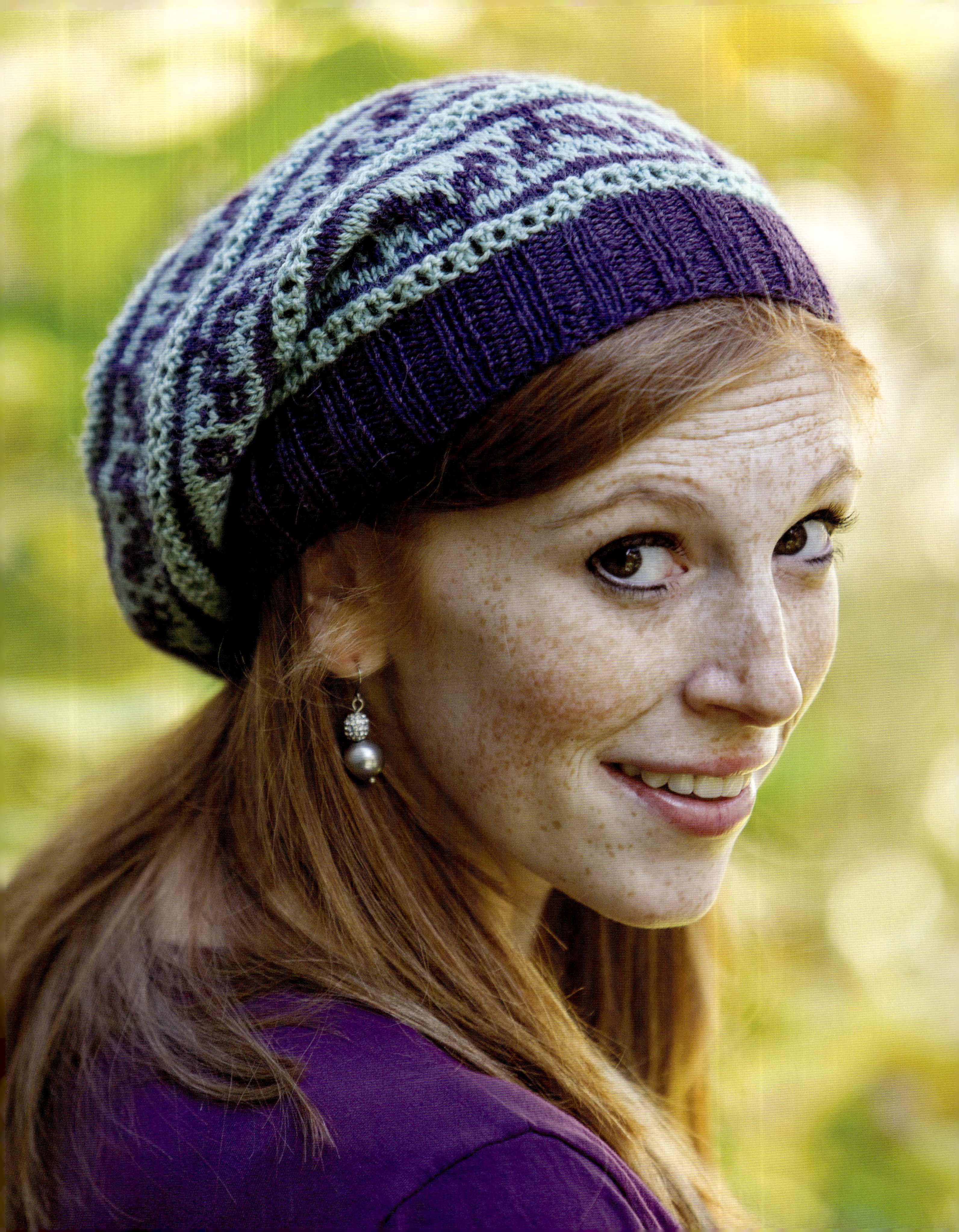

Bifoliate Slouch

For this hat I wanted to focus on the mosaic rather than the lace. By separating the bands of mosaic with simple lace a fabric was created that allows the hat to slouch as intended. The bamboo and silk content of the yarn assists with that goal. The simple, repeated mosaic motifs that appear in the band come together in the crown to develop into a visually complex whole reminiscent of a snowflake.

Finished Measurements: 15 (16.5)"/38 (42) cm circumference [stretches to 21 (23.25)"/53 (60) cm], 10.75"/27 cm tall

Sizes: S/M (M/L)

Yarn

Weight: Light Fingering

The Fibre Company Canopy Fingering; 50% baby alpaca, 30% merino, 20% viscose bamboo; 200 yd/183 m per 1.76 oz/50 g

Color A: Crocus (1 skein)

Color B: Fern (1 skein)

Needles: US size 4/3.5 mm and US size 2/2.75 mm, preferred needles for knitting in the round (see Knitting in the Round, page 105)

Notions: Stitch marker

Gauge in Stockinette over 4"/10 cm: 24 sts and 32 rows on larger needles (see A Note on Gauge, page 12)

Notes

- This project falls into the "unless directed otherwise" category. Please note that the lace band interrupts the striping pattern. After the lace band you will return to two row stripes.

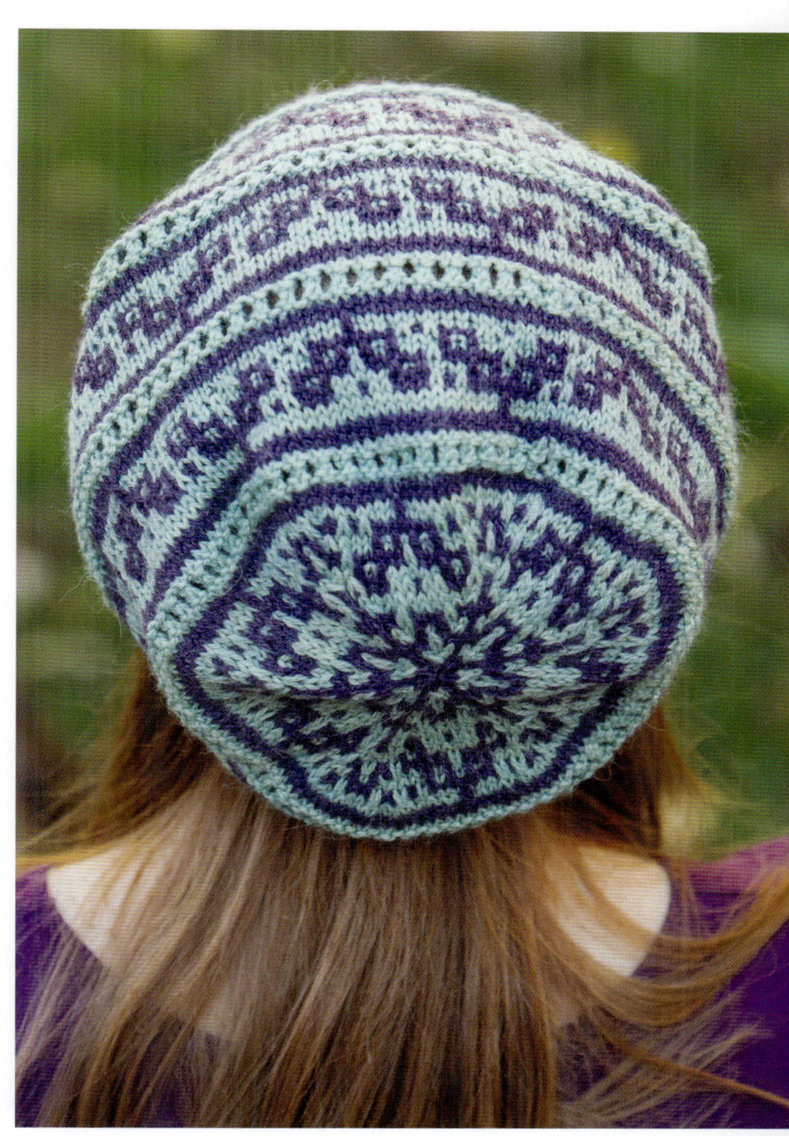

Instructions

Using Color A, two-strand variant of long tail cast-on method (see Cast-On/Bind-Off, page 109), smaller needle, and preferred method of knitting in the round, CO 108 (120) sts. Place marker to indicate beginning of round and join to work in the round, being careful not to twist sts.

Rounds 1–18: *K2, p2; rep from * to end of round.

INCREASE BAND

Switch to larger needle.
Round 1: With B, knit.
Round 2: Purl.

For S/M only:

Round 3: *K2tog, YO, k1, YO; rep from * to end of round. [144 sts]

For M/L only:

Round 3: *(K2tog, YO) twice, k1, YO; rep from * to end of round. [144 sts]

All sizes:

Round 4: Purl.

MOSAIC BAND

Work Chart A, repeating each round 6 times around.

Chart A

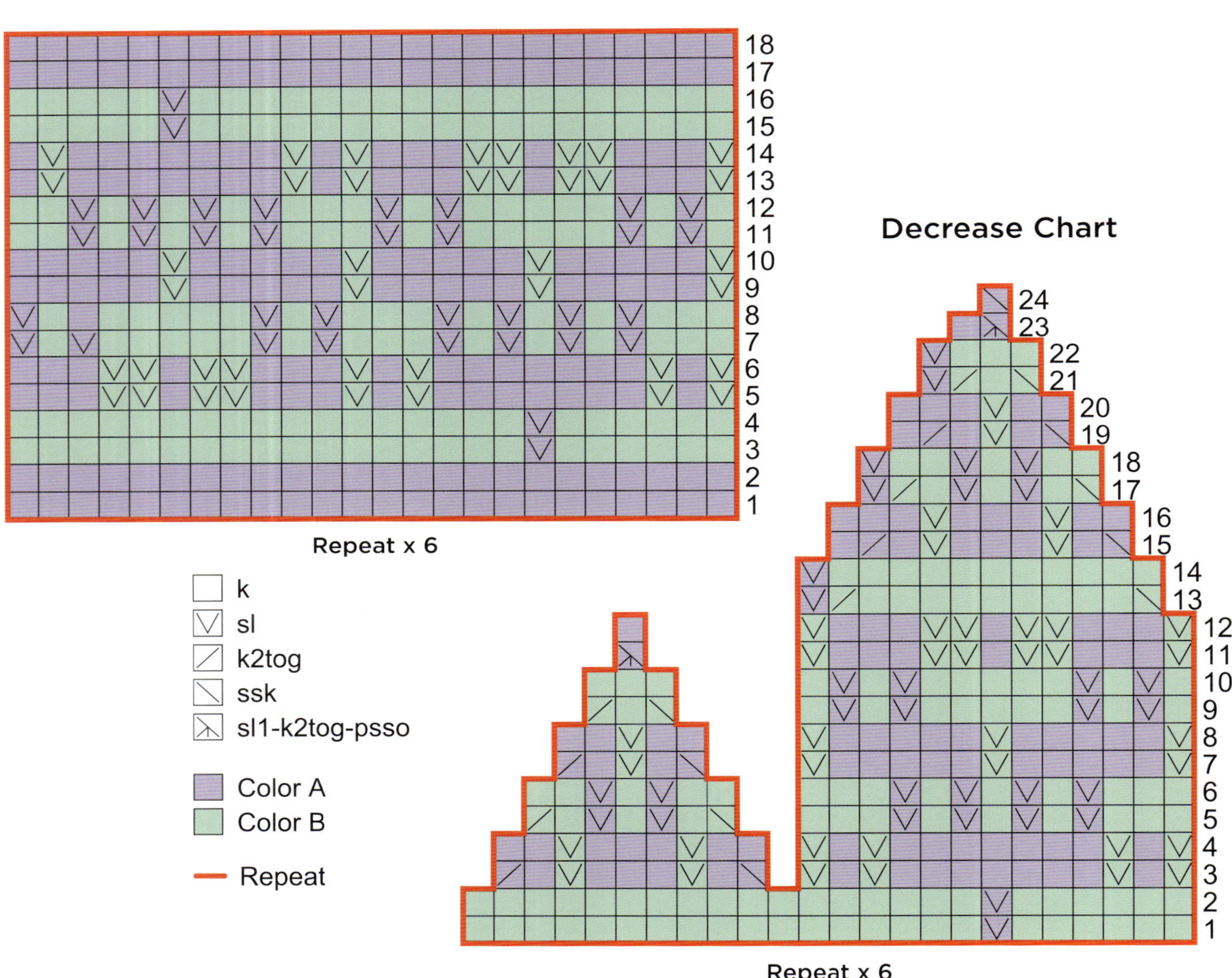

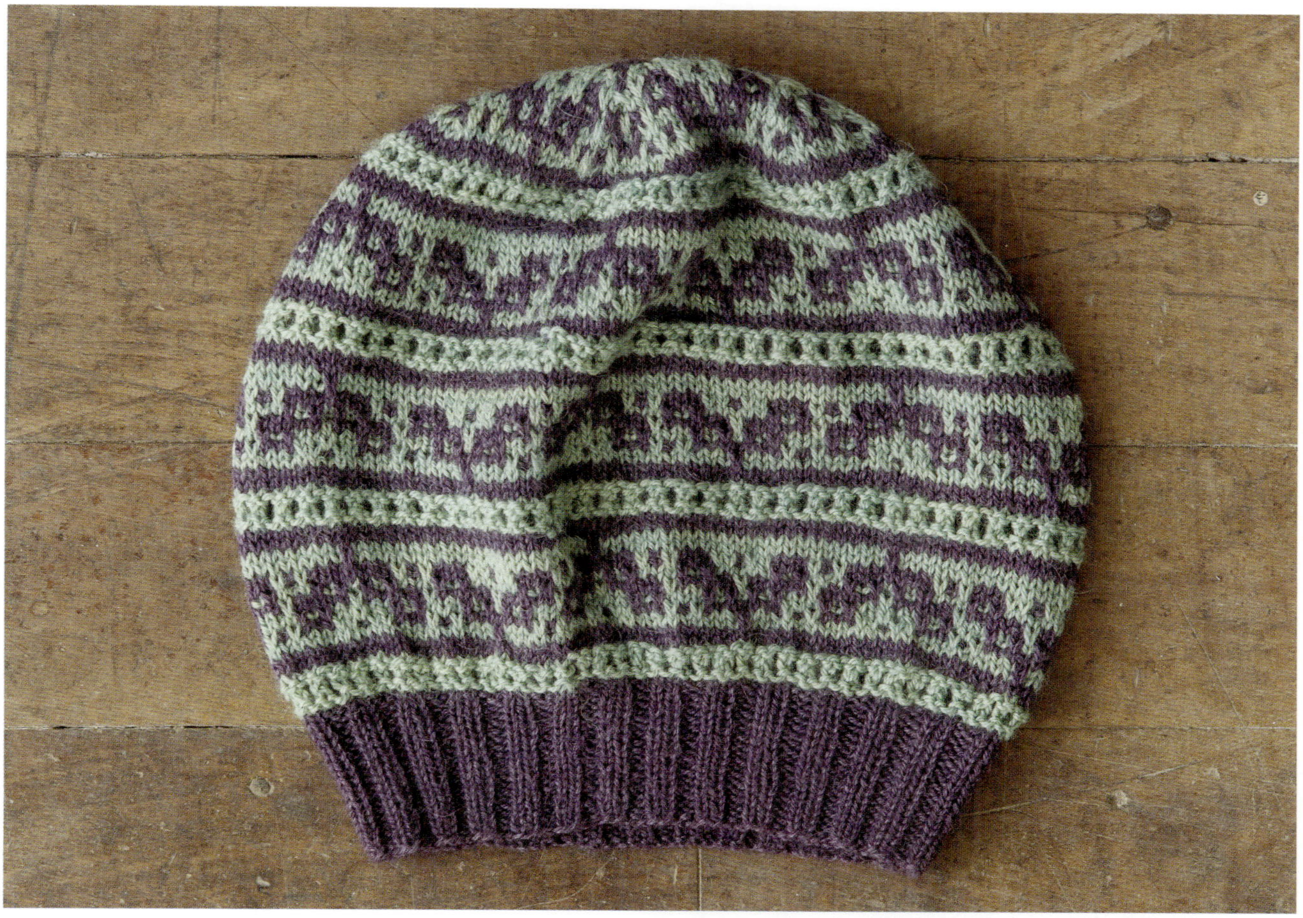

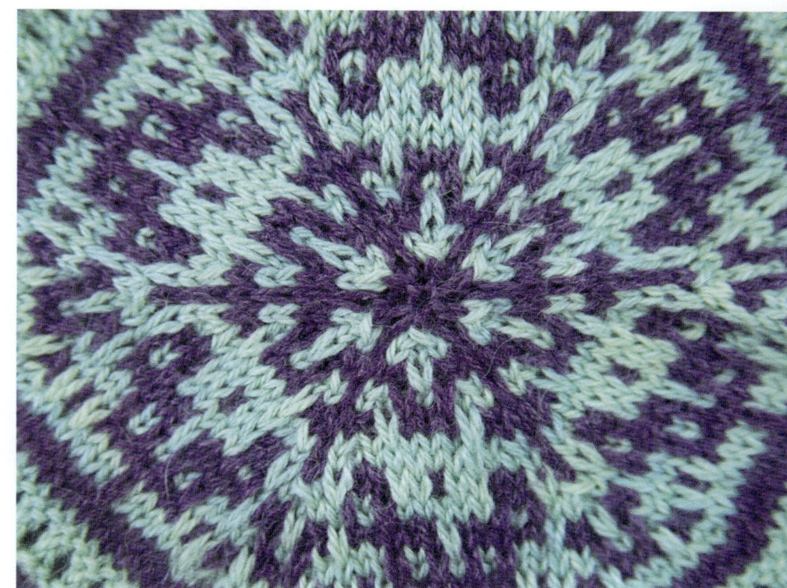

LACE BAND

Note: Work with Color B only; carry Color A loosely up the inside.

Rounds 1 and 2: With Color B only, knit.
Round 3: Purl.
Round 4: *K2tog, YO; rep from * to end of round.
Round 5: Purl.

Work [Mosaic Band, Lace Band] twice more for a total of three bands of each, not counting Increase Band.

CROWN

With A, knit 2 rounds.

Work Decrease Chart, repeating each round 6 times. [6 sts]

Cut yarn leaving a 7" tail.

Use a tapestry needle to transfer sts from needle to yarn tail. Pull tail to cinch tightly closed.

FINISHING

Weave in ends. Block over bowl or balloon, being careful to not stretch out the ribbing. Trim ends.

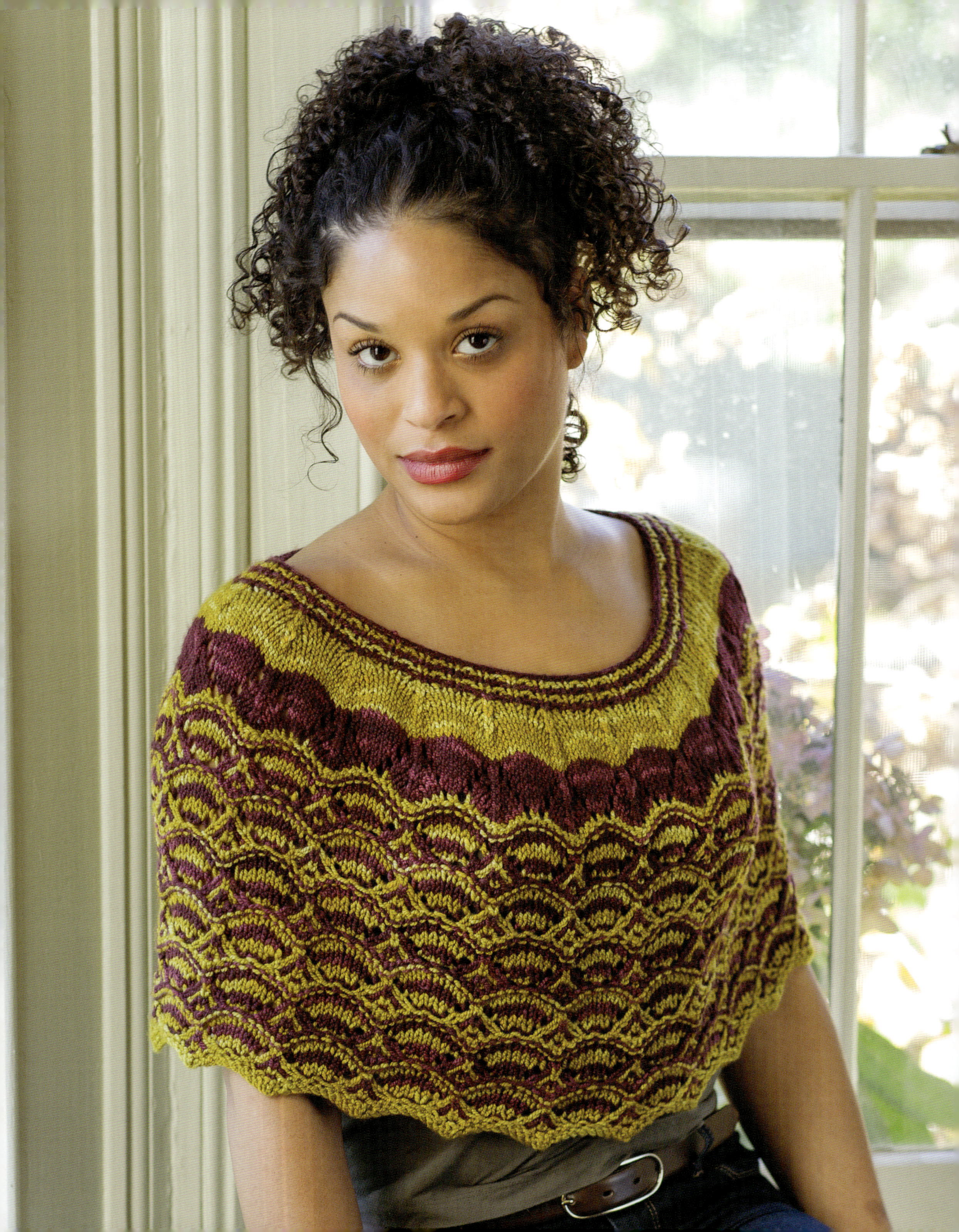

Isochronal Arc

Is it a poncho? Is it a cape? Is it a cowl? Whatever you think it is, it is an elegant addition to your wardrobe that will keep your shoulders warm. By placing the cast-on at the bottom, a subtle scalloped hem is created that opens up into interlocking arcs. The mosaic is prevented from getting too heavy by the lace elements, which allows the piece to hang beautifully. The decreases in the yoke echo the arcs from the mosaic lace, ending with a neckline that is ribbed to lie flat.

Finished Measurements: 13.5 (14.5)"/34 (37) cm long, 30"/76 cm circumference at neckline, 47.25 (54)"/120 (137) cm circumference at hem

Sizes: S/M (L/XL)

Yarn

  Weight: Worsted

  Berroco Artisan; 80% merino wool, 20% silk; 123 yd/112 m per 1.76 oz/50 g

  Color A: Maritime #6039 [2(3) skeins]

  Color B: Ocean Floor #6040 [2(3) skeins]

Needles: US size 9/5.5 mm circular needle, 40"/100 cm in length, and US size 8/5 mm circular needle, 40"/100 cm in length (see Knitting in the Round, page 105)

Notions: Stitch marker

Gauge in Stockinette over 4"/10 cm: 16 sts and 22 rows on larger needle (see A Note on Gauge, page 12)

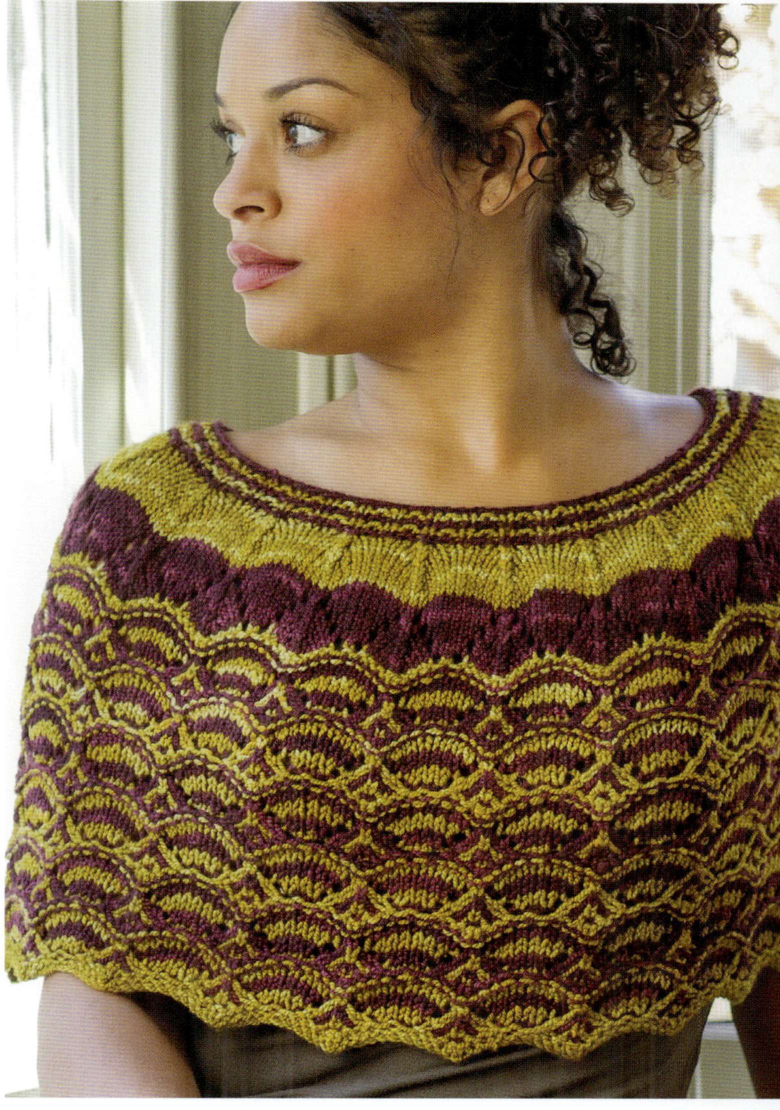

Instructions

Using cable cast-on method (see Cast-On/Bind-Off, page 105), larger needle, Color B, and your preferred method of knitting in the round, CO 210 (240) sts. Place marker to indicate beginning of round and join to work in the round, being careful not to twist sts.

Purl two rounds.

Join in Color A and work Chart A three total times, repeating each round 21 (24) times around.

With A and smaller needles, work Chart B once, repeating each round 21 (24) times around.

For L/XL only:
Knit two rounds.

All sizes:
With B, knit four rounds.

DECREASE SECTION
Round 1: *K4, CDD, k3; rep from * to end of round. [168 (192) sts]
Round 2: Knit.
Round 3: *K3, CDD, k2; rep from * to end of round. [126 (144) sts]
Round 4: Knit.

For S/M only:
Round 5: With A, *k2, CDD, k1; rep from * to end of round. [84 sts]
Round 6: *K1, p1; rep from * to end of round.

Chart A

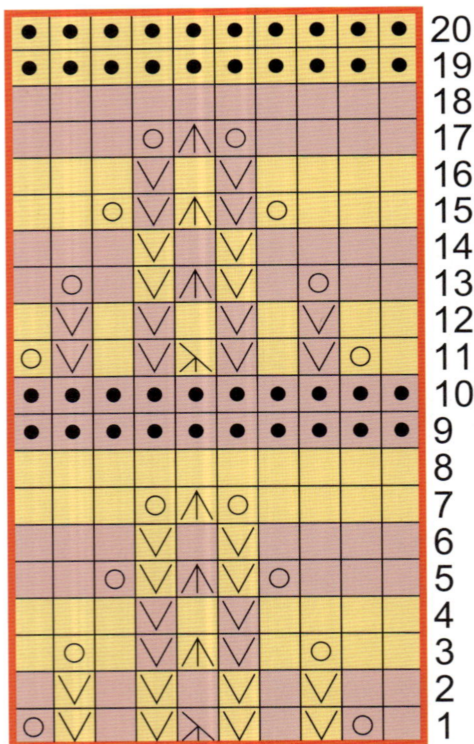

Repeat x 21 (24)

Chart B

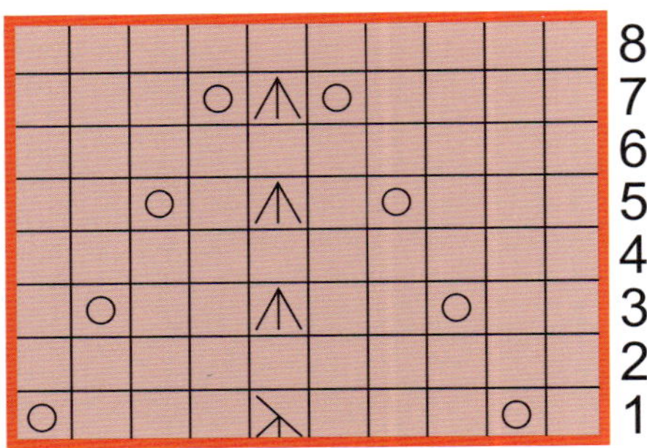

Repeat x 21 (24)

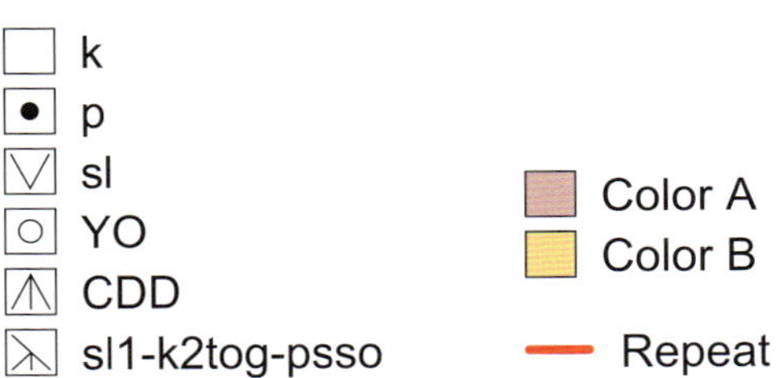

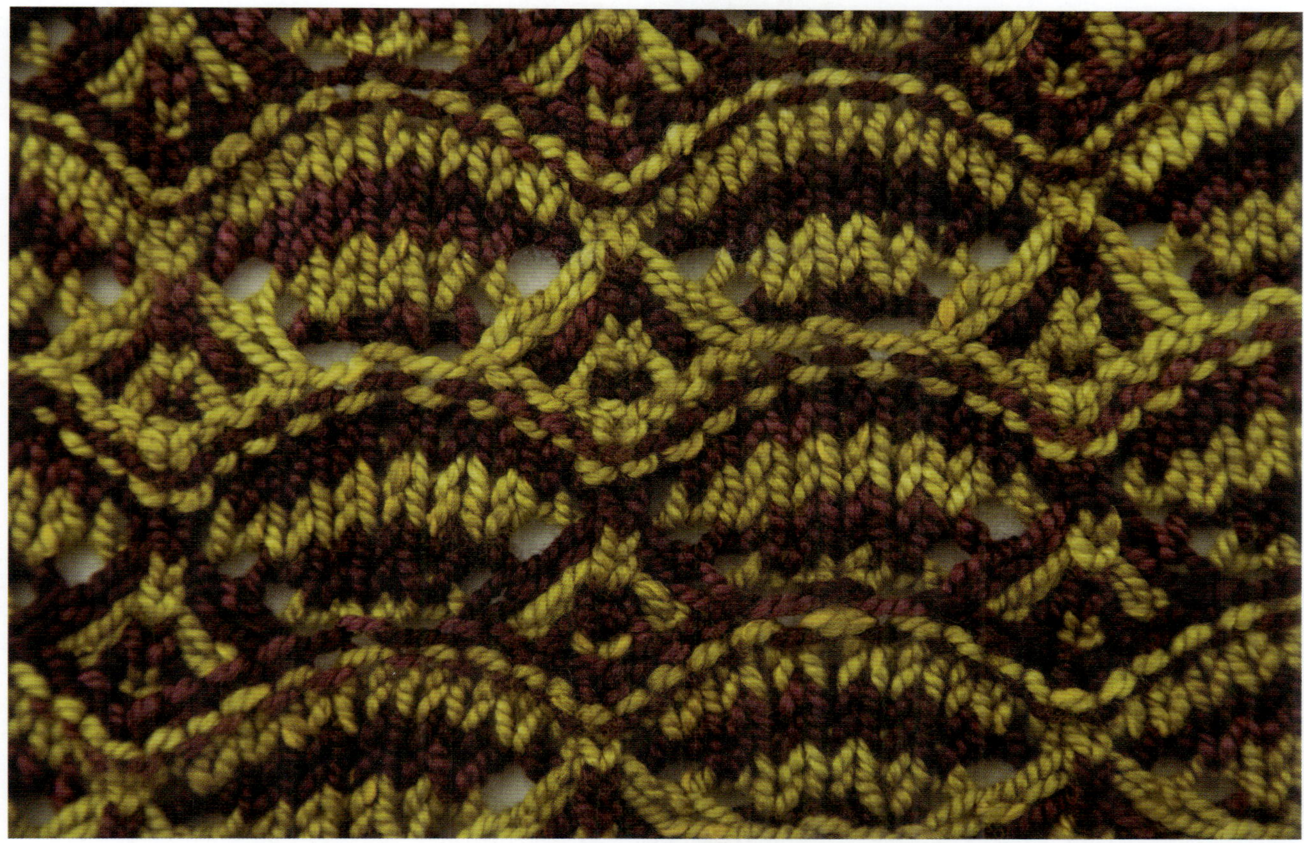

For L/XL only:

Round 5: *K2, CDD, k1; rep from * to end of round. [96 sts]

Round 6: Knit.

Round 7: With A, *k2, skp, k4; rep from * to end of round. [84 sts]

Round 8: *K1, p1; rep from * to end of round.

RIBBING SECTION

Round 1: With B, knit.

Round 2: *K1, p1; rep from * to end of round.

With A, repeat Rounds 1 and 2.

With B, repeat Rounds 1 and 2.

With A, knit 1 round.

Using the knit/purl stretchy bind-off method (see Cast-On/Bind-Off, page 110), BO all sts.

FINISHING

Weave in ends. Block assertively to shape, tapering to match where the decrease section begins. If you have crease lines where piece was blocked flat, refold so that they are flattened out, steam, and pat lightly to remove crease. Trim ends.

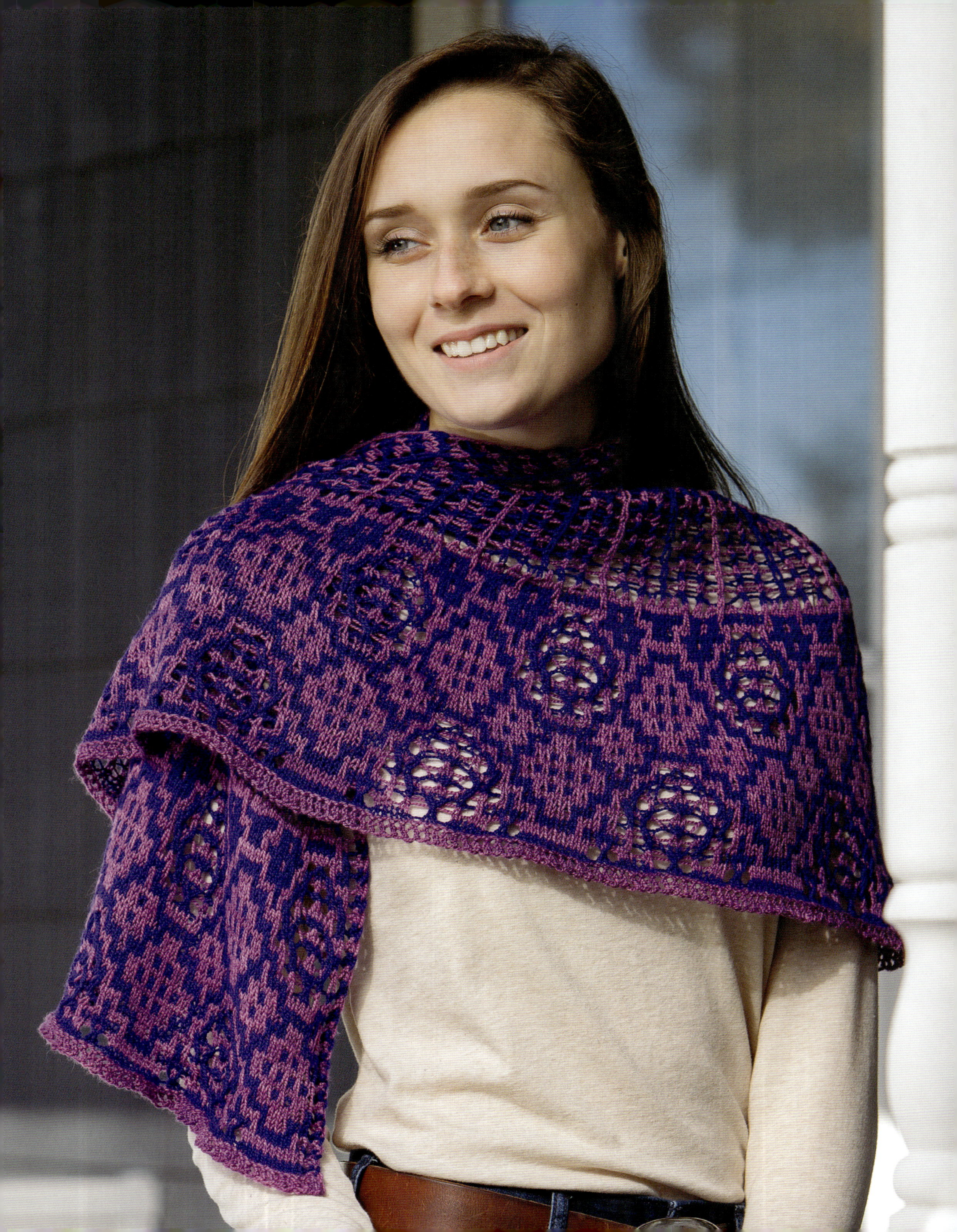

Rhipis

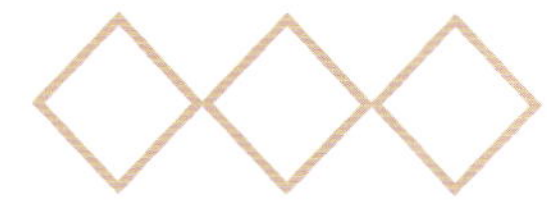

The fine lace body of this shawl pushes the limit of how much lace I have been able to incorporate while still maintaining discernable colorwork. By using pi-shawl shaping I was able to expand the overall lace out until the final increase row sets the stage for the wide, intricate mosaic lace border. It might be hard to believe, but the lace motifs that interlock with the mosaic elements have the same color patterning. If you were to choose not to work the lace in the border you would have a band of the mosaic motifs that alternate which color is dominant.

Finished Measurements: 19.5"/49.5 cm long, 47.5"/120.5 cm wingspan

Sizes: One size

Yarn

Weight: Fingering

Baah! La Jolla; 100% superwash merino; 400 yd/366 m per 3.53 oz/100 g

Color A: Iris (1 skein)

Color B: Lilac (1 skein)

Note: You will need approximately 300 yd/275 m per color

Needles: US size 6/4 mm

Notions: Stitch markers

Gauge in Stockinette over 4"/10 cm: 20 sts and 28 rows (see A Note on Gauge, page 12)

Notes

- When a slipped stitch occurs between two yarn overs, it is necessary to treat the yarn overs as if they were a double yarn over (see Mosaic Lace, page 5). To do so, you must knit into the first YO and purl the second YO.
- This project falls into the "unless directed otherwise" category. In the trim there are places where you slip three stitches in a row. Be mindful of these stitches and keep the yarn that runs behind the stitches at an even, relaxed tension.

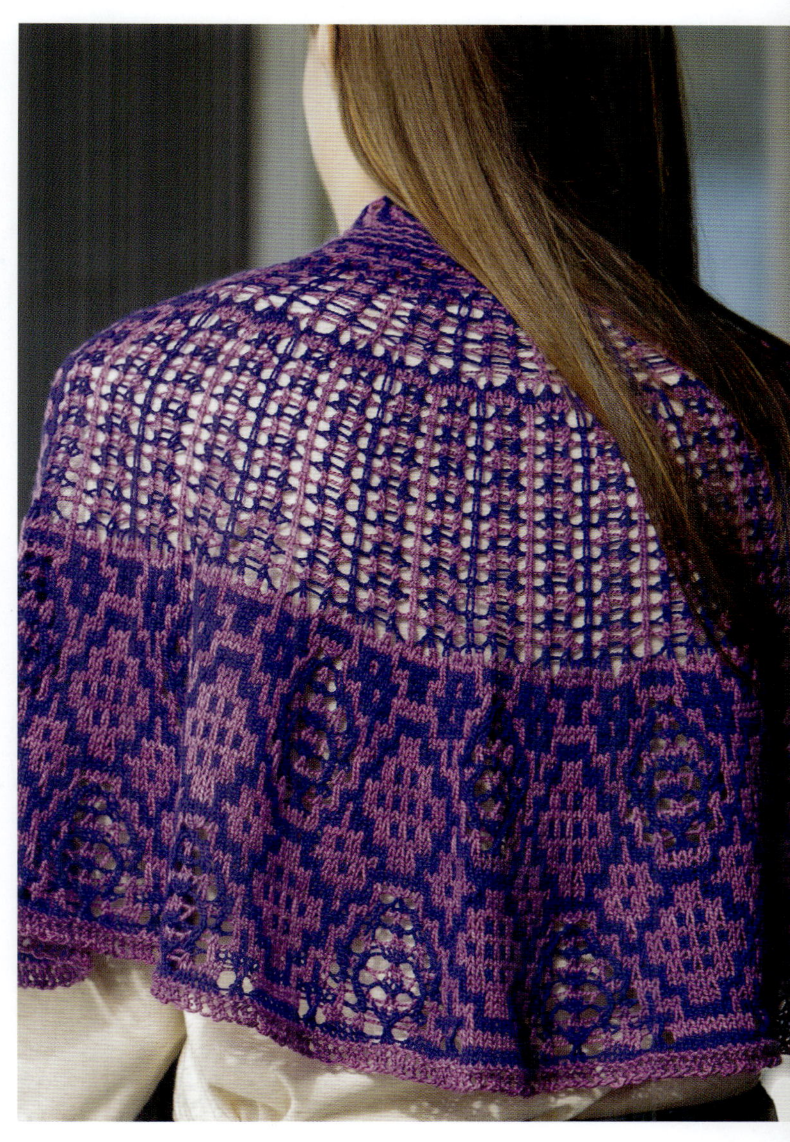

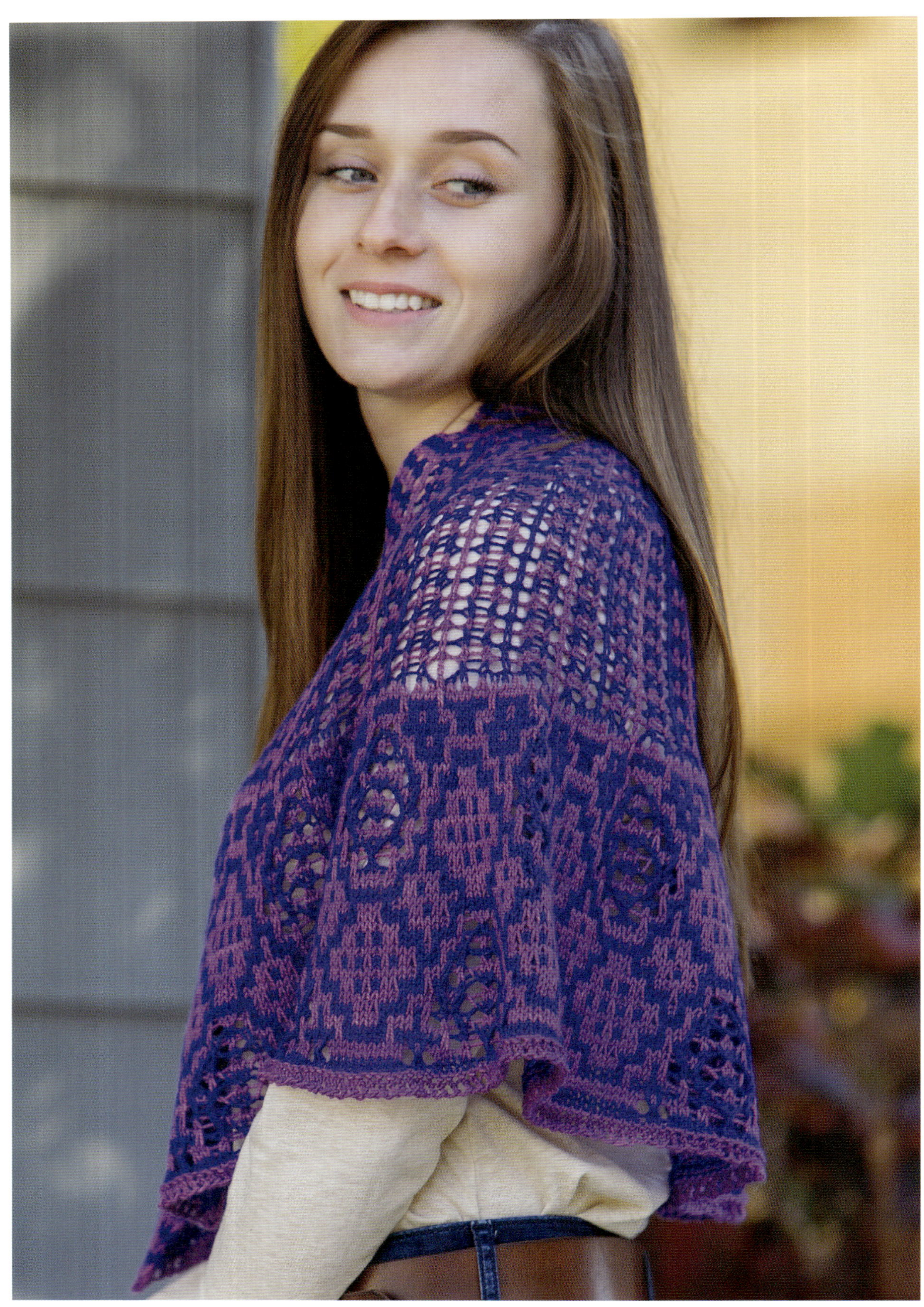

Instructions

Using Color A and long tail cast-on method (see Cast-On/Bind-Off, page 107), CO 4 sts.

SET UP
Row 1 (RS): K1, YO, k2, YO, k1. [6 sts]
Rows 2 and 4 (WS): Knit.
Row 3: K1, YO, k1, M1R, k2, M1L, k1, YO, k1. [10 sts]

Join in Color B.

Row 5: With B, k2, YO, (k1, M1R) twice, k2, (M1L, k1) twice, YO, k2. [16 sts]
Rows 6 and all even rows: Sl1-wyif, knit to last st, sl1-wyif.
Row 7: With A, k1, k2tog, YO, knit to last 3 sts, YO, ssk, k1.
Row 9: With B, k1, k2tog, YO, k1, M1R, pm, (k1, M1L, k2, M1R, pm, k1) twice, M1L, k1, YO, ssk, k1. [22 sts]
Row 11: With A, k1, k2tog, YO, knit to last 3 sts, YO, ssk, k1.
Row 13: With B, k1, k2tog, YO, knit to marker, M1R, sm, (k1, M1L, knit to marker, M1R, sm, k1) twice, M1L, knit to last 3 sts, YO, ssk, k1. [6 sts increased]
Rows 14–25: Rep Rows 10–13 four times. [46 sts]
Row 26: Sl1-wyif, k2, purl to last 3 sts, k2, sl1-wyif.

Remove markers before proceeding to the body.

BODY
Rows 27–34: Work Chart A twice, repeating indicated sts 4 times.
Row 35: With A, k1, k2tog, YO, *k1, YO; rep from * to last 4 sts, kfb, YO, ssk, k1. [86 sts]
Row 36: Sl1-wyif, k2, purl to last 3 sts, k2, sl1-wyif.
Row 37: With B, k1, k2tog, YO, k7, (sl1, k9) seven times, sl1, k2, YO, ssk, k1.
Row 38: Sl1-wyif, k2, slipping all contrasting color sts wyif purl to last 3 sts, k2, sl1-wyif.
Rows 39–50: Work Chart A 3 times, repeating indicated sts 8 times.

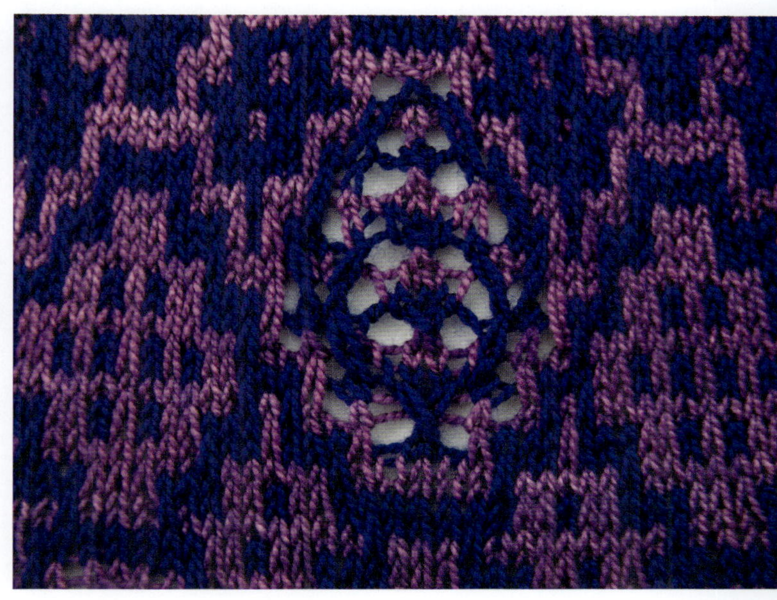

Chart A

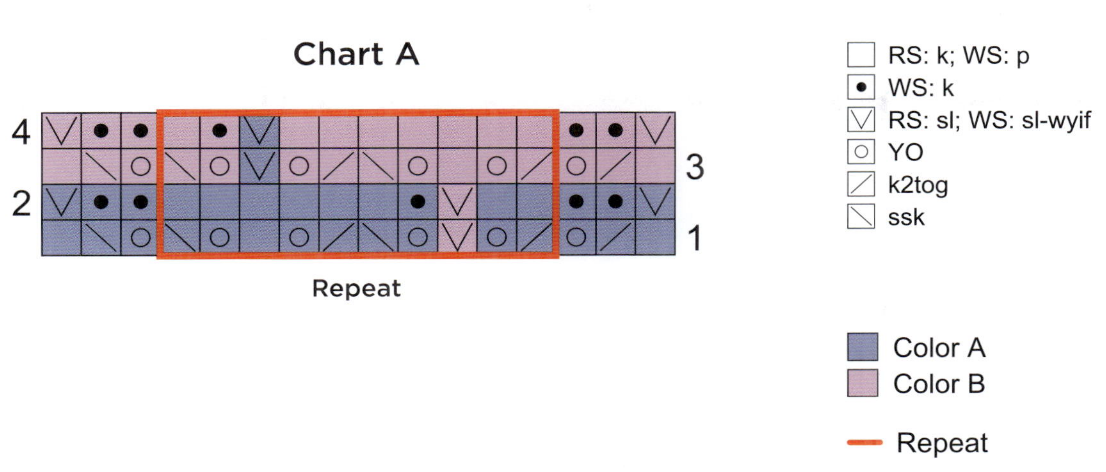

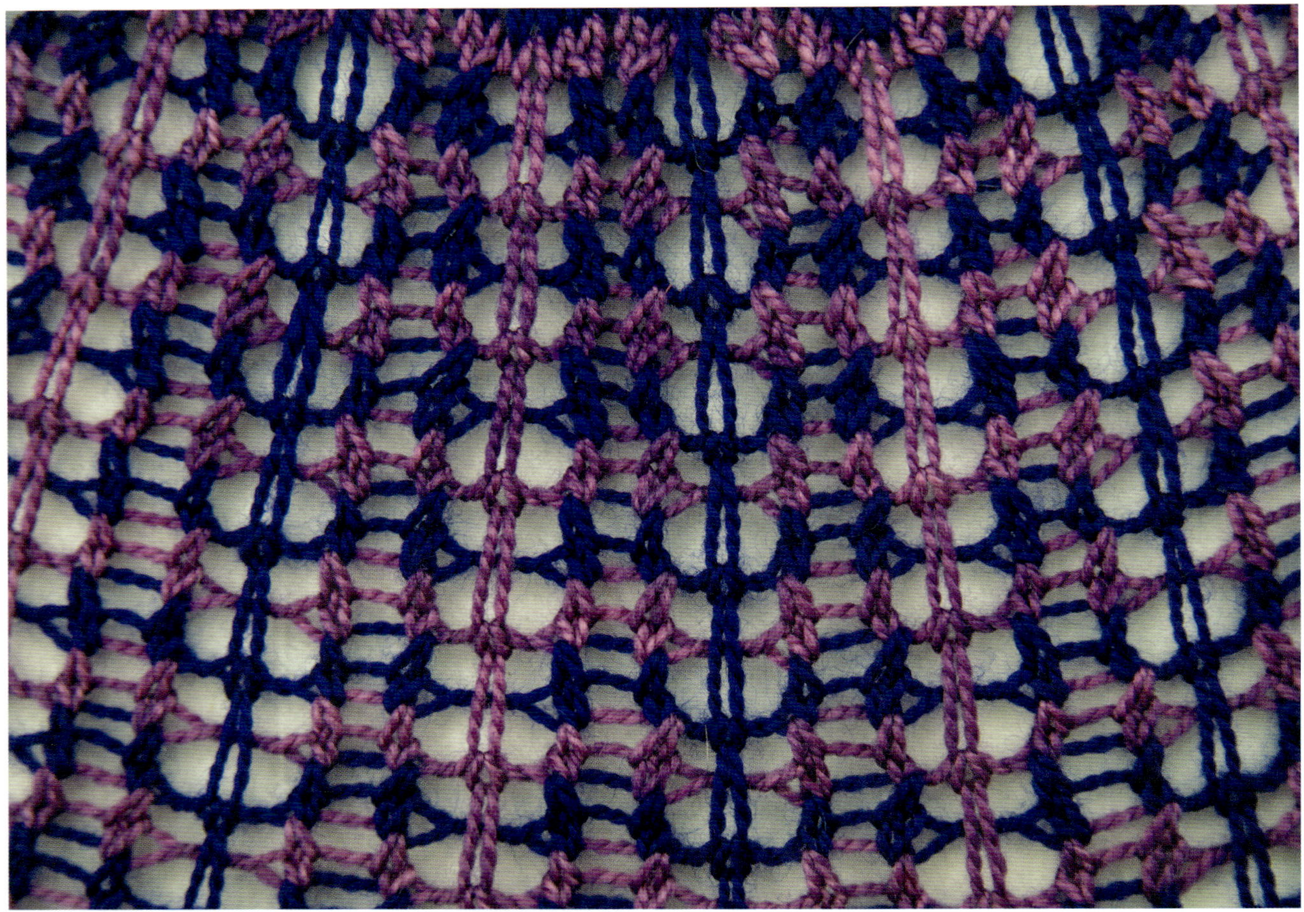

Row 51: With A, k1, k2tog, YO, *k1, YO; rep from * to last 4 sts, kfb, YO, ssk, k1. [166 sts]

Row 52: Sl1-wyif, k2, purl to last 3 sts, k2, sl1-wyif.

Row 53: With B, k1, k2tog, YO, k7, (sl1, k9) 15 times, sl1, k2, YO, ssk, k1.

Row 54: Sl1-wyif, k2, slipping all contrasting color sts wyif purl to last 3 sts, k2, sl1-wyif.

Rows 55–82: Work Chart A 7 times repeating indicated sts 16 times.

Rows 83 and 84: Work Rows 1–2 of Chart A repeating indicated sts 16 times.

Row 85: With B, k1, k2tog, YO, kfb, YO, *k1, YO; rep from * to last 4 sts, kfb, YO, ssk, k1. [327 sts]

Row 86: Sl1-wyif, k2, purl to last 3 sts, k2, sl1-wyif.

Rows 87–146: Work Chart B repeating indicated sts 12 times.

Using the expandable lace bind-off, knit variant method (see Cast-On/Bind-Off, page 109), BO all sts.

FINISHING

Weave in ends. The cast-on edge will form a dip in the upper edge of the shawl. To close this gap, lay the piece flat and take the first and last sts of the dip and align them with each other so that the dip forms a vertical seam. Using the yarn tail, close this gap neatly with your tapestry needle. Block aggressively. Trim ends.

Chart B

Chart B
60 59 58 57 56 55 54 53 52 51 50 49 48 47 46 45 44 43 42 41 40 39 38 37 36 35 34 33 32 31 30 29 28 27 26 25 24 23 22 21 20 19 18 17 16 15 14 13 12 11 10 9 8 7 6 5 4 3 2 1
Repeat x 12
RS: k; WS: p
WS: k
RS: sl; WS: sl-wyif
YO
k2tog
ssk
CDD
sl1-k2tog-psso
Color A
Color B
Repeat

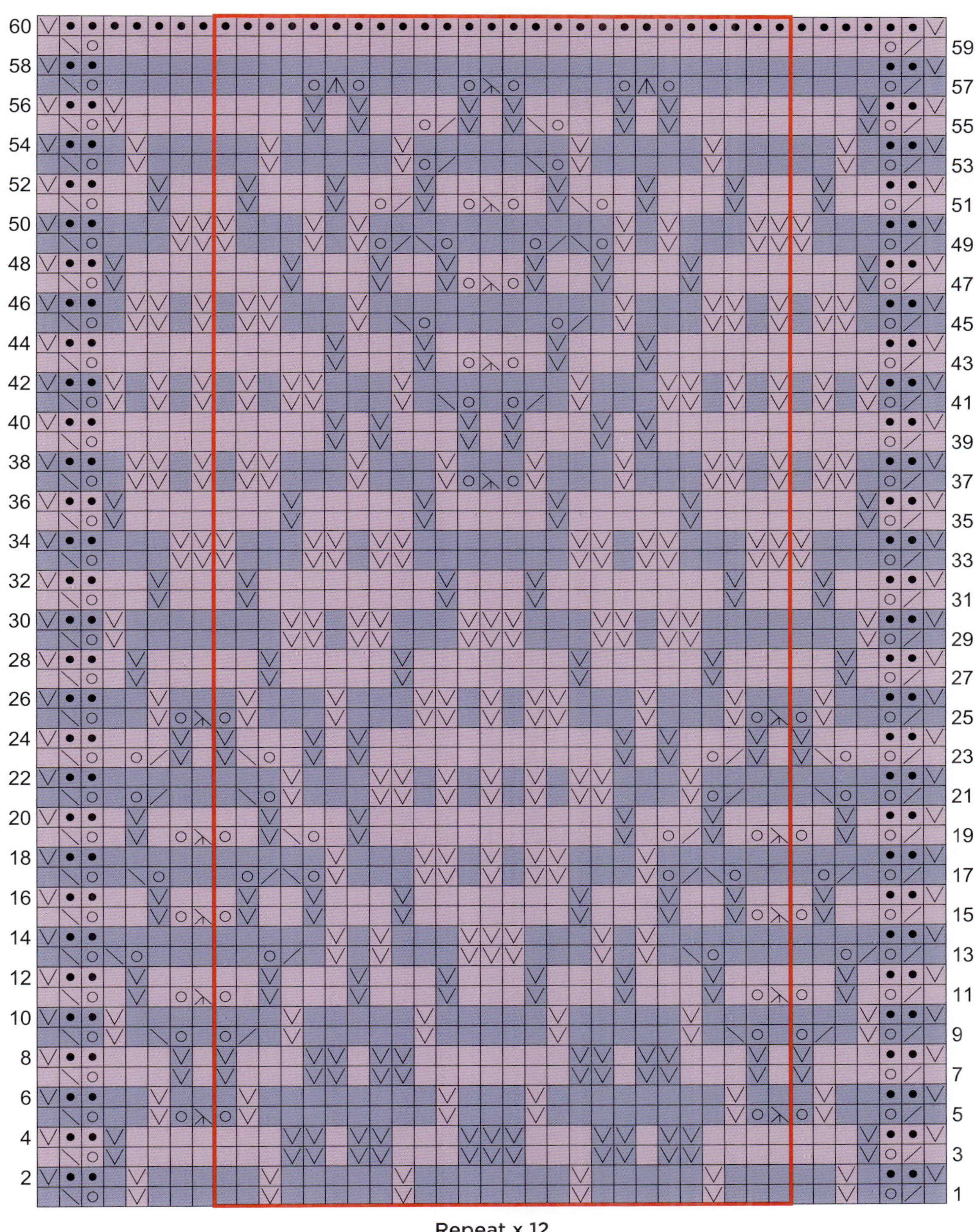

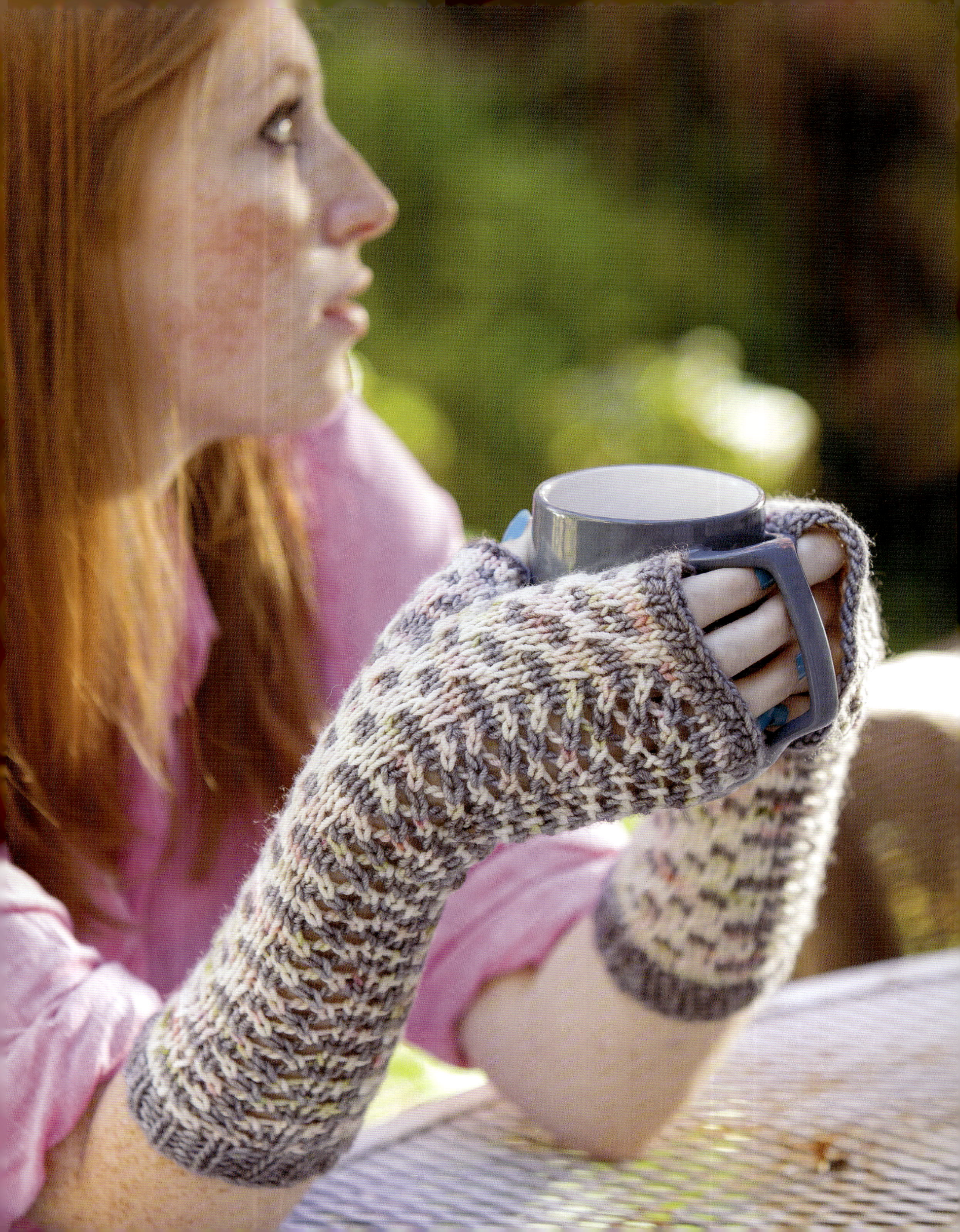

Punctatus Mitts

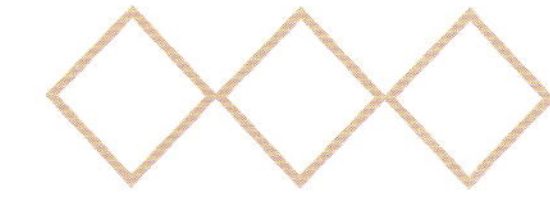

The beautiful yarn in this pattern posed particular challenges. It has excellent stitch definition and when combined with variegation it becomes a very "noisy" yarn for the purposes of mosaic. Best to keep things simple. The overall colorwork pattern is one of the simplest possible mosaics and the lace benefits from the stitch definition. The complexity in this piece comes from offsetting the lace so that it wraps around the side of the hand without venturing onto the palm. This detail is why there is a true left and right for these mitts.

Finished Measurements: 7"/18 cm hand circumference, 12.5"/32 cm long

Sizes: One size

Yarn

Weight: Worsted

Phydeaux Sportif Eight-ply Worsted Weight; 100% superwash merino wool; 218 yd/199 m per 3.53 oz/100 g

Color A: Direwolf (1 skein)

Color B: Ghost (1 skein)

Note: You will need approximately 110 yd/100 m per color

Needles: US size 7/4.5 mm, preferred needles for working small circumference (see Knitting in the Round, page 105)

Notions: Stitch marker

Gauge in Stockinette over 4"/10 cm: 20 sts and 26 rows (see A Note on Gauge, page 12)

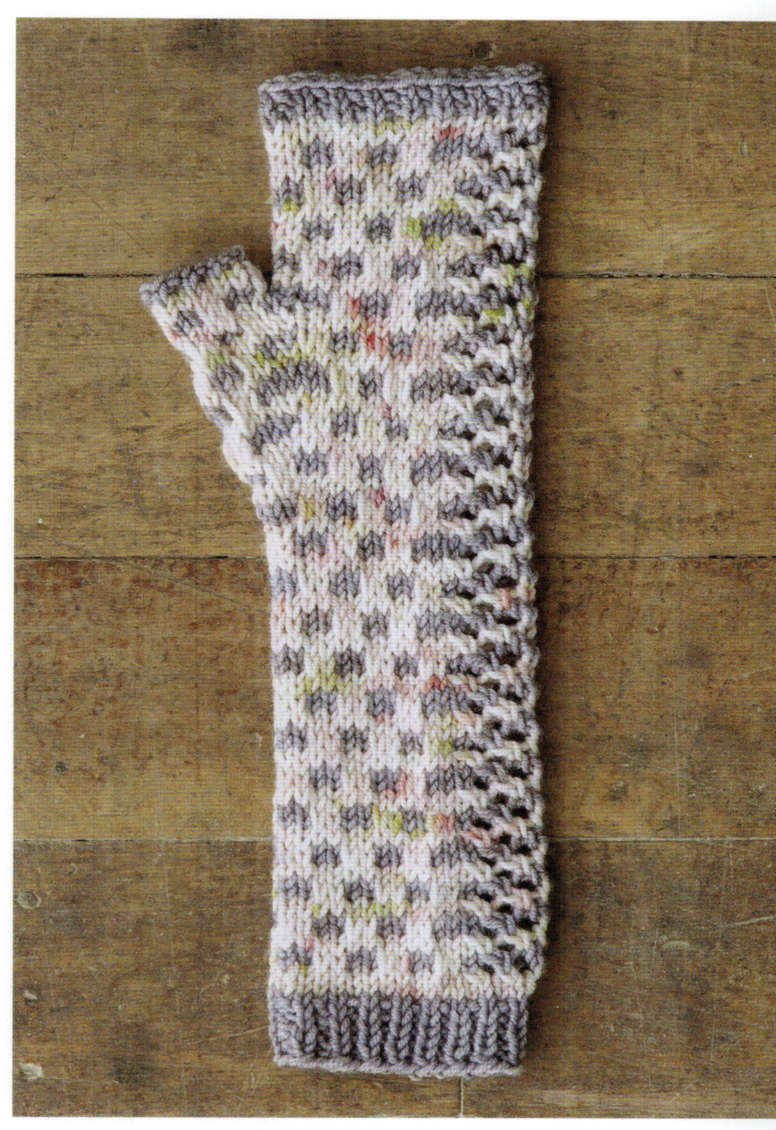

Instructions

Using Color A, long tail cast-on method (see Cast-On/Bind-Off, page 107), and your preferred method of knitting in the round, CO 32 sts. Place marker to indicate beginning of round and join to work in the round, being careful not to twist sts.

Rounds 1–5: *K1, p1; rep from * to end of round.
Increase Round: With B, k12, YO, knit to end of round. [33 sts]

BODY

Next Round: Work Chart A twice, work Chart B once, then work Chart A 4 times.

Continue in pattern until you have worked Rounds 1–8 of Charts A and B 6 times.

GUSSET

Right Hand

Next Round: Work Chart A twice, work Chart B once, work Chart A twice, work Thumb Gusset Chart placing marker as shown, then work Chart A once. [35 sts]

Continue in this pattern through Row 20 of Thumb Gusset Chart, ending on Round 4 of Charts A and B. [47 sts]

Next Round: Using Round 5 of Charts A and B, work Chart A twice, work Chart B once, work Chart A twice, work first two sts of Chart A, transfer thumb gusset sts to waste yarn, using backwards loop method (see Cast-On/Bind-Off, page 105) CO 2 sts, then work Chart A once more. [33 sts]

Chart A

Repeat

Chart B

k
sl
YO
M1R
M1L
k2tog
ssk

Color A
Color B

Stitch Marker
Repeat

pm = Place Marker

Thumb Gusset Chart

pm   pm

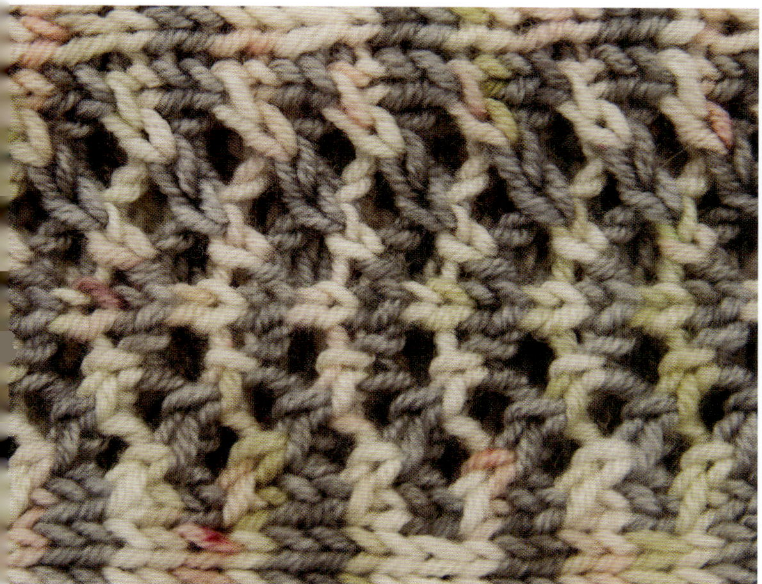

Next Round: Using Round 6 of Charts A and B, work Chart A twice, work Chart B once, work Chart A twice, k4, work Chart A once. Work Rounds 7 and 8 as established.

Left Hand

Next Round: Work Chart A twice, work Chart B once, work Chart A 3 times, work Thumb Gusset Chart placing marker as shown. [35 sts]

Continue in this pattern through Row 20 of Thumb Gussett Chart, ending on Round 4 of Charts A and B. [47 sts]

Next Round: Using Round 5 of Charts A and B, work Chart A twice, work Chart B once, work Chart A 3 times, work first two sts of Chart A, transfer thumb gusset sts to waste yarn, using backwards loop method (see Cast-On/Bind-Off, page 105) CO 2 sts. [33 sts]

Next Round: Using Round 6 of Charts A and B, work Chart A twice, work Chart B once, work Chart A 3 times, k4.

Work Rounds 7 and 8 as established.

Both Hands

Next Round: Work Chart A twice, work Chart B once, then work Chart A 4 times.

Continue in pattern until you have worked Rounds 1–8 twice.

END

Round 1: With A, k2tog, knit to end of round.
Rounds 3 and 4: *K1, p1; rep from * to end of round.

Using knit/purl stretchy bind-off method (see Cast-On/Bind-Off, page 110), BO all sts.

THUMB

Transfer held sts to needle. [16 sts]

With A, pick up and knit 1 st from each side of the thumb gap, place marker to indicate beginning of round. [18 sts]

Round 1: *K2, sl2; rep from * to end of round.
Round 2: K2tog, *sl2, k2; rep from * to last 2 sts, ssk.
Rounds 3 and 4: With B, knit.
Rounds 5 and 6: With A, sl1, *k2, sl2; rep from * to last 3 sts, k2, sl1.
Rounds 7 and 8: With B, knit.
Round 9: With A, knit.

Using knit/purl bind-off method (see Cast-On/Bind-Off, page 109), BO all sts.

FINISHING

Weave in ends using the yarn tails to neaten up any holes at the thumb joins. Block. If you have crease lines where piece was blocked flat, refold so that they are flattened out, steam, and pat lightly to remove crease. Trim ends.

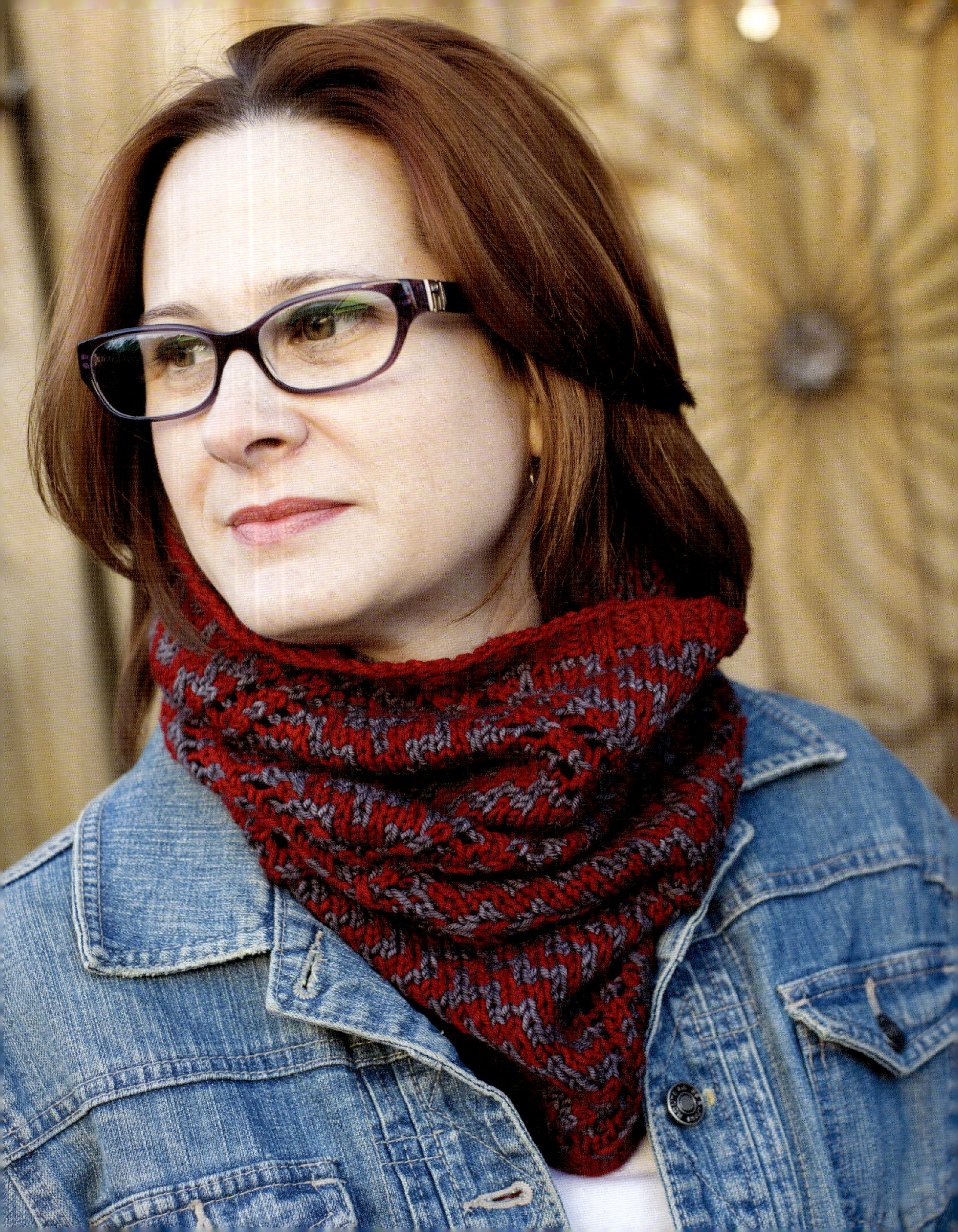

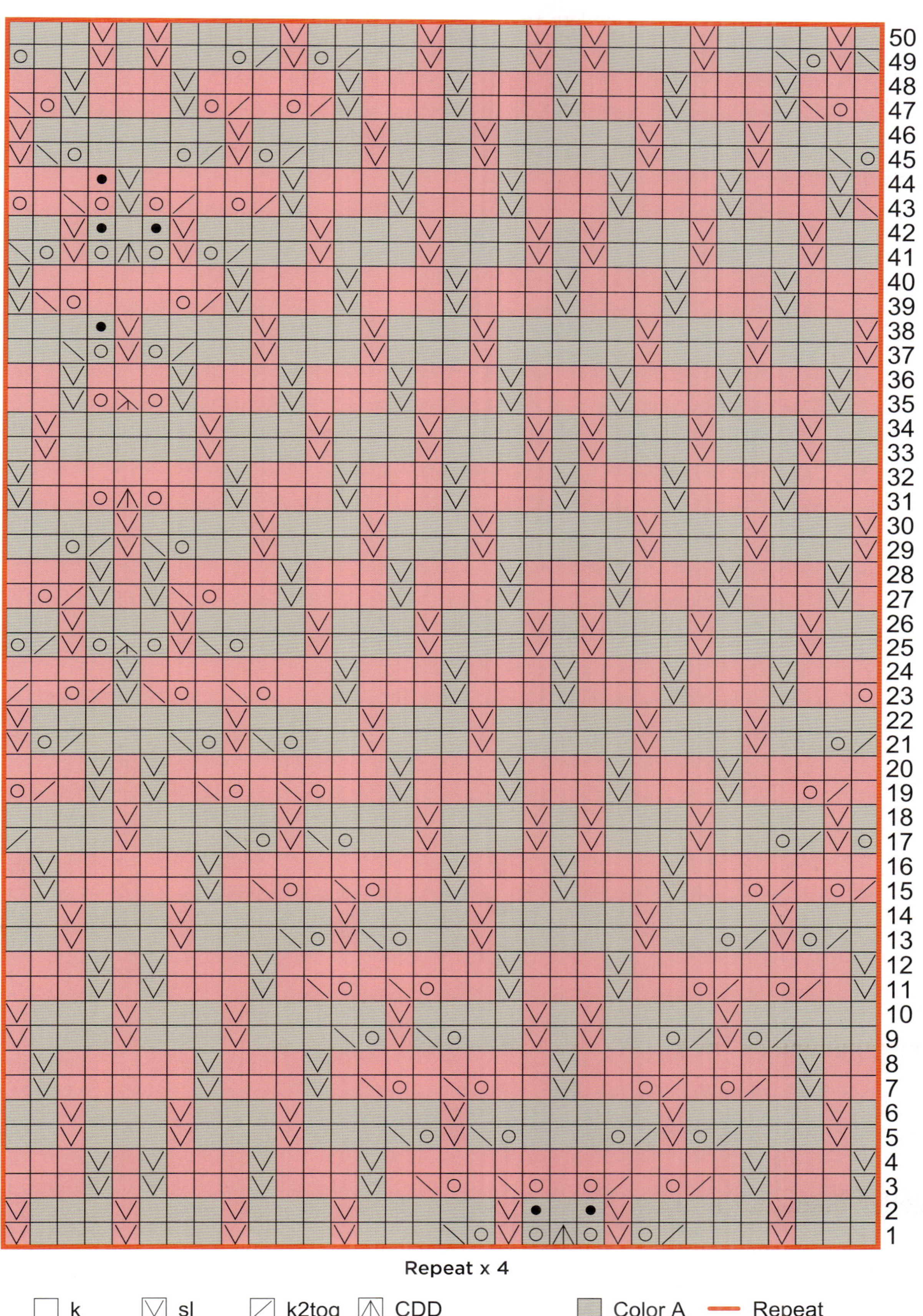

50
49
48
47
46
45
44
43
42
41
40
39
38
37
36
35
34
33
32
31
30
29
28
27
26
25
24
23
22
21
20
19
18
17
16
15
14
13
12
11
10
9
8
7
6
5
4
3
2
1
Repeat x 4
k
p
sl
YO
k2tog
ssk
CDD
sl1-k2tog-psso
Color A
Color B
Repeat

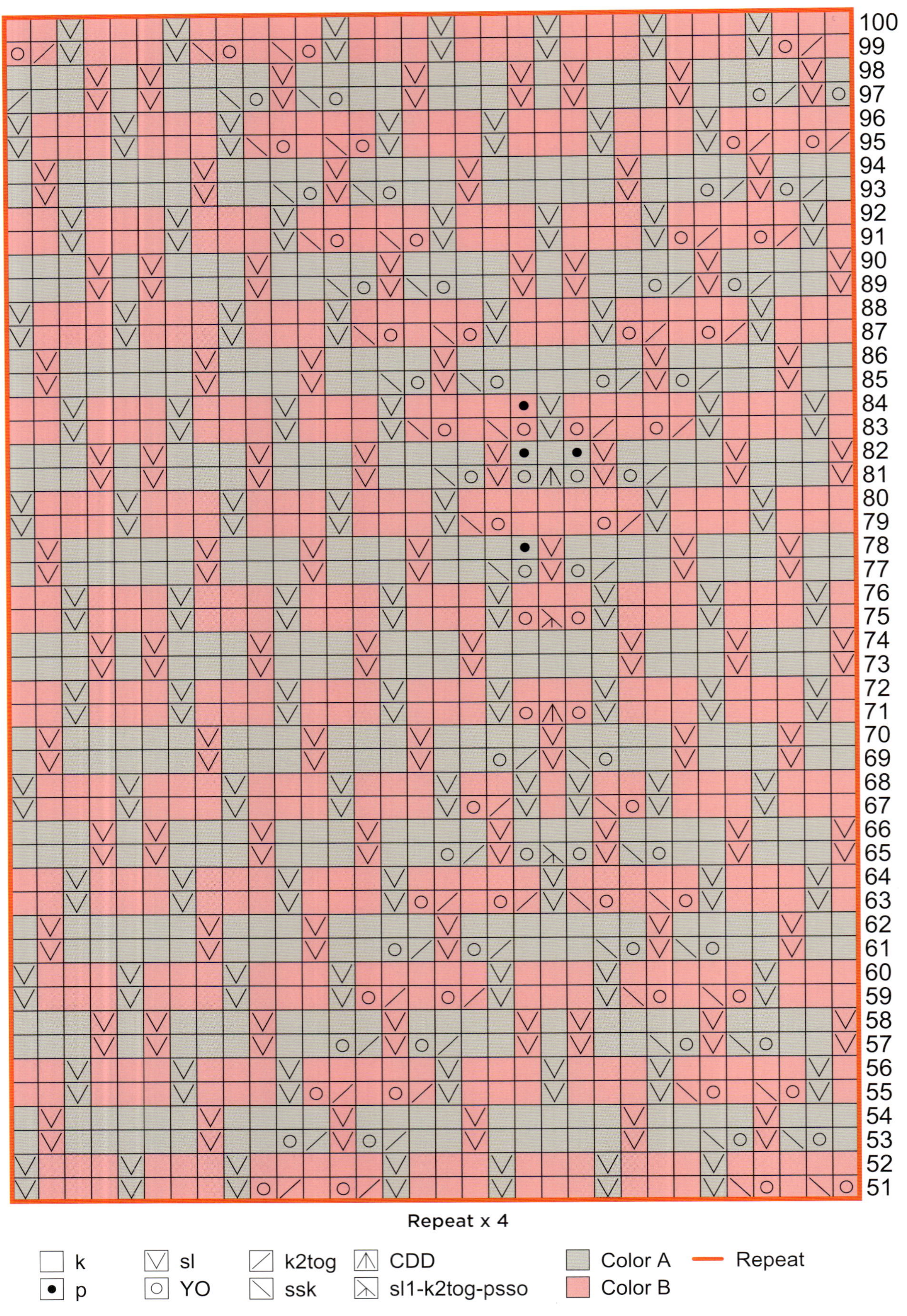
Repeat x 4
k
p
sl
YO
k2tog
ssk
CDD
sl1-k2tog-psso
Color A
Color B
Repeat

Chart C

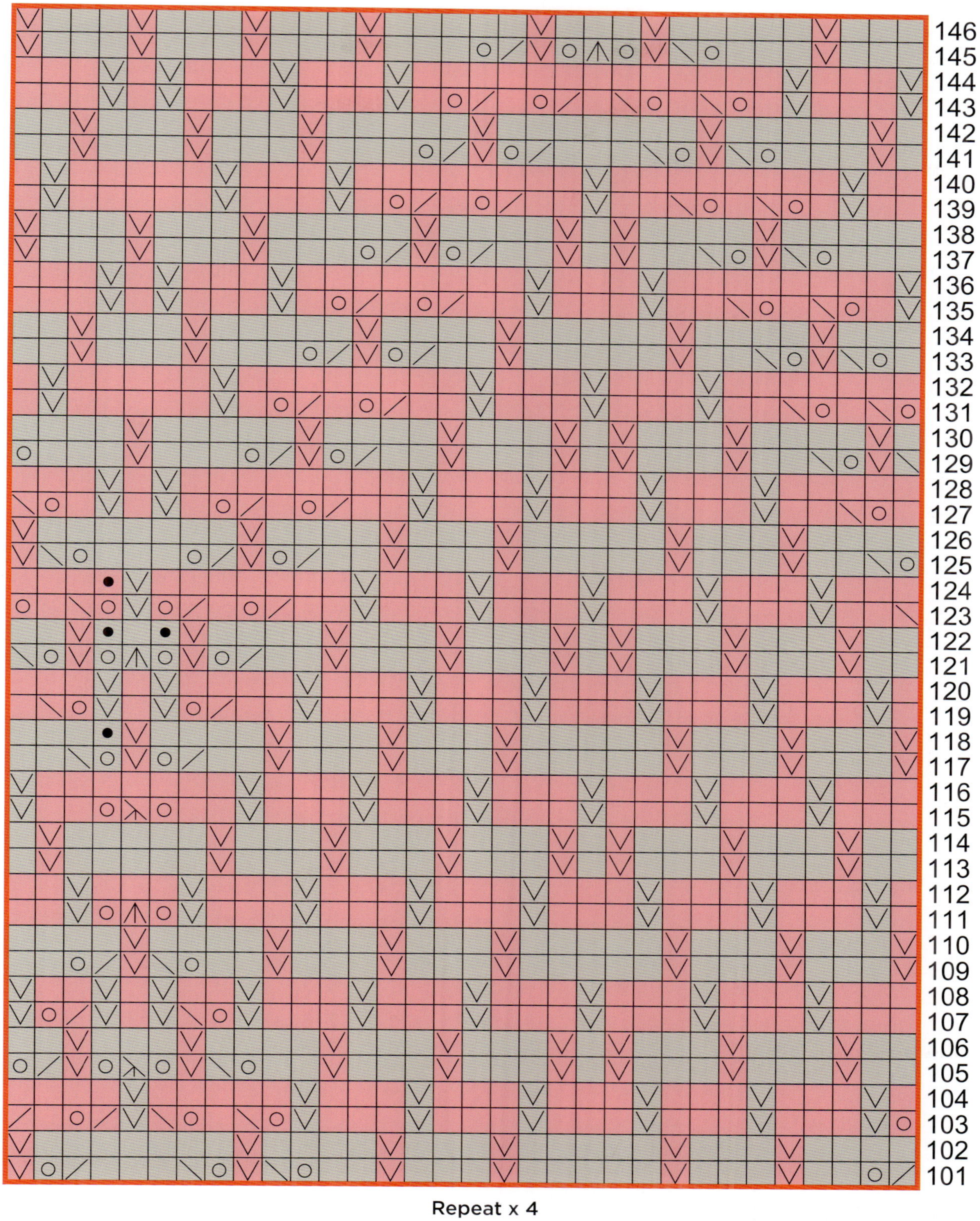

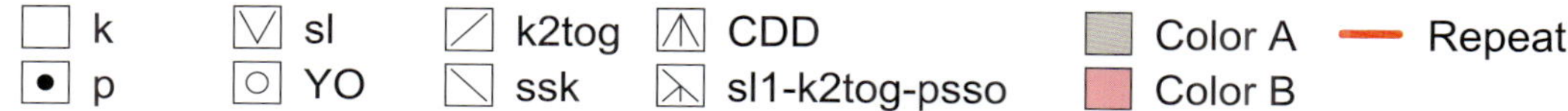

Repeat x 4

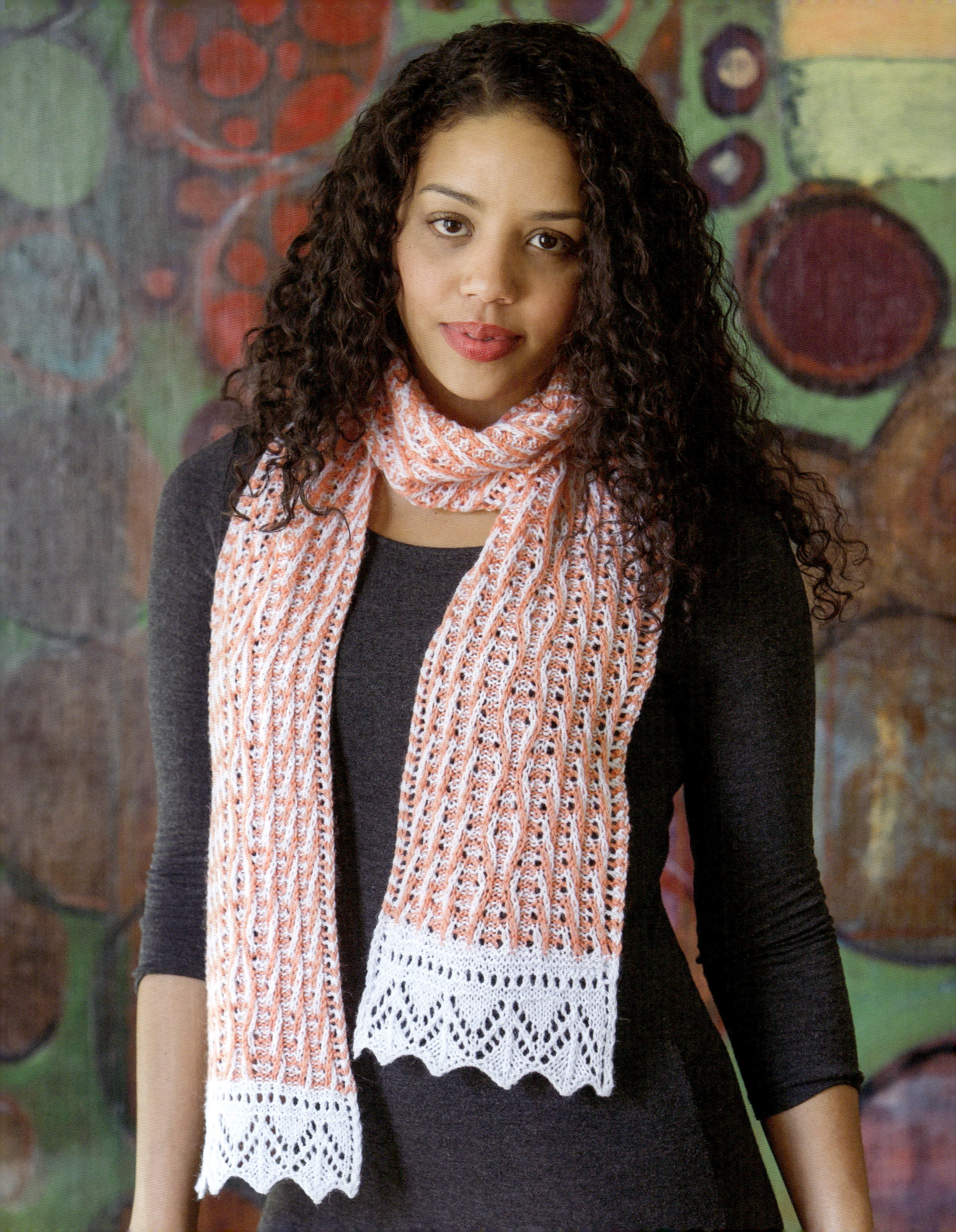

Tamiami Trail

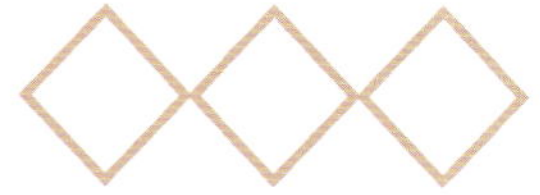

A delicate lace border sets the stage for the sinuous movement of the mosaic lace in this lovely scarf. Although it looks like complex cabling, it is all a trick of the combination of lace and slipped stitches. The body of this pattern contains nothing more complex than yarn overs and single decreases, once again tapping into my desire to create something that *looks* like you did something difficult when in fact you did not.

Finished Measurements: 6.5"/16.5 cm wide, 70.5"/179 cm long

Sizes: One size

Yarn

Weight: Fingering

Knit Picks Palette; 100% wool; 231 yd/211 m per 1.76 oz/50 g

Color A: Conch (1 skein)

Color B: Clarity (1 skein)

Note: The yardage on Color A is tight. If you think you might stray from gauge it would be a good idea to have a second ball handy just in case. You can make the scarf as long as you like by doing more repeats, but you will need more yarn.

Needles: US size 3/3.25 mm

Gauge in Stockinette over 4"/10 cm: 24 sts and 34 rows (see A Note on Gauge, page 12)

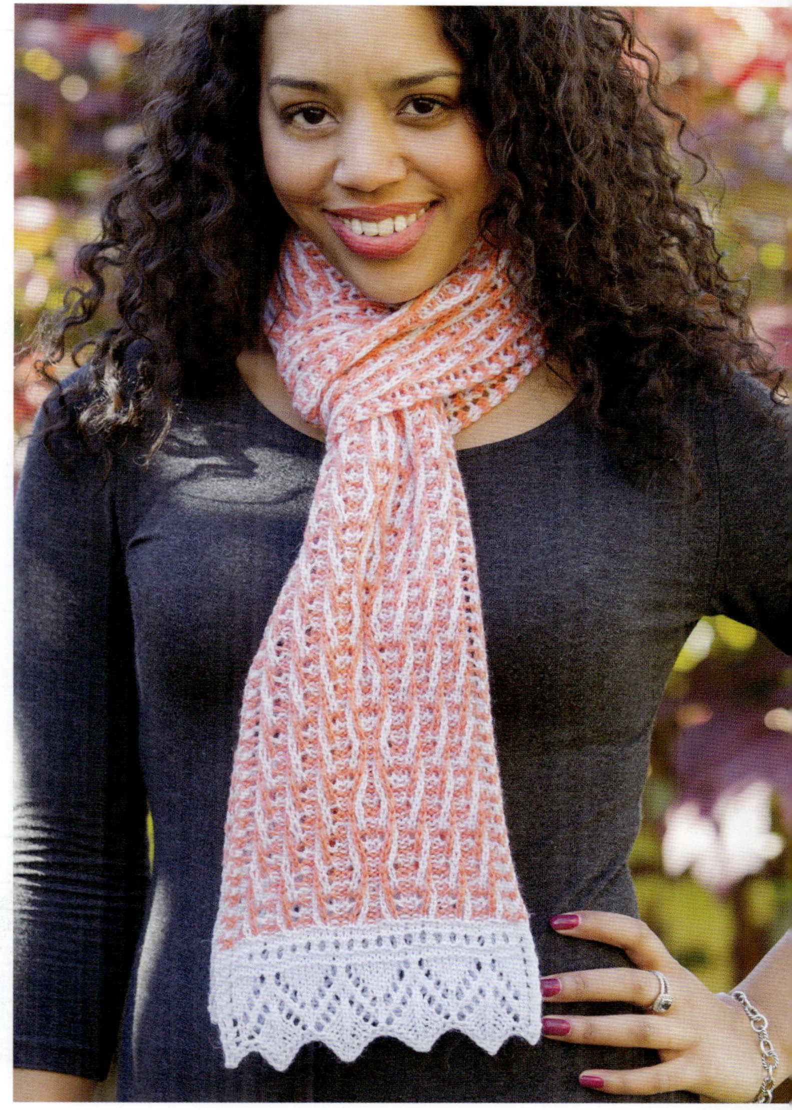

Instructions

LACE EDGE

Using Color B and knitted cast-on method (see Cast-On/Bind-Off, page 107), CO 47 sts.

Knit 2 rows.

Work Edging Chart.

TRANSITION ROWS

Row 1 (RS): K1, k2tog, YO, knit to last 3 sts, YO, ssk, k1.

Row 2 (WS): Sl1-wyif, knit to last st, sl1-wyif.

Row 3: K1, *k2tog, YO; rep from * to last 4 sts, k1, YO, ssk, k1.

Row 4: Sl1-wyif, k2, k2tog, knit to last st, sl1-wyif. [46 sts]

Row 5 : K1, k2tog, YO, knit to last 3 sts, YO, ssk, k1.

Row 6: Sl1-wyif, knit to last st, sl1-wyif.

Row 7: Repeat Row 5.

Row 8: Repeat Row 6.

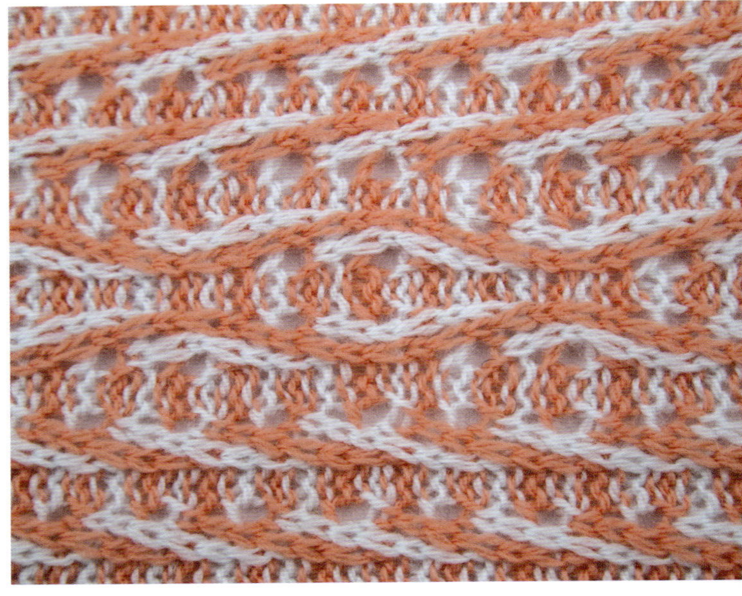

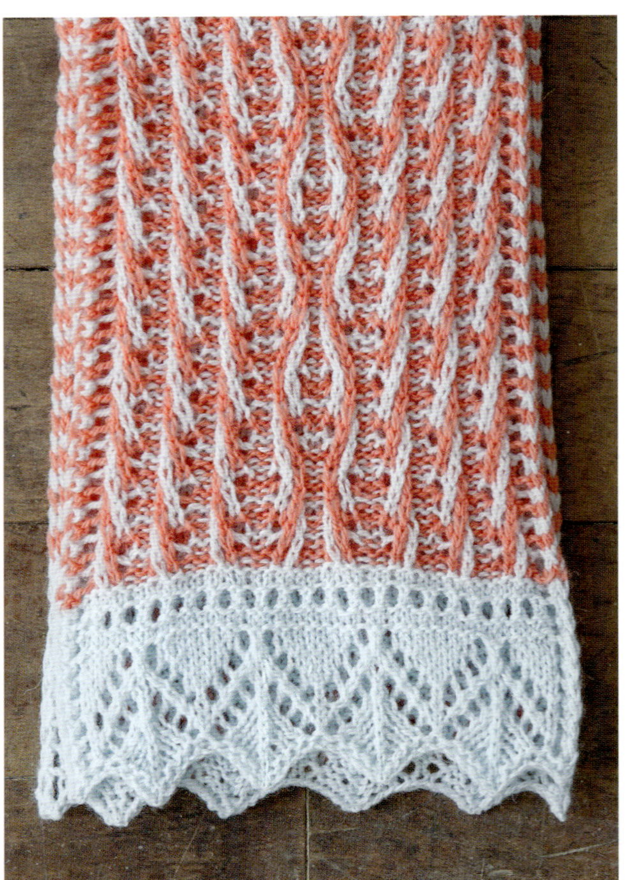

BODY

Join in Color A.

(Work Chart A, work Chart B) 22 times.

Transfer live sts to waste yarn or stitch holder. Cut yarn leaving a tail to weave in later.

LACE EDGE

Using Color B and knitted cast-on method, CO 47 sts.

Knit 2 rows.

Work Edging Chart.

TRANSITION ROWS

Work Transition Rows 1–5 as previously.

Cut yarn leaving tail 3–4 times the length of the width of the scarf.

With RS facing and using Kitchener stitch (see Joining Techniques, page 110), graft live stitches.

FINISHING

Weave in ends. Block assertively to size. Trim ends.

Edging Chart

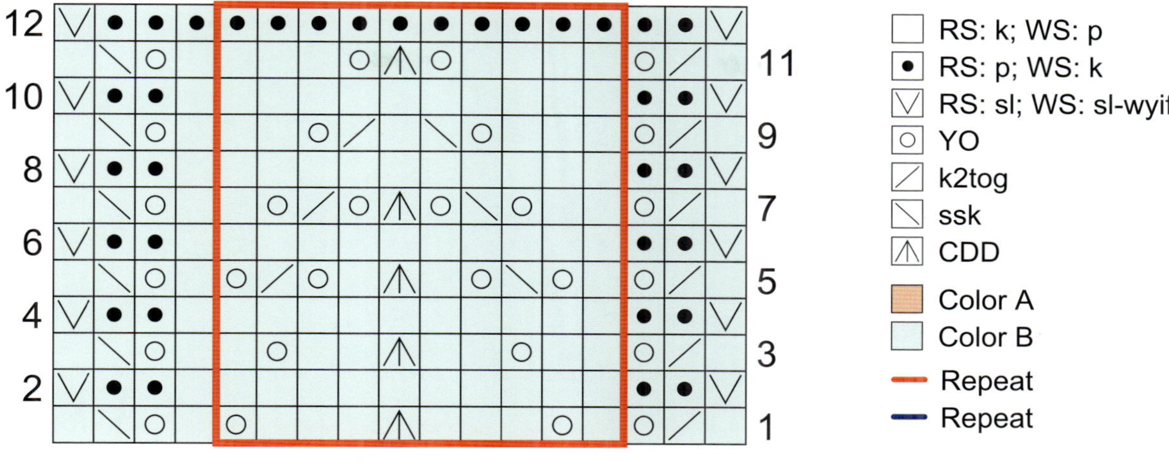

Chart A

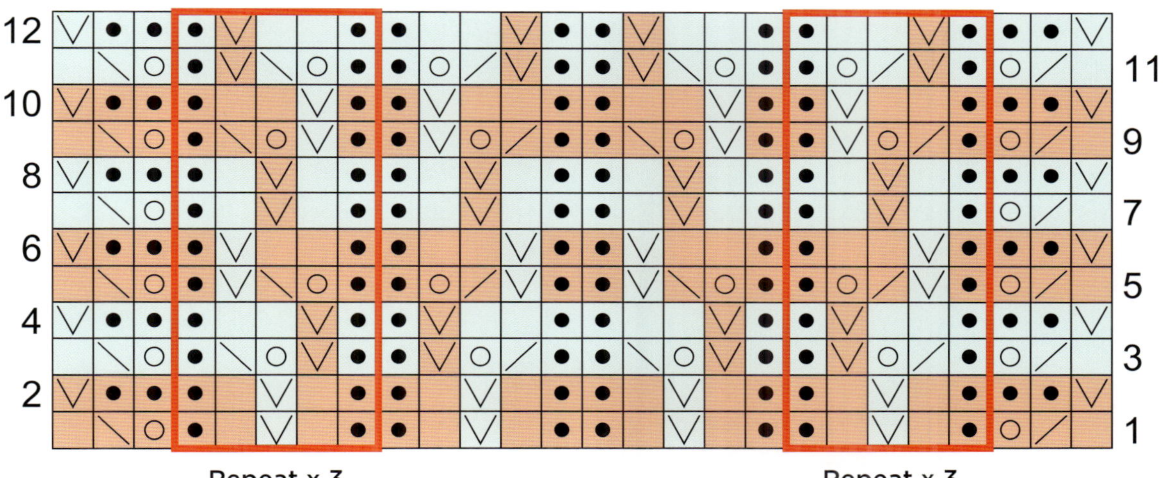

Chart B

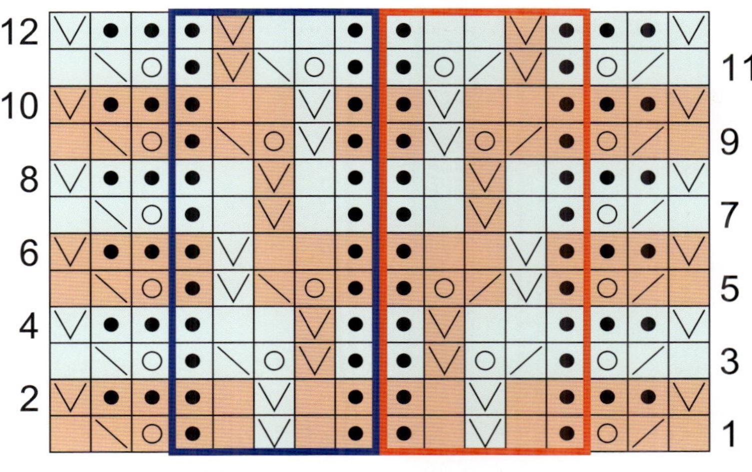

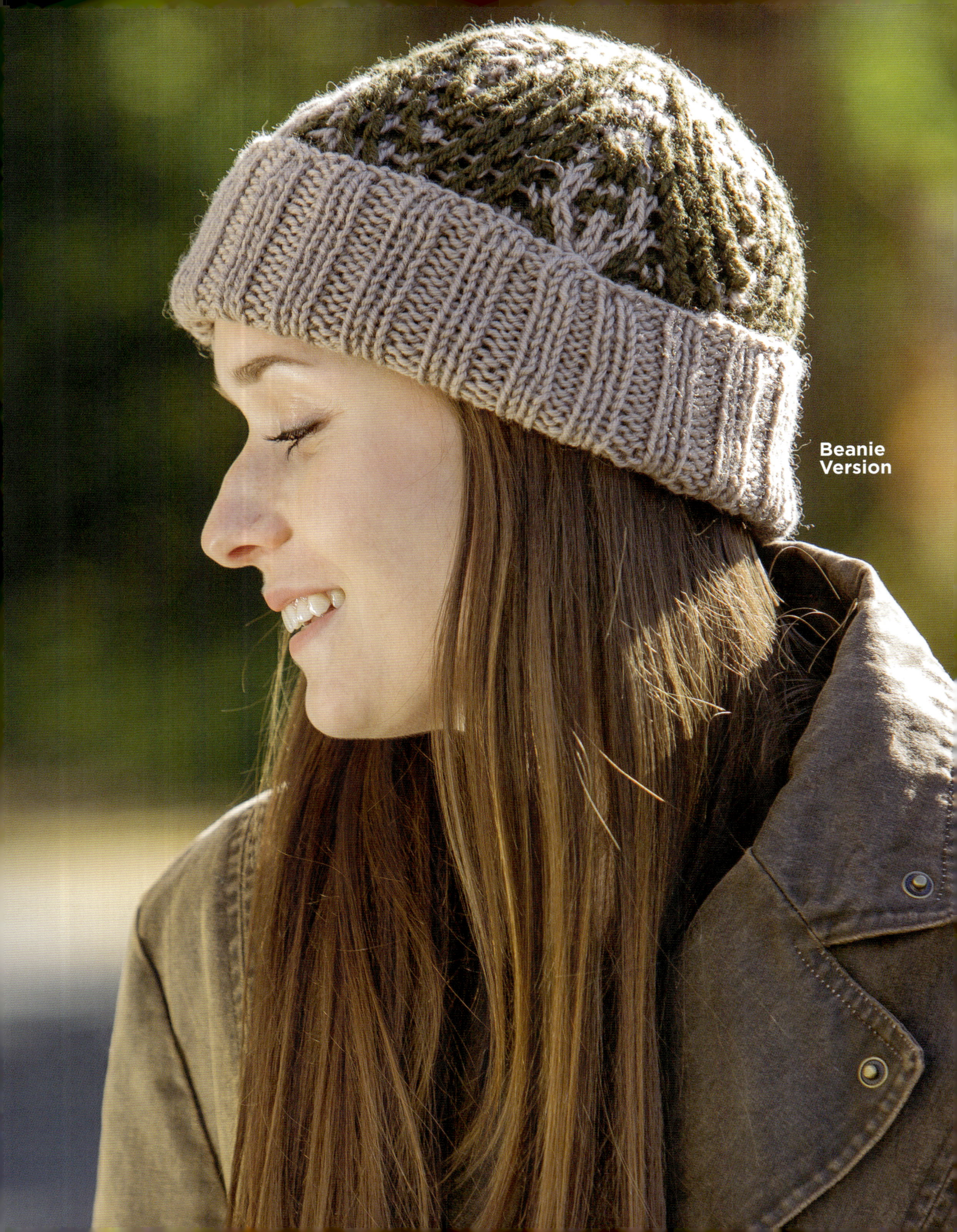
Beanie
Version

Quatrefoil Cap

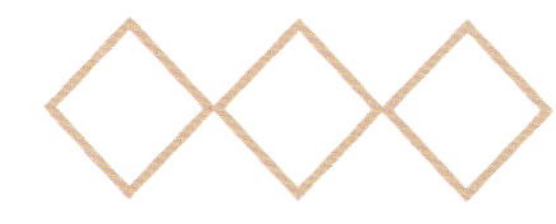

Starting off a hat at the crown opens up a whole world of options when it comes to design. By careful control of the interplay of increases and mosaic lace, this pattern grows a beautiful counterpane from the top down. At that point, you can choose a slouchy or fitted cap—the beanie—and work the appropriate number of repeats. Upon deciding to knit both versions as samples, I also thought it would be good fun to swap the colors to demonstrate how drastically such a change affects the final product.

Finished Measurements: Slouch: 19"/48 cm around brim (stretches to 22"/56 cm), 10.5"/26.5 cm tall
Beanie: 18"/46 cm around brim (stretches to 24"/31 cm), 10"/25.5 cm tall
Sizes: Slouch and Beanie
Yarn
  Weight: DK
  Patons Classic Wool DK Superwash; 100% wool; 125 yd/144 m per 1.75 oz/50 g
  Color A: Deep Olive (1 skein)
  Color B: Latte (1 skein)
Needles: US size 7/4.5 mm, preferred needles for knitting in the round (see Knitting in the Round, page 105)
Notions: Stitch marker
Gauge in Stockinette over 4"/10 cm: 14 sts and 24 rows (see A Note on Gauge, page 12)

Notes
- With the circular cast-on you will have two ends in a very small space and yarn management is going to be a bit tricky. I found that tying the dangling ends in a neat bow and tucking them inside the piece helped keep them in line.
- When joining in Color B to begin charts, use a slip knot in place of the first YO so that the yarn is secure.
- Because there are decreases that bridge the rounds there are spots where it is necessary to juggle the stitches a bit at the beginning of some rounds.

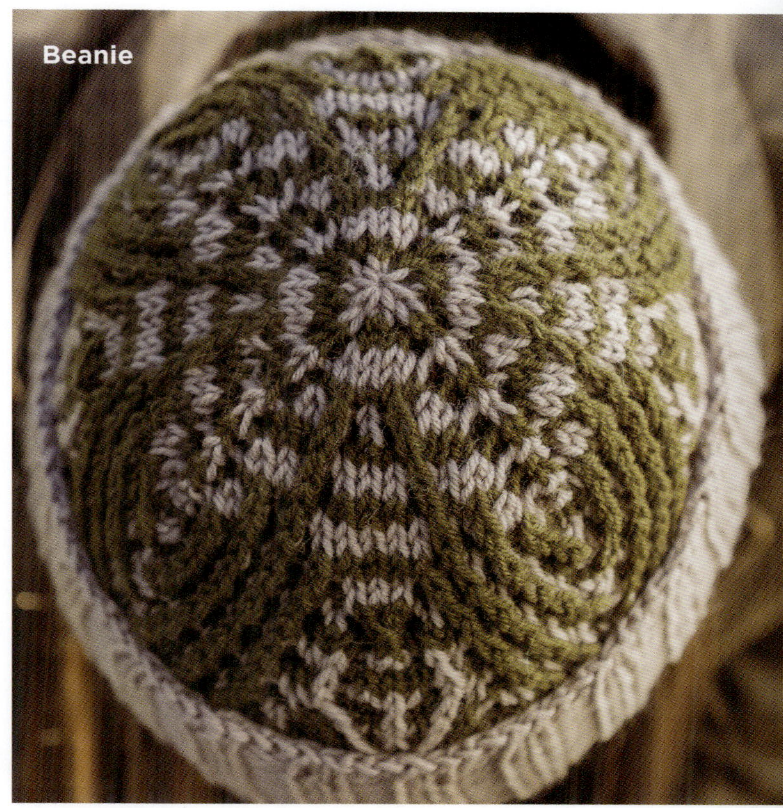

Special Stitch
ssk-pssf-sl: slip, slip, knit - pass slipped stitch forward - slip; ssk then return knit stitch to LH needle, pass the next stitch forward over the knit stitch and drop off the front of the needle, slip the knit stitch purl-wise back to RH needle. [2 stitches decreased]

Instructions

Using Color A, circular cast-on method (see Cast-On/Bind-Off, page 106), and preferred method of knitting in the round, CO 8 sts. Place marker to indicate beginning of round and join to work in the round, being careful not to twist sts.

Knit 2 rounds.

Work Chart A, repeating each round 4 times around. [88 sts]

SLOUCH ONLY:

Work Chart B twice, repeating each round 4 times around.

Work Chart C once, repeating each round 4 times around.

Brim

Round 1: With A, knit.
Rounds 2–11: *K2, p2; rep from * to end of round.

Using the 2 x 2 ribbing bind-off method (see Cast-On/Bind-Off, page 109), BO all sts.

Note for Slouch: Begin Round 3 of both Charts B and C by removing beginning of round marker, slipping first st, replacing marker, then working chart as shown. This first stitch needs to be "borrowed" for the last decrease of the round.

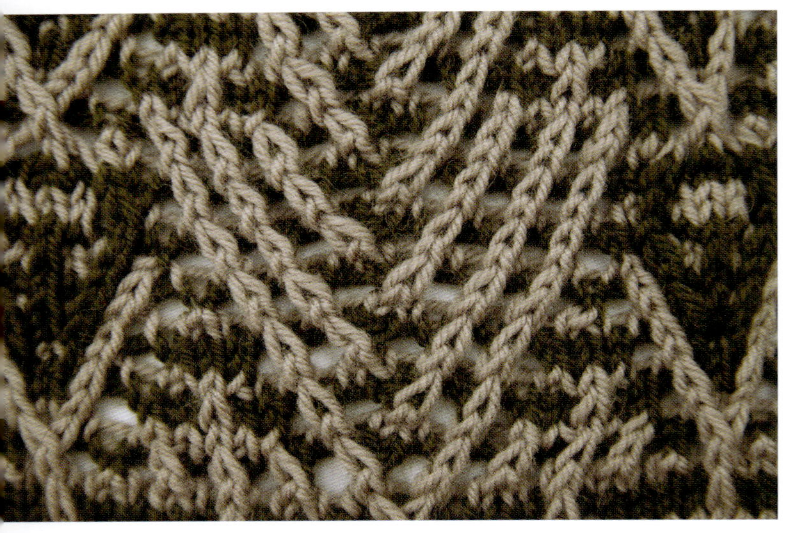

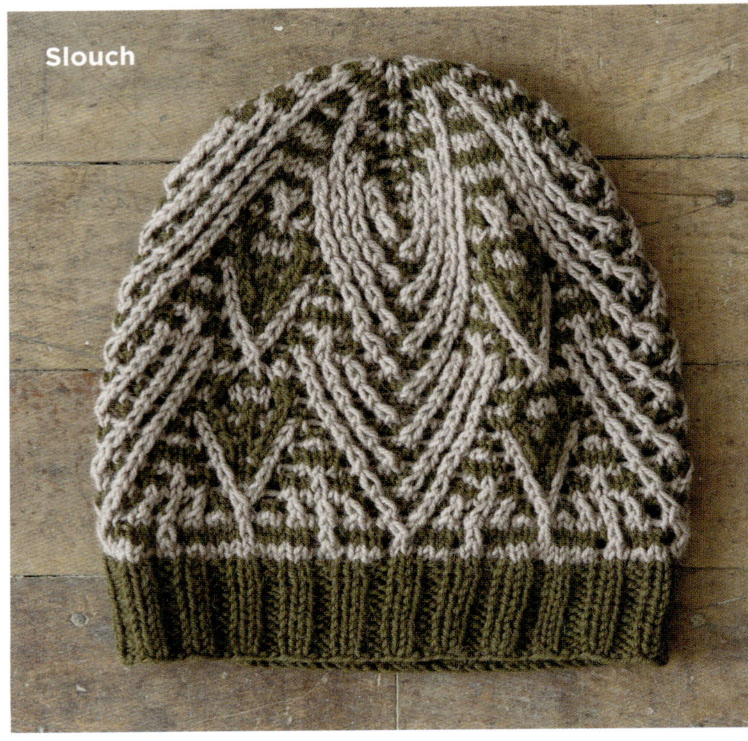

Slouch

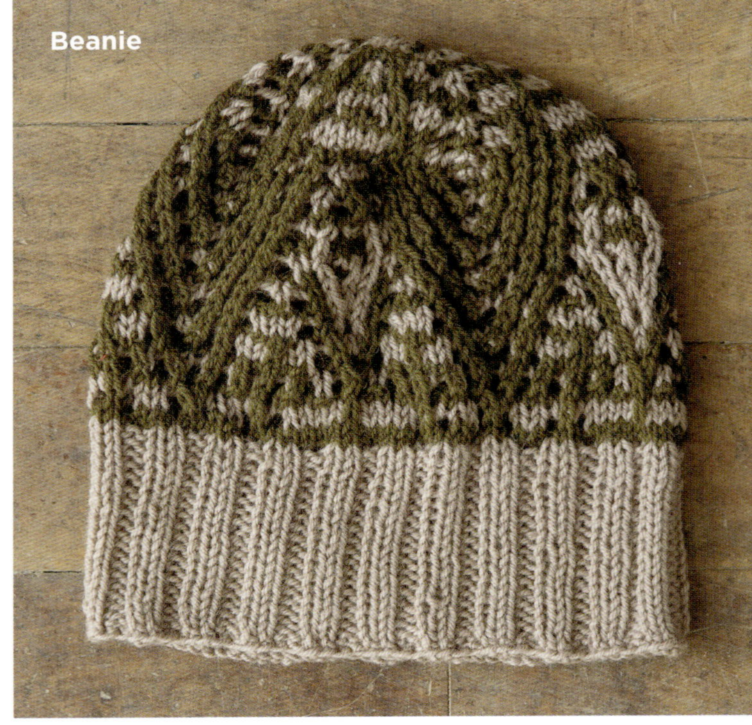

Beanie

Work Chart B once, repeating each round 4 times around.

Work Chart C once, repeating each round 4 times around.

Brim

Round 1: With A, knit.
Rounds 2–18: *K2, p2; rep from * to end of round.

Using the expandable lace bind-off, knit/purl variant method (see Cast-On/Bind-Off, page 109), BO all sts.

Notes for Beanie:
- *The color positions are reversed for the knitted sample. To match sample, cast on in Color B and swap A and B in charts.*
- *Begin Round 3 of both Charts B and C by removing beginning of round marker, slipping first st, replacing marker, then working chart as shown. This first stitch needs to be "borrowed" for the last decrease of the round.*

FINISHING

Weave in ends. Block assertively over bowl or balloon, being careful to not stretch out ribbing. Trim ends.

Chart A

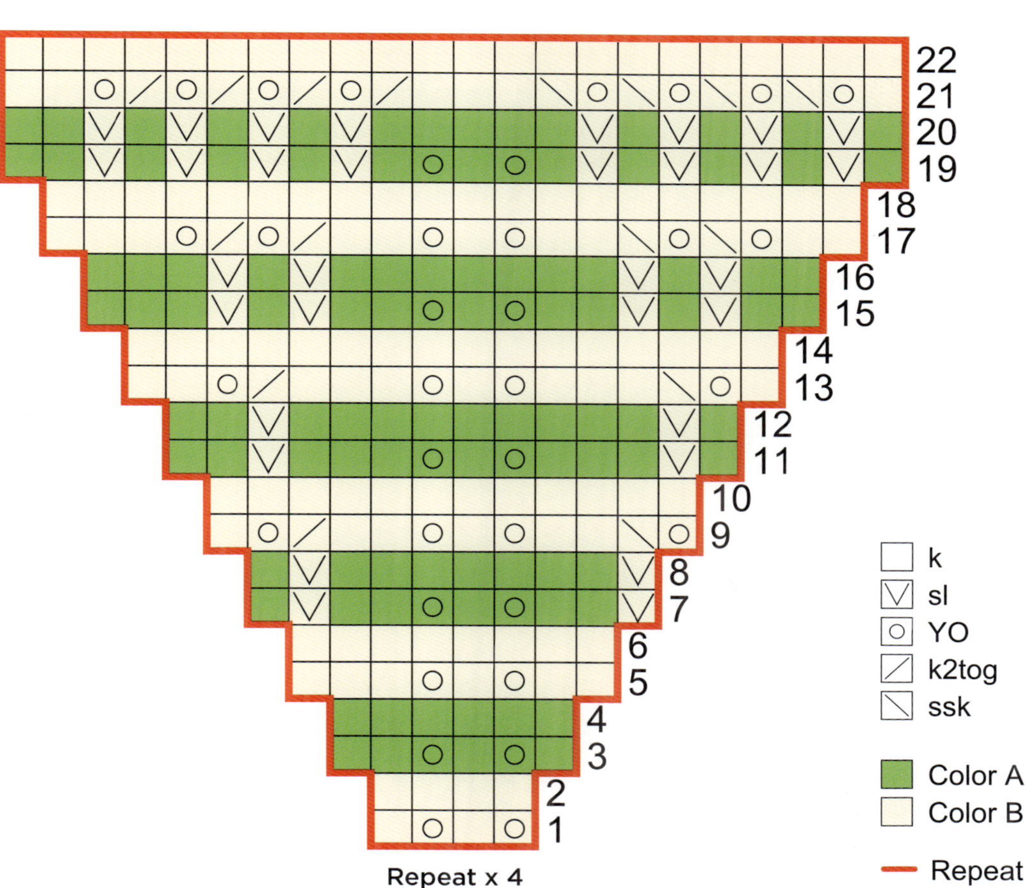

Chart B

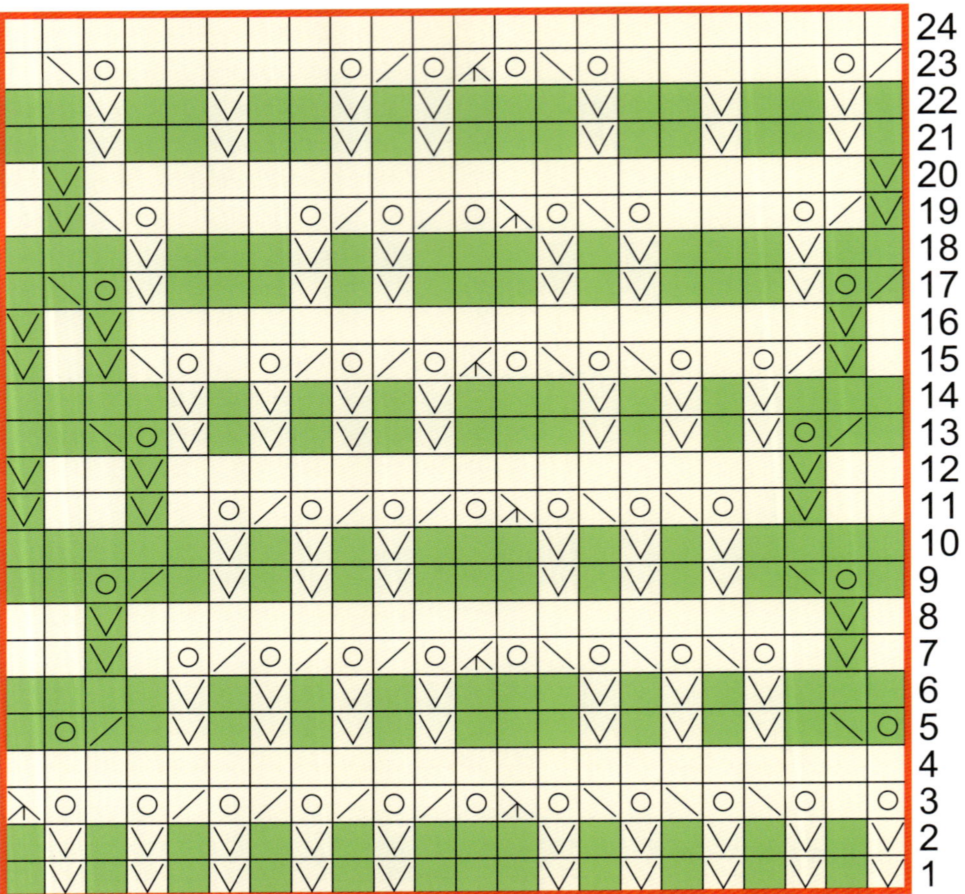

Repeat x 4

Chart C

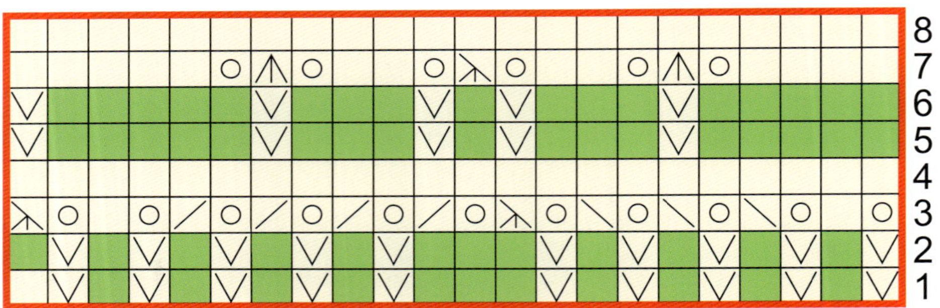

Repeat x 4

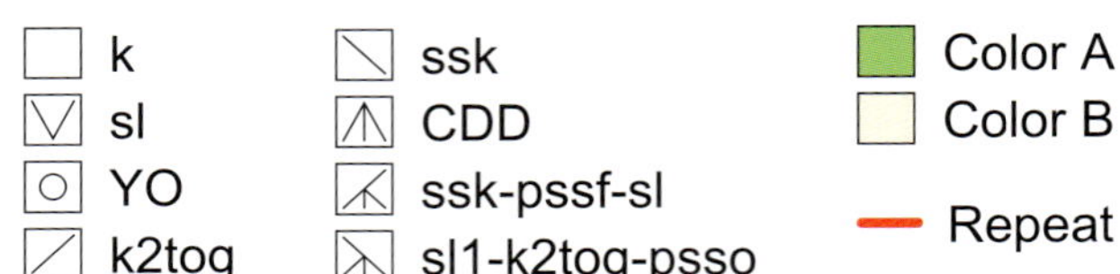

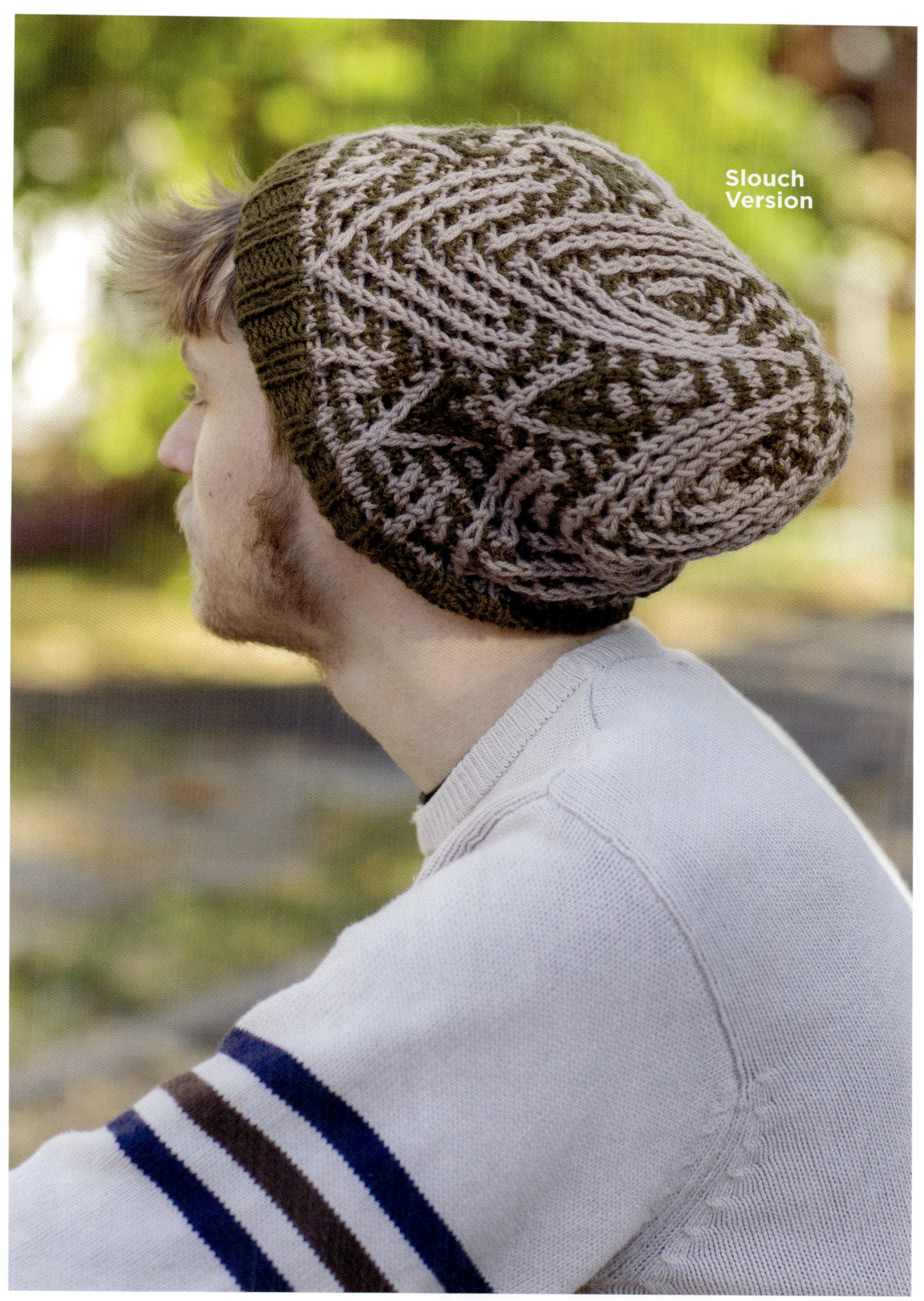
Slouch
Version

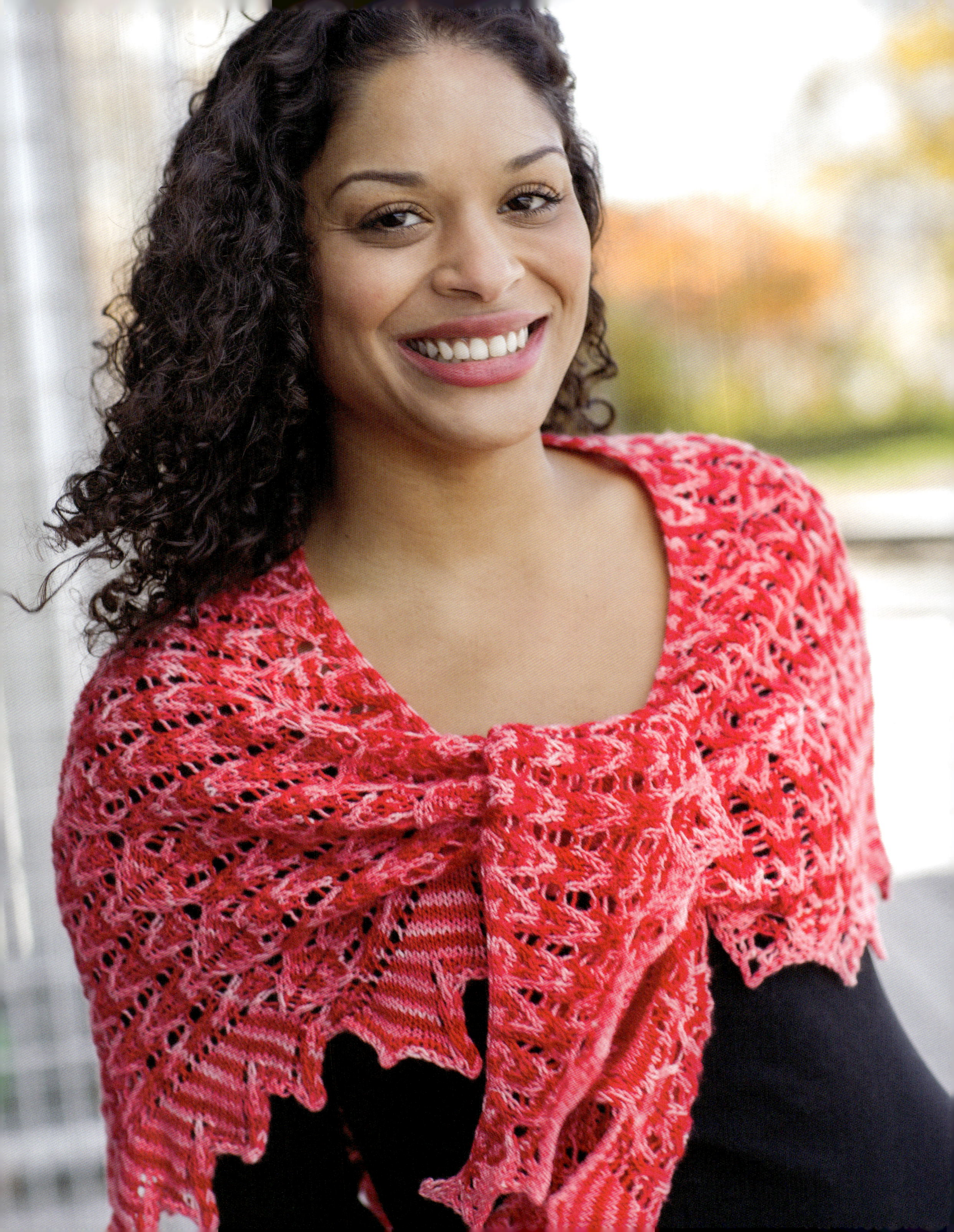

Ves

Collaborations always push me in directions that I probably would have never gone on my own. This shawl was developed as a joint project between myself and the dyer Miss Babs. She asked me to design a shawl using her yarn and Sri Lanka as my inspiration. I spent a lot of time searching the Internet for pictures of all things Sri Lankan and became entranced by the elaborate Ves costumes worn by Sri Lanka's traditional Kandyan dancers. One element of the garb is a heavily embossed headdress with vertical columns tapering to points. I used the unique properties of mosaic lace to mimic the depth of texture and intricacies of the embossing. The end result could not please me more.

Finished Measurements: 21"/53 cm long,
40"/101.5 cm wingspan
Sizes: One size
Yarn
  Weight: Fingering
  Miss Babs Yummy 2-ply; 100% superwash
    merino wool; 400 yd/366 m per 4 oz/113 g
  Color A: Manel (1 skein)
  Color B: Lotus (1 skein)
Needles: US size 5/3.75 mm
Notions: Stitch markers
Gauge in Stockinette over 4"/10 cm: 20 sts and
  26 rows (see A Note on Gauge, page 12)

Notes
• When a slipped stitch occurs between two
  yarn overs it is necessary to treat the yarn
  overs as if they were a double yarn over (see
  Mosaic Lace/Yarn Overs, page 5). To do so
  you must knit into the first YO and purl the
  second YO.

Special Stitch
kfYOb: knit front, yarn over, knit back; knit into
  the front leg of the next stitch but do not
  remove the stitch from the LH needle, wrap
  the working yarn around the RH needle once
  and then knit into the back loop of the same
  stitch. [2 stitches increased]

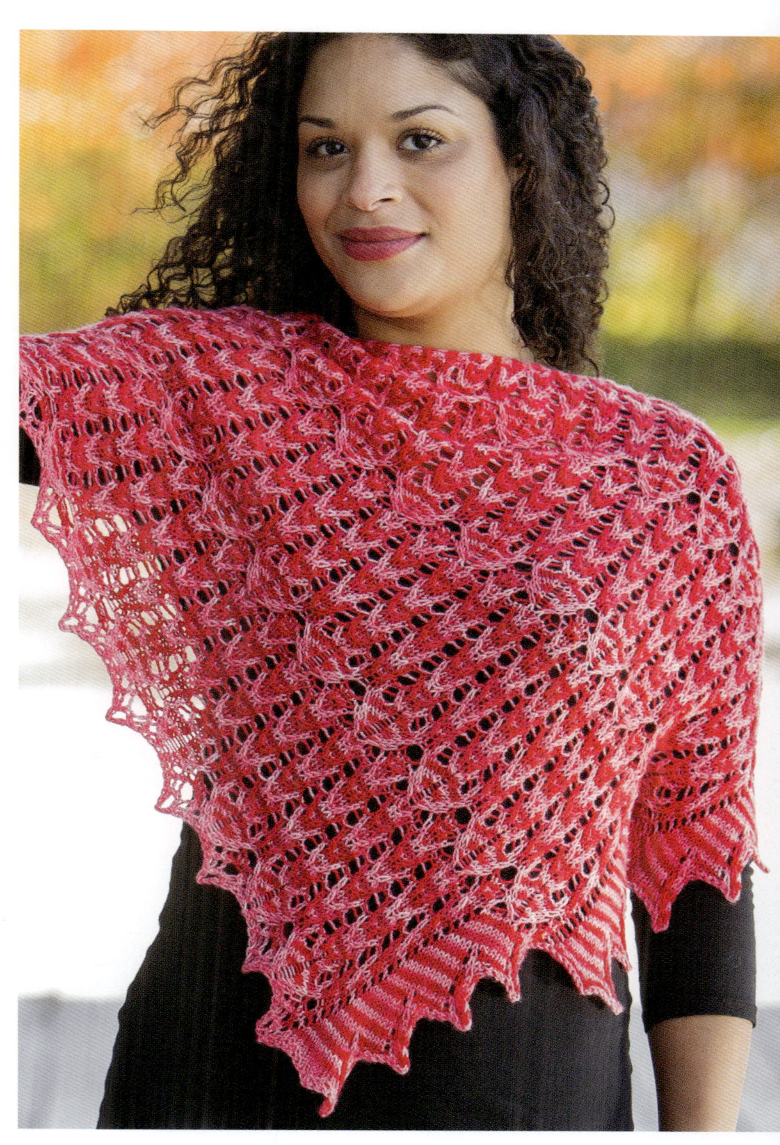

Instructions

Using Color A and long tail cast-on method (see Cast-On/Bind-Off, page 107), CO 3 sts.

SET UP

Knit one row.

Work Set Up Chart once. On the final row, place marker (pm) as indicated. [21 sts]

BODY–PART 1

Work Chart A three times. [36 sts increased]

Notes:
- *To work Chart A, begin with Row 1 and repeat indicated sts until you have one st before the marker.*
- *On Row 12, when binding off, slip first st, *k1, insert LH needle through front legs of sts on RH needle, k2tog; rep from * 5 times for a total of 6 sts bound off. You will have one st remaining on RH needle and 11 sts before the marker.*

BODY–PART 2

Work Chart B, repeating indicated sts until you have one st before the marker.

Work [Part 1, Part 2] four more times for a total of 5 full repeats. [201 sts]

Work Part 1 once more and then work Rows 37–42 of Chart B. [246 sts]

Work Chart C once. [254 sts]

Using the expandable lace bind-off, knit variant method (see Cast-On/Bind-Off, page 109) and treating each YO in a double YO as individual sts, BO all sts.

---

*Note: On Row 48, when binding off, slip first st, *k1, insert LH needle through front legs of sts on RH needle, k2tog* rep from * seventeen times for a total of eighteen sts bound off. Purl 11 sts and place marker for a total of 12 sts between marker and edge of piece.*

FINISHING

Weave in ends. Block just enough to pull open the lace portions, being careful that you don't overstretch the texture out of the piece. Trim ends.

Set Up Chart

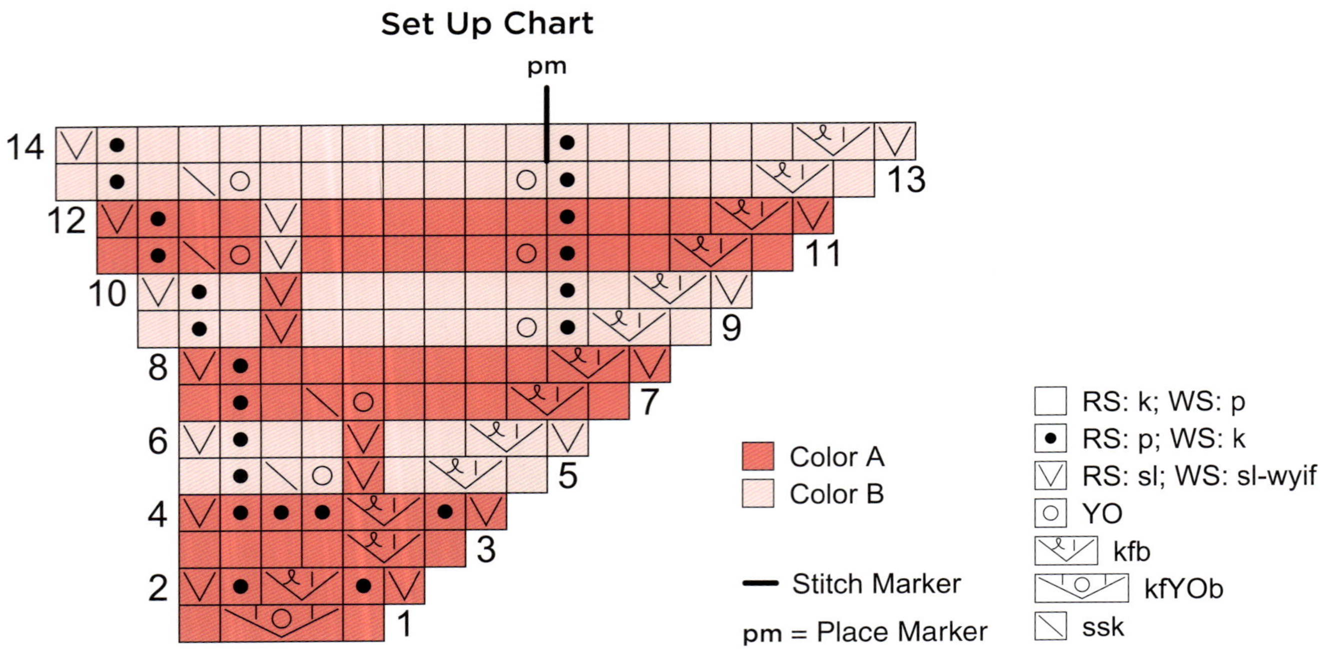

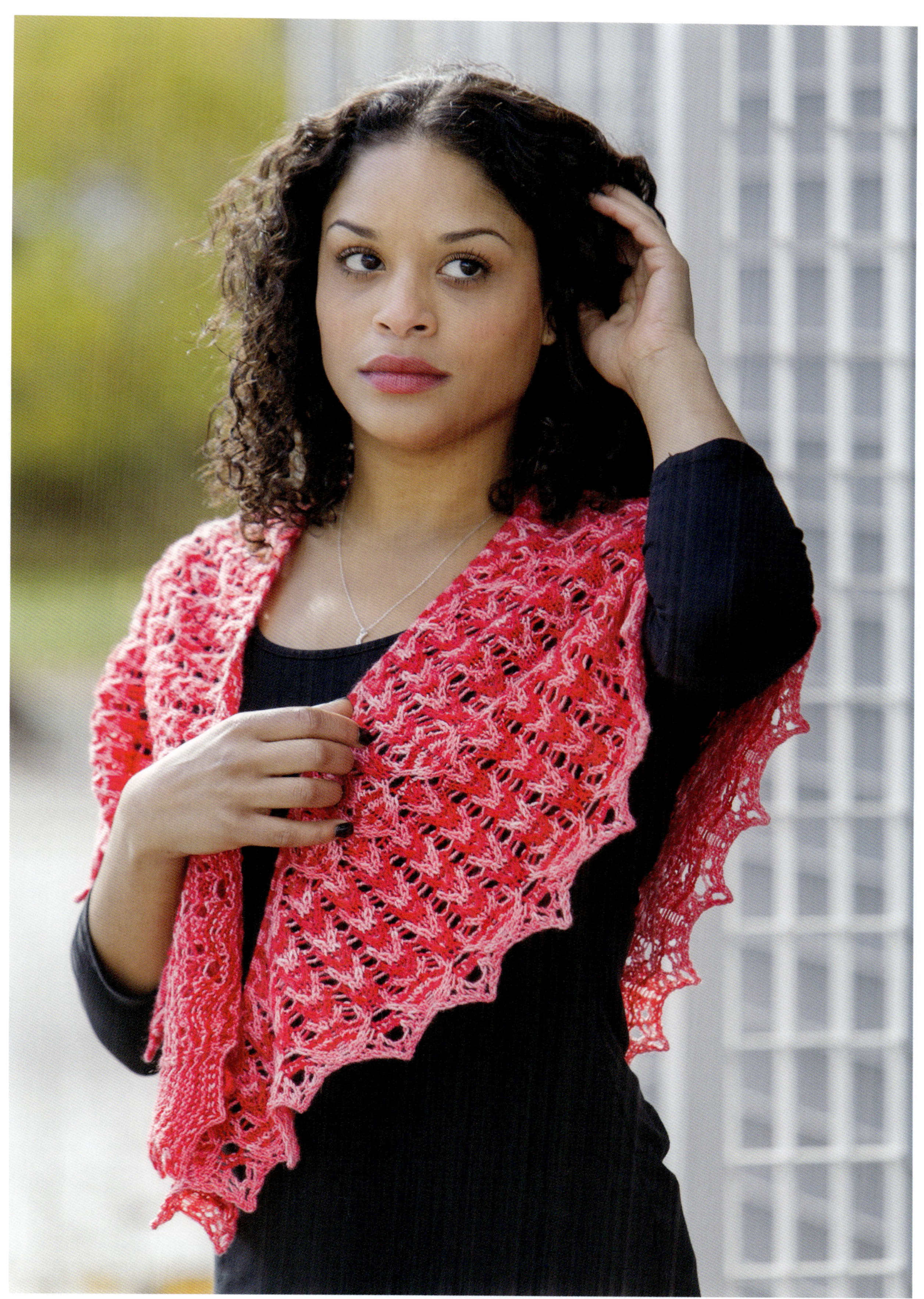

Chart A

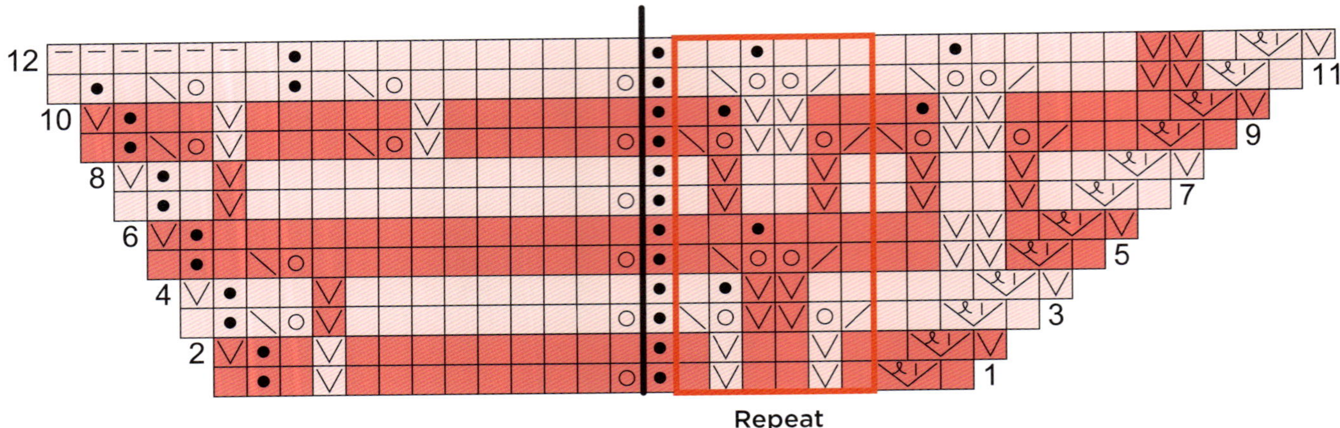

Chart B

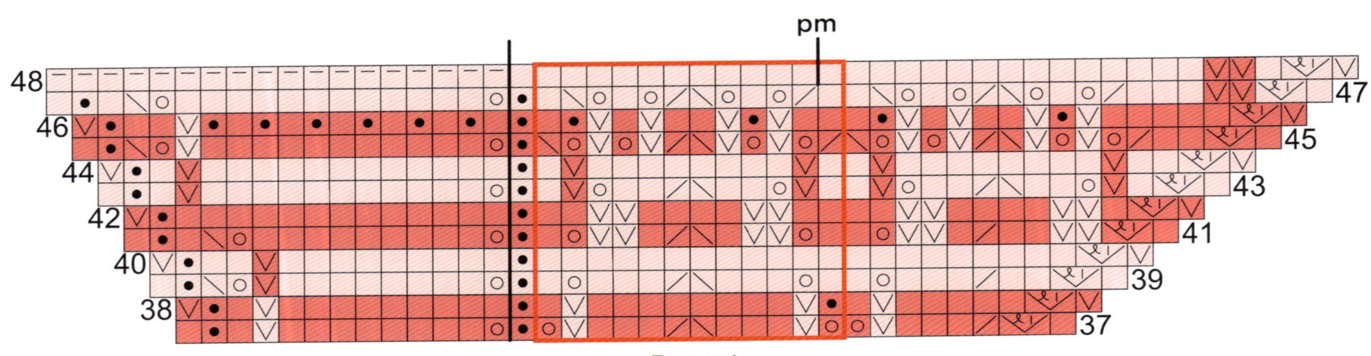

Chart C

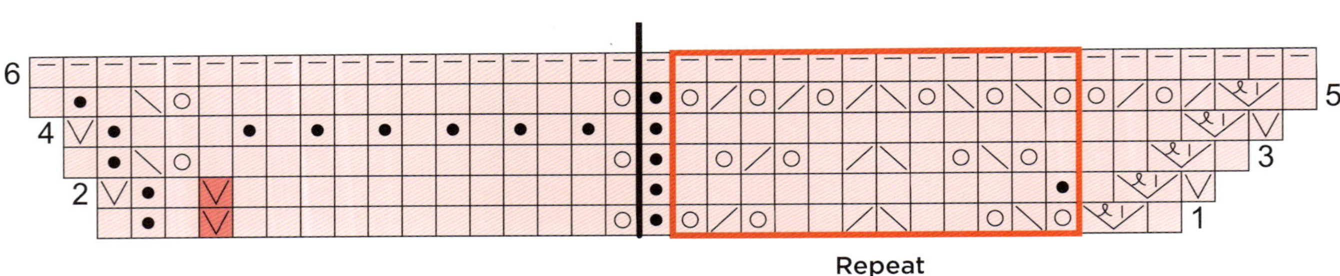

□ RS: k; WS: p	⧄ k2tog
• RS: p; WS: k	⧅ ssk
⋁ RS: sl; WS: sl-wyif	— WS: BO
○ YO	
kfb	

Color A
Color B
— Repeat
— Stitch Marker

pm = Place Marker

Pinwheel Market Bag

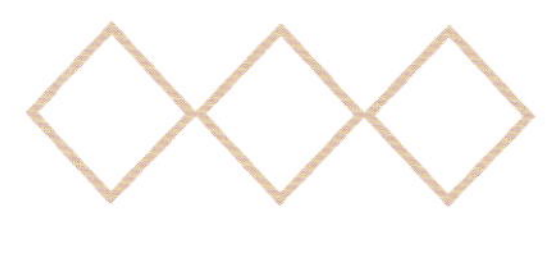

Just because something is supremely functional doesn't mean it cannot be attractive too. The durability of cotton yarn makes it perfect for creating a market bag for carrying everything from vegetables to beach toys (and maybe even more yarn). I chose to begin with a solid base to avoid items falling out the bottom and then went with an expandable lace pattern to make the bag roomy. The mosaic top and handle bring both beauty and stability to the top of the piece.

Finished Measurements: 27"/68.5 cm
  circumference, 26"/66 cm long.
Sizes: One size
Yarn
  Weight: DK
  Tahki Cotton Classic; 100% mercerized cotton;
   108 yd/100 m per 1.75 oz/50 g
  Color A: Grey #3009 (2 skeins)
  Color B: Butter Yellow #3548 (2 skeins)
Needles: US size 6/4 mm, preferred needles
  for knitting in the round (see Knitting in the
  Round, page 105)
Notions: Stitch holder or waste yarn, stitch
  marker
Gauge in Stockinette over 4"/10 cm: 18 sts and
  28 rows (see A Note on Gauge, page 12)

Notes
• With the circular cast-on you will have
  two ends in a very small space and yarn
  management is going to be a bit tricky. I found
  that tying the dangling ends in a neat bow
  and tucking them inside the piece helped keep
  them in line.

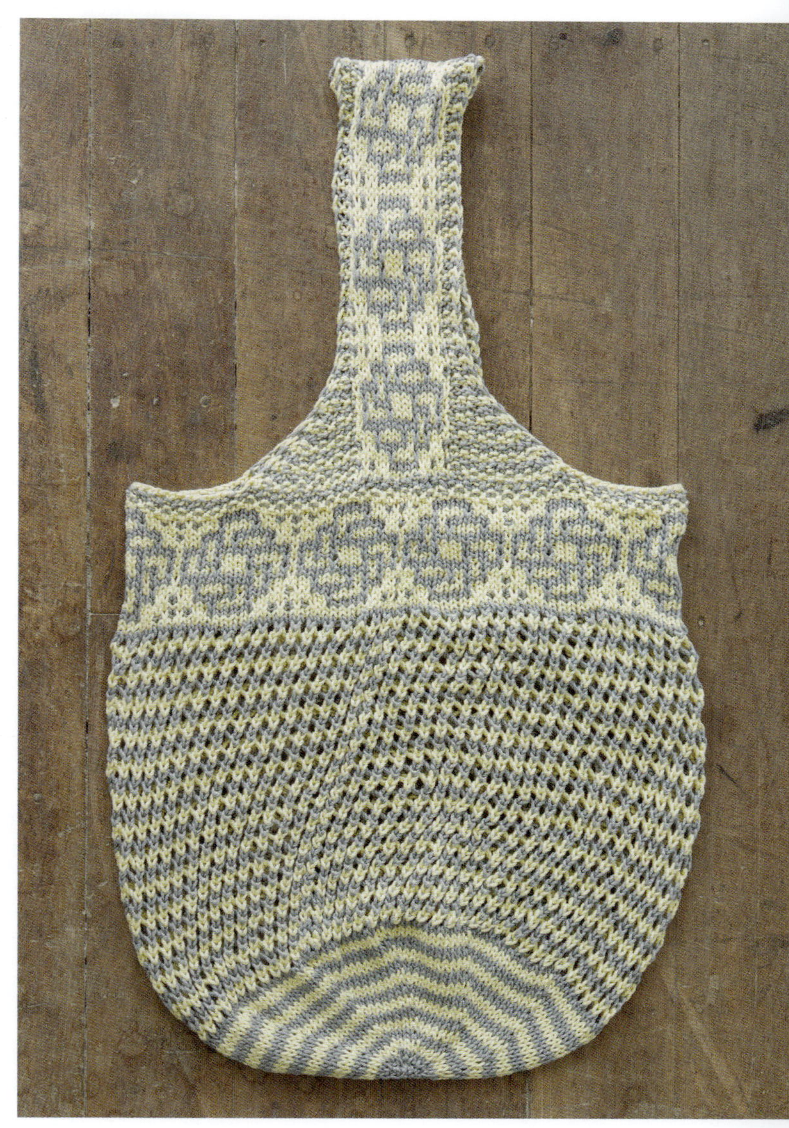

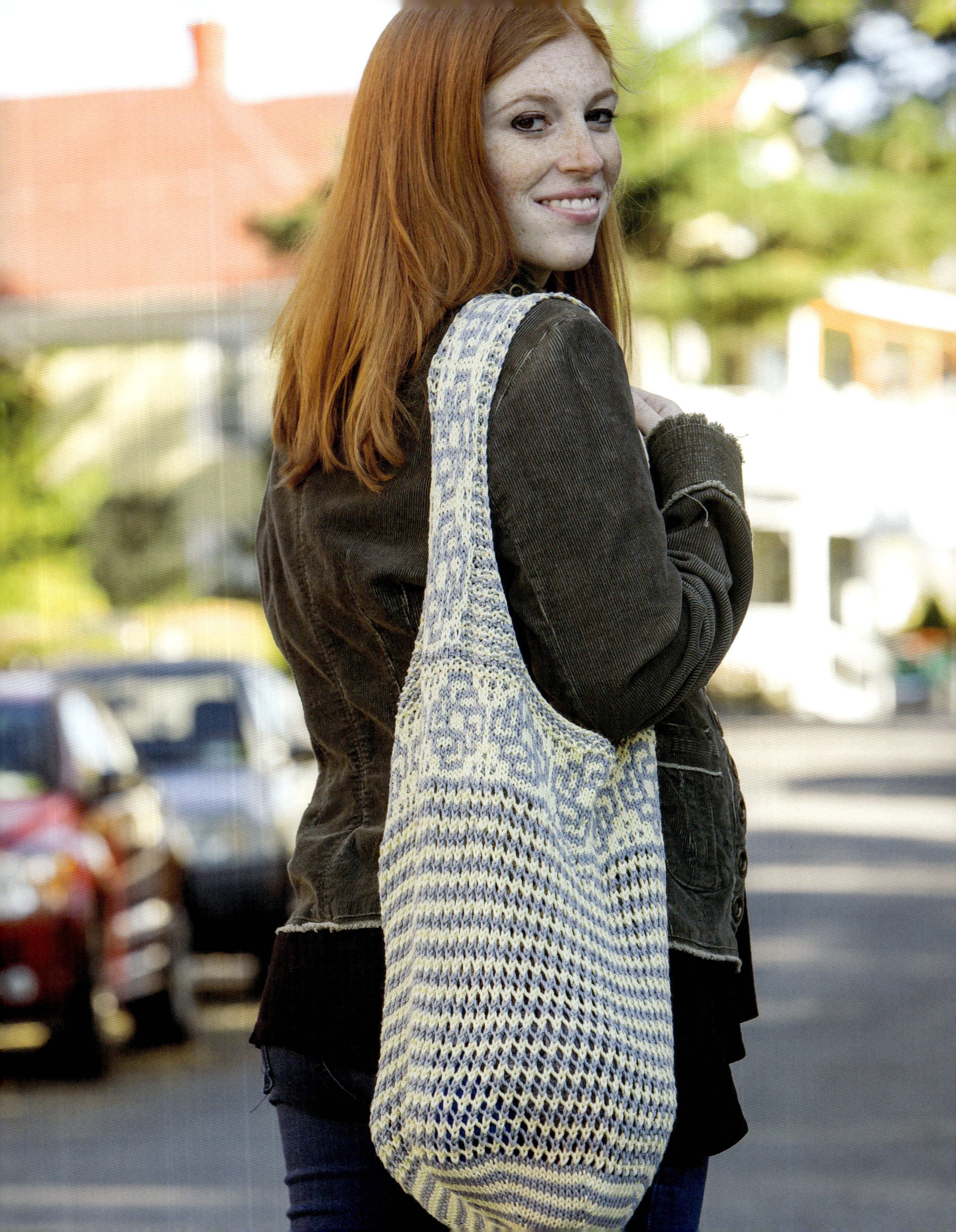

Instructions

BOTTOM INCREASE SECTION

Using Color A, circular cast-on method (see Cast-On/Bind-Off, page 106), and preferred method of knitting in the round, CO 5 sts. Place marker to indicate beginning of round and join for knitting in the round, being careful not to twist sts.

Round 1: Kfb 5 times. [10 sts]

Rounds 2 and 4: Knit.

Round 3: Kfb 10 times. [20 sts]

Round 5: With B, *k2, YO, pm; rep from * to end of round. [10 sts increased]

Round 6: Knit, knitting all YO through the back loop.

Round 7: With A, *knit to marker, YO, sm; rep from * to end of round. [10 sts increased]

Round 8: Knit, knitting all YO through the back loop.

Repeat Rounds 5–8 five more times. [140 sts] On repeats of Round 5 do not place new markers, simply knit to marker, yo, sm instead.

LACE BODY

Round 1: With B, *YO, k2tog; rep from *to end of round.

Round 2: Knit.

Rounds 3 and 4: With A, rep Rounds 1 and 2.

Repeat Rounds 1–4 thirteen more times for a total of 56 rounds (28 stripes).

TRANSITION

With B, knit 2 rounds.

MOSAIC TOP

Work Rounds 1–26 of Chart A once, repeating each round 10 times around.

	k
∨	sl

	Color A
	Color B
—	Repeat

HANDLE SET UP

Round 1: With B, knit.

Round 2: *K1, p1; rep from * to end of round.

Round 3: With A, *p1, k1; rep from * to end of round.

Round 4: *K1, p1; rep from * to end of round.

Round 5: With B, *p1, k1; rep from * to end of round.

*Note: On bind-offs in Round 6, bind off in pattern as follows: k1, *p1, lift rightmost stitch on RH needle up, over and off the tip of the needle, k1, lift rightmost stitch on RH needle up, over and off the tip of the needle, rep from * until 27 sts have been bound off.*

Chart A

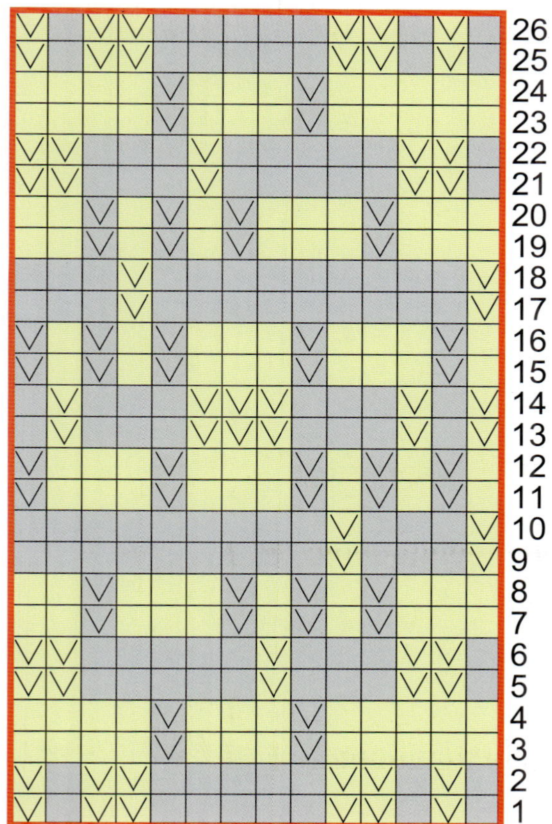

Repeat x 10

Round 6: K8, (k1, p1) seven times, BO 27 sts, (k1, p1) six times, k17, (p1, k1) six times, p1, BO 27 sts, k1, (p1, k1) six times, k7. Slip the 22 sts from beginning of round to first BO section onto RH needle. Transfer 43 live sts between the bound off sections to waste yarn.

Cut both yarns, leaving tails to weave in.

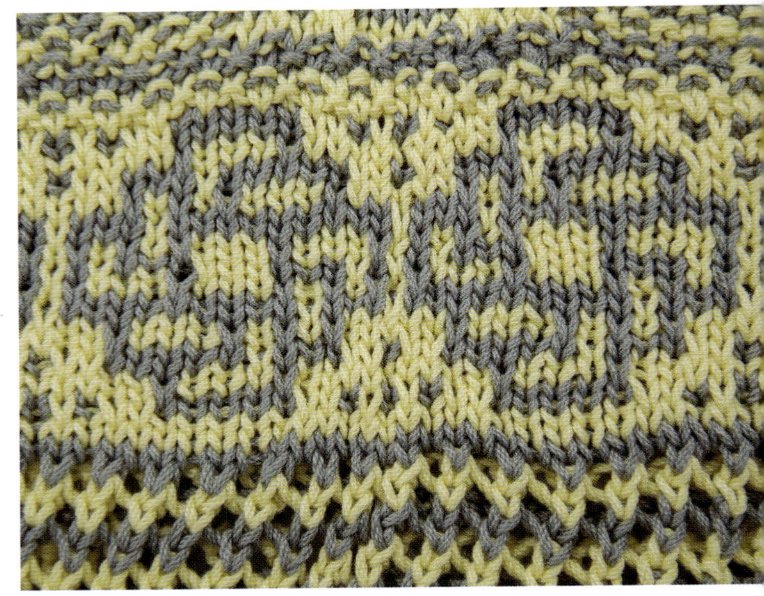

Handle Decrease Chart

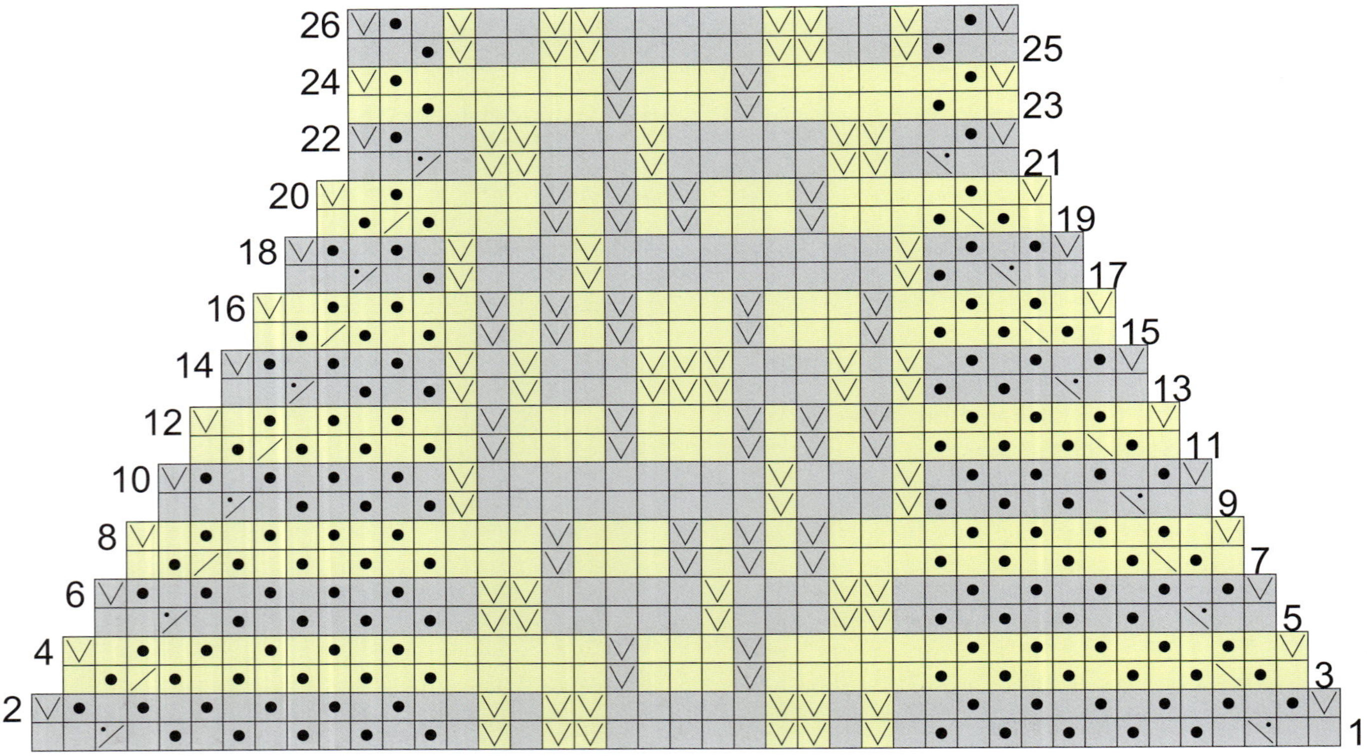

	RS: k; WS: p		ssk		Color A
•	RS: p; WS: k		p2tog		Color B
∨	RS: sl; WS: sl-wyif		ssp		
∕	k2tog				

HANDLES (WORKED FLAT)

Work Handle Decrease Chart once. [21 sts]

Work Handle Chart twice.

Next row (RS): K2, p1, k15, p1, k2.

Cut yarns and transfer sts to waste yarn.

Pick up remaining live sts and repeat Handle Instructions for second side.

FINISHING

Weave in ends. Fold bag so that handles are flat and laying on top of each other. Block assertively to shape. If you have crease lines where piece was blocked flat, refold so that they are flattened out, steam, and pat lightly to remove creases.

With WS facing, transfer held sts to needles and graft handles together using Color B and Kitchener stitch (see Joining Techniques, page 110).

Handle Chart

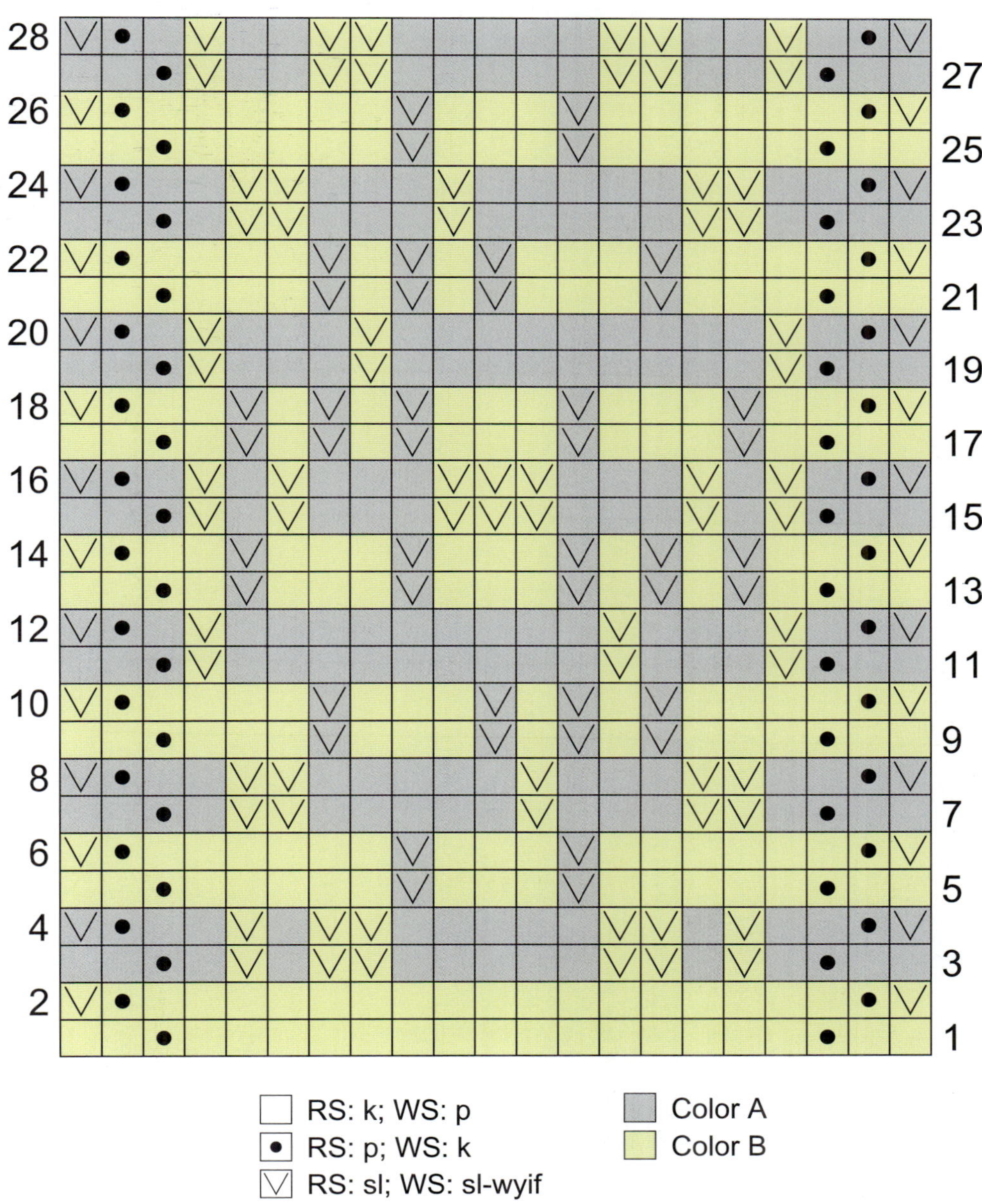

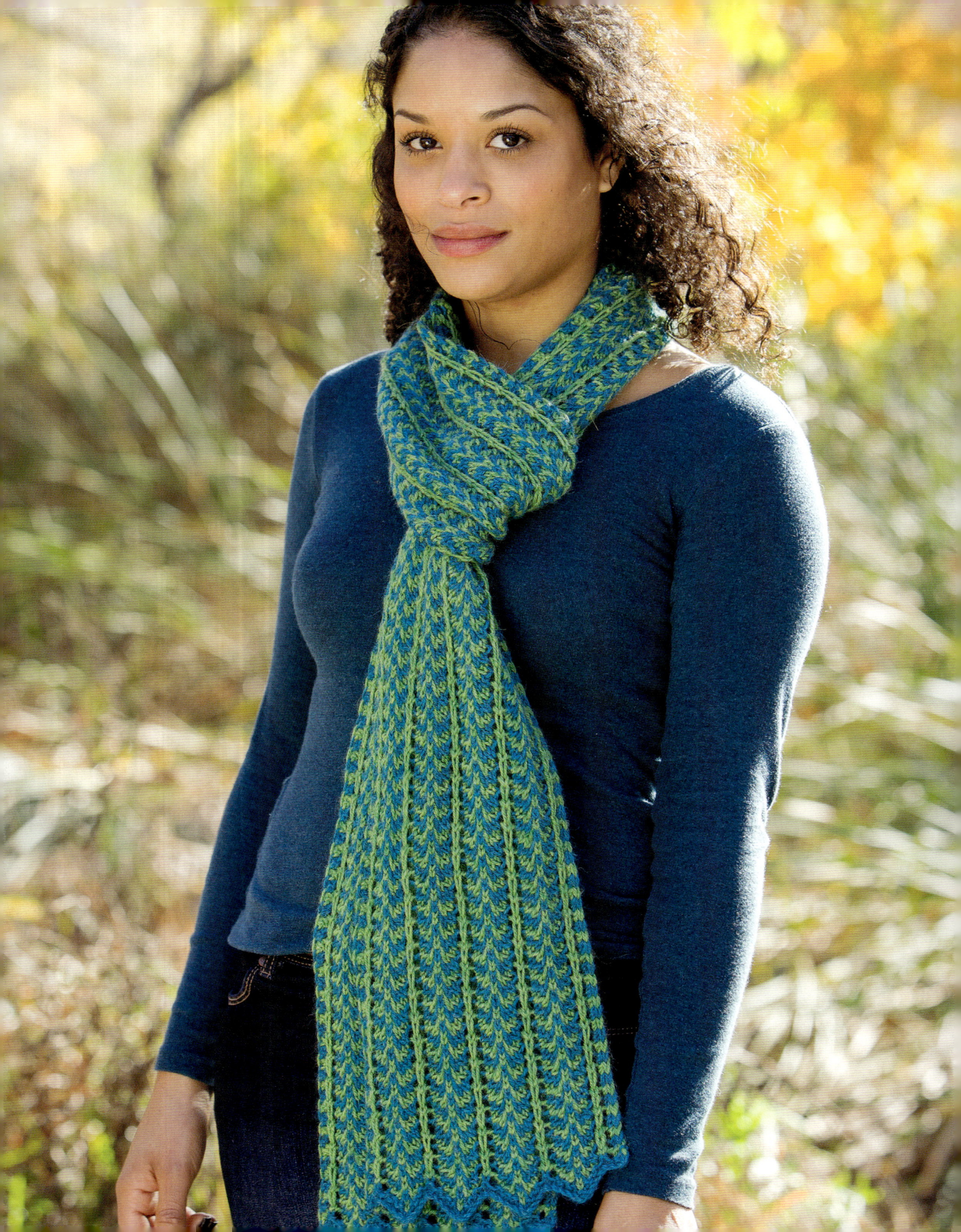

Clupeidae

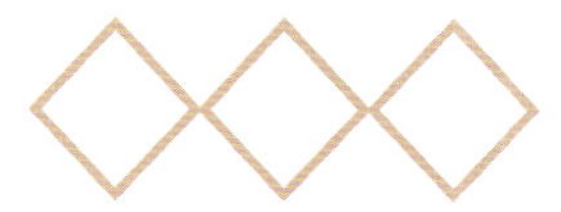

One of my favorite ways to wear a scarf is by doubling it over and then pulling the ends through the created loop, but that technique has one undesirable result. One of the "tails" will always have the wrong side facing the world. This scarf is my solution to that problem. By creating two separate tails you can then join them together with the right sides both facing out. Once joined, the pattern is continued until you have enough length to double over and form a loop. I think of it as a "self-styling" scarf. Put it on, pull the tails through the loop and you are ready to go.

Finished Measurements: 7"/18 cm wide, 50"/127 cm long

Sizes: One size

Yarn

  Weight: Sport

  Berroco Ultra Alpaca Light; 50% super fine alpaca, 50% Peruvian wool; 144 yd/132 m per 1.76 oz/50 g

  Color A: Caribbean Mix #42186 (1 skein)

  Color B: Seedling Mix #42187 (1 skein)

Needles: US size 8/5 mm

Notions: Stitch holder or waste yarn

Gauge in Stockinette over 4"/10 cm: 16 sts and 22 rows (see A Note on Gauge, page 12)

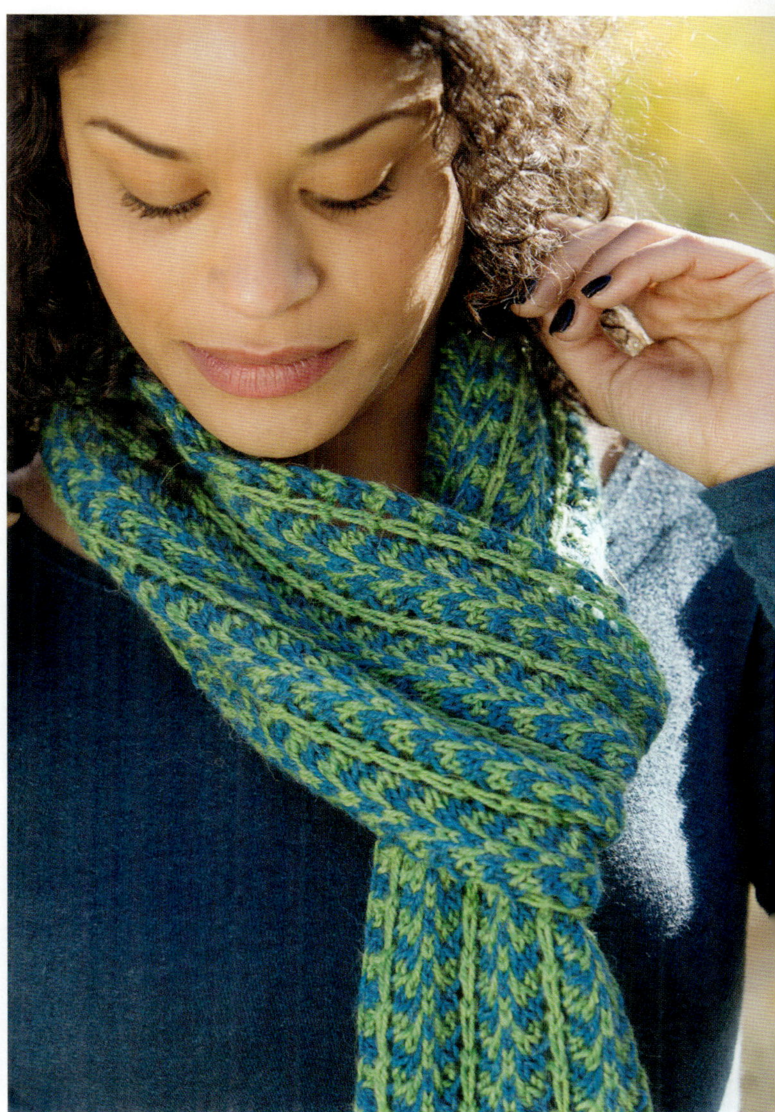

"

Instructions

FIRST HALF

Using Color A and cable cast-on method (see Cast-On/Bind-Off, page 105), CO 47 sts.

Set Up
Knit 2 rows.

Tail One
Join in Color B.

Work Chart A 60 times, then work Row 1 of Chart A once more.

Transfer sts to waste yarn or stitch holder. Cut yarn leaving tails for weaving in.

SECOND HALF

Using Color A and cable cast-on method, CO 47 sts.

Set Up
Knit 2 rows.

Tail Two
Join in Color B.

Work Chart A 58 times, then work Row 1 of Chart A once more. Do not cut yarn.

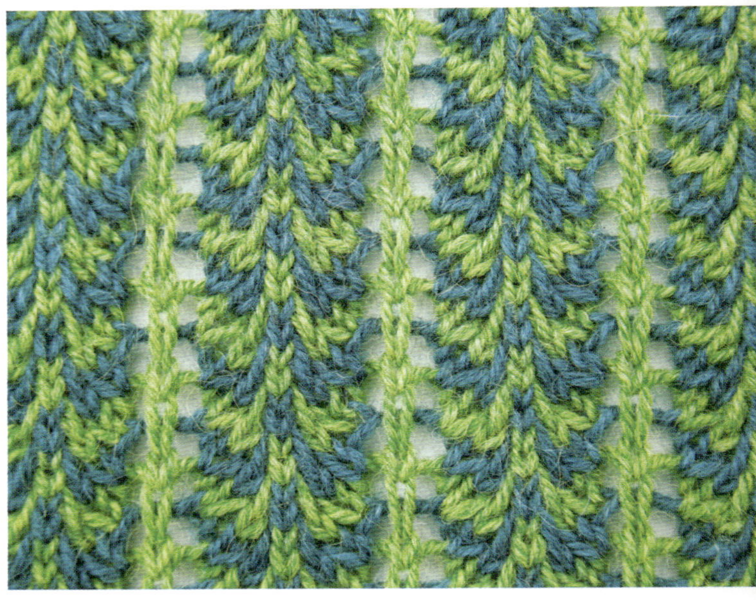

ATTACH TAILS

Transfer stitches from Tail One to a third needle so that the point of the needle is positioned ready to knit the wrong side. Position this panel of scarf with wrong side facing you between you and the panel currently on the needles (both wrong sides will be facing you). Work Row 2 of Chart A, working through the aligned sts from both panels simultaneously as follows.

Chart A

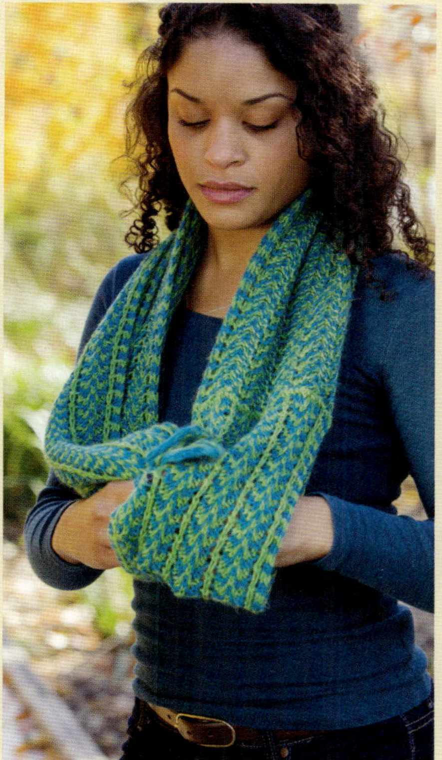 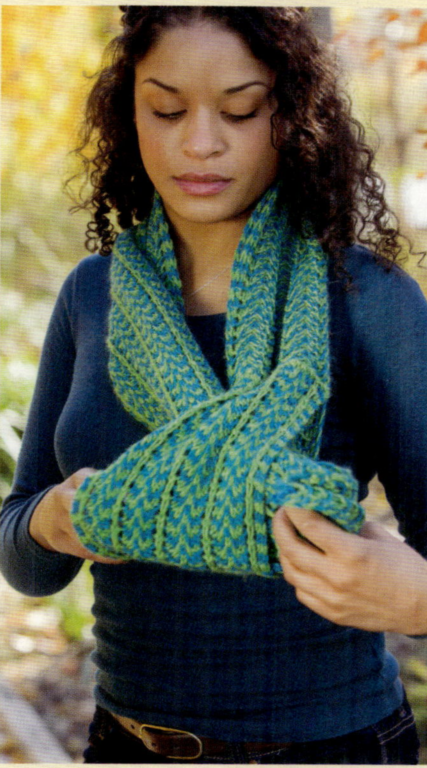 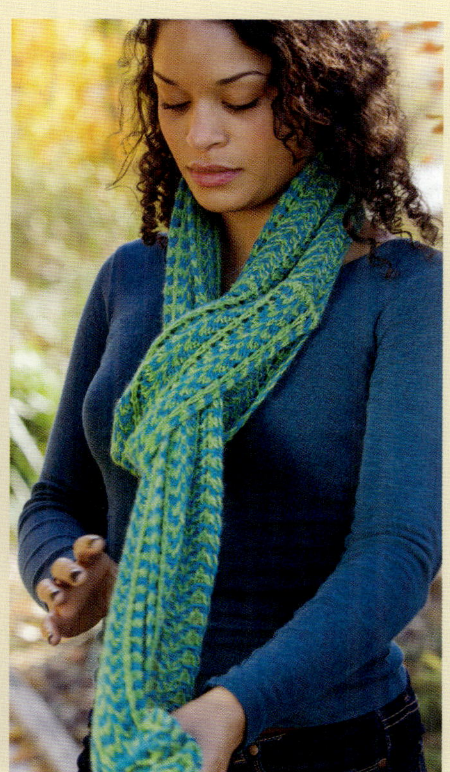

Transfer the first stitch from the back needle to the front needle and then work them together. Slip the first sts on both panels to RH needle (with yarn held in front of the sts) then knit through the front legs of the next sts on both panels as if working a k2tog, work through the front legs of the next sts on both panels as if to p2tog—address each pair of sts in this same manner to the end of the row. If a stitch is to be slipped, slip as usual (purl-wise with yarn held in front of stitch).

LOOP

Turn work as usual and proceed to Row 3, treat each pair of slipped sts from previous row as one st. Complete Chart A.

Work Chart A 24 additional times.

Using Color B, knit one additional row and then BO from the WS using expandable lace bind-off method, knit variant (see Cast-On/Bind-Off, page 109).

FINISHING

Weave in ends and block flat.

Fold bound-off end to join line and, using whip-stitch, sew the end down to form a loop. Trim ends.

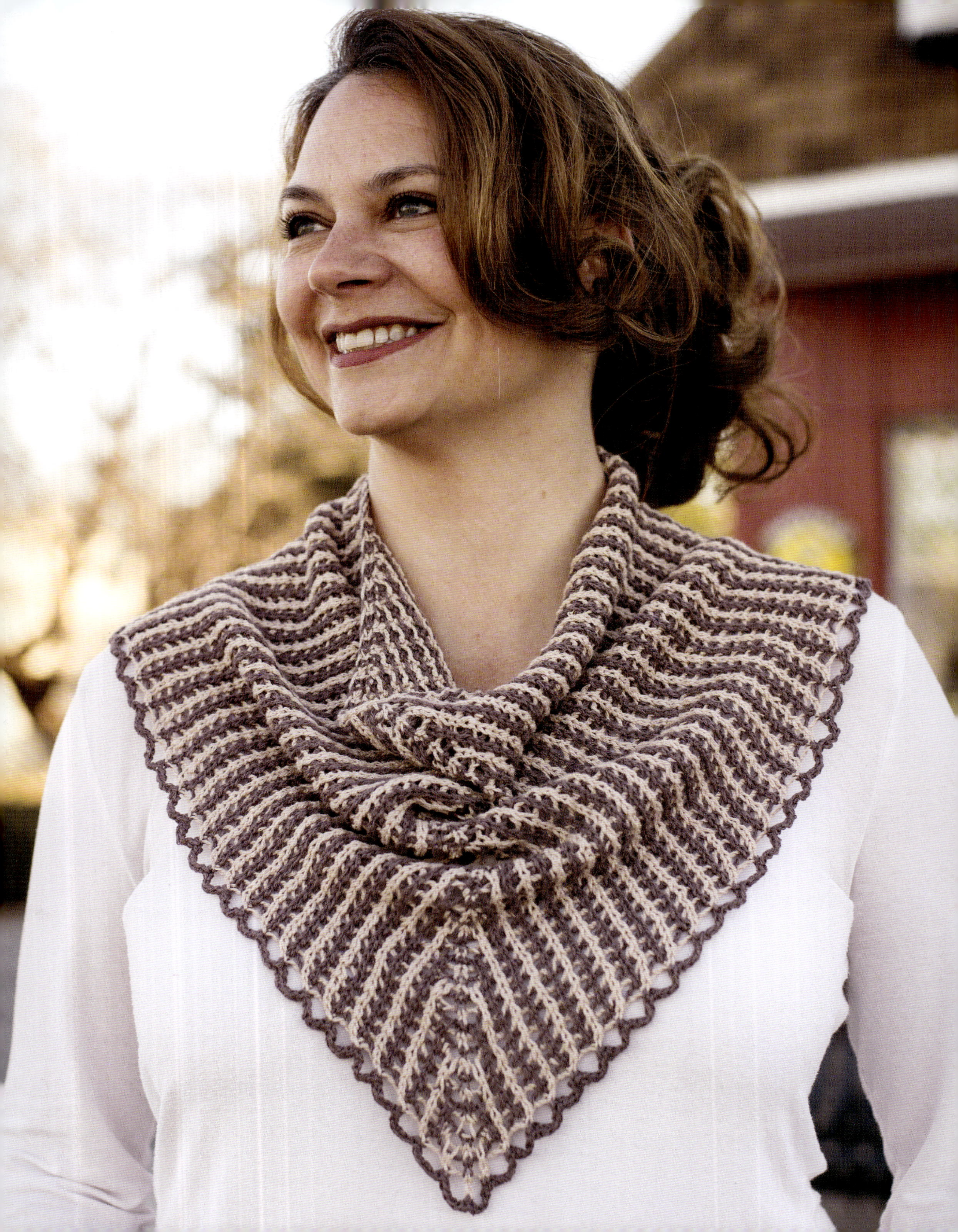

Lacy Pinstripe Cowlette

Your basic knitted lace mesh consists of yarn overs and single decreases, that's pretty much it. And because single decreases are directional, the fabric tends to bias. Of course, I had to figure out how to work slipped stitches into the mix and this light and lacy cowlette is the result. I wanted to make sure there were pieces in this book for every season so I chose to work this piece in a wonderful linen/cotton blend to create an accessory that you can wear in spring and even into summer. The neutral palette that I chose will match just about anything, but you can shake the colors up to your heart's content.

Finished Measurements: 24"/61 cm circumference at neck, 18"/46 cm tall in front, 8.5"/53.5 cm tall in back

Sizes: One size

Yarn

  Weight: Fingering

  Knit Picks Lindy™ Chain; 70% linen, 30% Pima cotton; 180 yd/165 m per 1.76 oz/50 g

  Color A: Plum (1 skein)

  Color B: Linen (1 skein)

Needles: US size 5/3.75 mm circular needle, 24"/60 cm in length (see Knitting in the Round, page 105)

Notions: Stitch marker

Gauge in Stockinette over 4"/10 cm: 18 sts and 28 rows (see A Note on Gauge, page 12)

Special Stitch

ssk-pssf-sl: slip, slip, knit - pass slipped stitch forward - slip; ssk then return knit stitch to LH needle, pass the next stitch forward over the knit stitch and drop off the front of the needle, slip the knit stitch purl-wise back to RH needle. [2 stitches decreased]

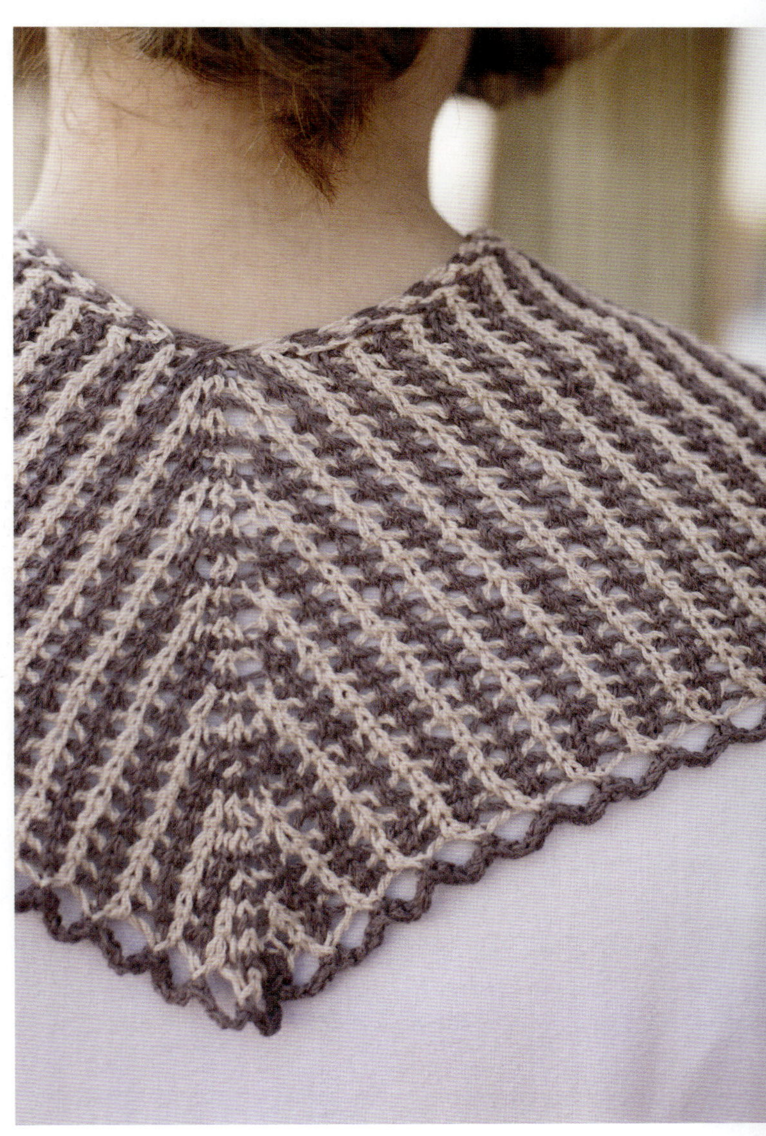

Instructions

Using the long tail cast-on method (see Cast-On/Bind-Off, page 107) and Color B, CO 7 sts.

SET UP

Row 1 (RS): K2, (YO, k1) four times, k1. [11 sts]

Row 2 (WS): Sl1-wyif, k3, p3, k3, sl1-wyif.

Row 3: With A, k2, (YO, k1, sl1, k1, YO, k1) twice, k1. [15 sts]

Row 4: Sl1-wyif, k3, sl1-wyif, p5, sl1-wyif, k3, sl1-wyif.

Row 5: With B, k2, YO, k1, sl1, YO, ssk, sl1, YO, pm, k1, YO, sl1, k2tog, YO, sl1, k1, YO, k2. [19 sts]

Row 6: Sl1-wyif, k3, sl1-wyif, p2, sl1-wyif, p3, sl1-wyif, p2, sl1-wyif, k3, sl1-wyif.

FLAT SECTION

Work Chart A using the following method.

Rows 1 and 7: Work across row, repeating first indicated section until you reach the marker, YO as shown in chart, sm, work to end of row, repeating second indicated section to three sts from end of row, and then finish chart.

Rows 3 and 9: Work across row, repeating first indicated section until you reach one st before marker, k1, YO as shown in chart, sm, work to end of row, repeating second indicated section to four sts from end of row, and then finish chart.

Rows 5 and 11: Work across row, repeating first indicated section until you reach the marker, YO as shown in chart, sm, work to end of row, repeating second indicated section to four sts from end of row, and then finish chart.

Stitch Count Table for Flat Section

Repeat Number	1	2	3	4	5
Stitch Count	43	67	91	115	139

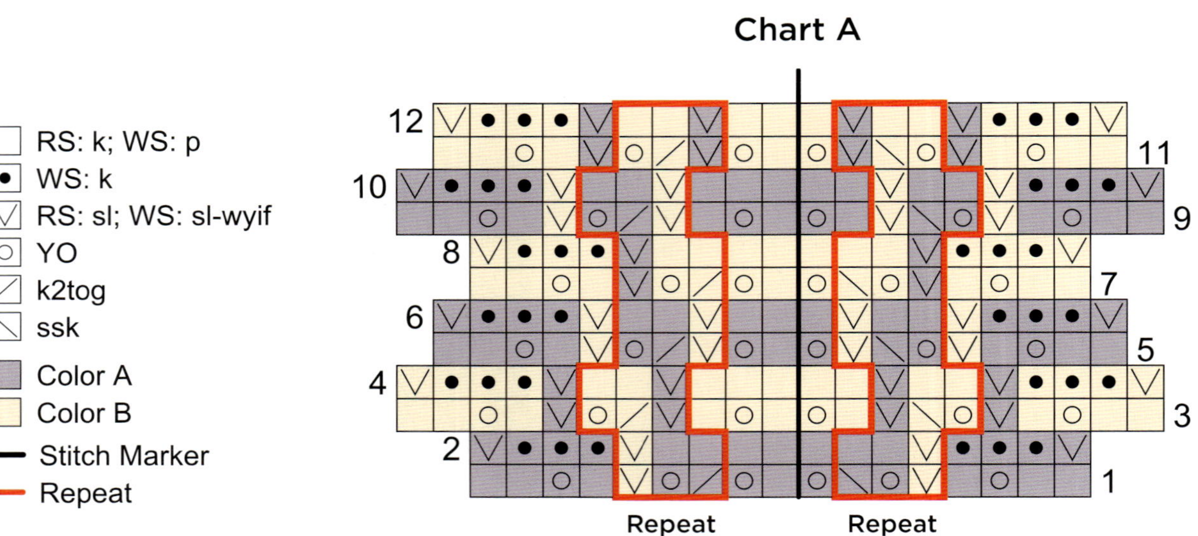

Work all wrong side rows as charted.

Work Chart A a total of 5 times. [139 sts]

Work Rows 1–5 one additional time, stopping one stitch short of finishing Row 5. [151 sts]

Use the following technique to join to work in the round. Cross the last st of Row 5 with the first st of the next round in the following manner. Insert LH needle through front leg of final st on RH needle and slip st onto LH needle. Insert RH needle through back leg of what is now the second st on the LH needle and slip st to RH needle. Place marker to indicate beginning of round.

Work Round 6 by knitting all same color sts and slipping all contrasting sts to last st, kfb. [152 sts]

IN THE ROUND SECTION

Work Chart B using the following method.

Rows 1 and 7: Work across row, repeating first indicated section until you reach the first marker, YO as shown in chart, sm, work to end of row, repeating second indicated section to one st from end of row marker, and then finish chart.

Rows 3 and 9: Work across row, repeating first indicated section until you reach one st before the first marker, k1, YO as shown in chart, sm, work to end of row, repeating second indicated section to one st from end of row marker and then finish chart.

Rows 5 and 11: Work across row, repeating first indicated section until you reach the first marker, YO as shown in chart, sm, work to end of row, repeating second indicated section to three sts from end of row marker, and then finish chart.

Work all even rounds as charted.

Stitch Count Table for In the Round Section					
Repeat Number	1	2	3	4	5	6
Stitch Count	164	176	188	200	212	224

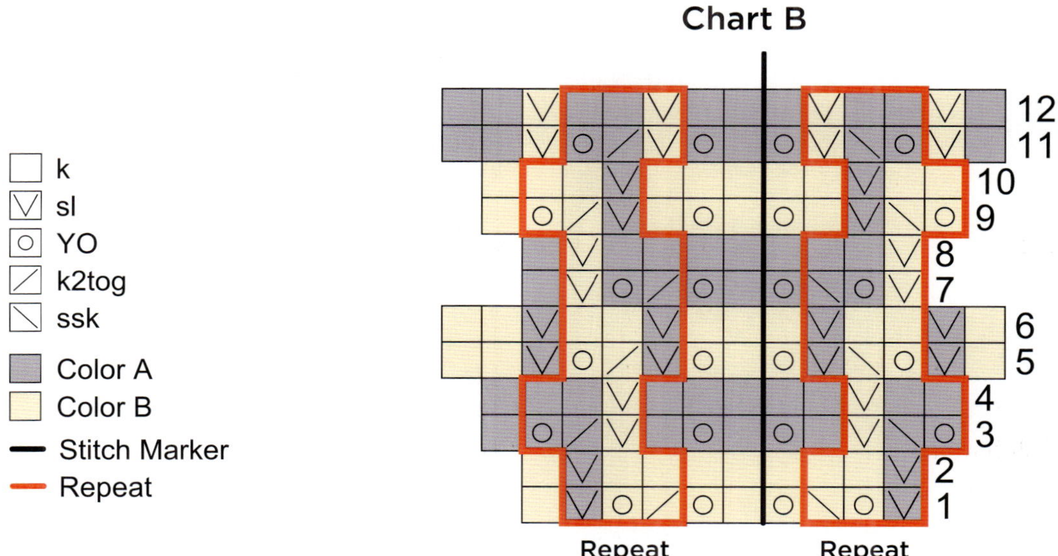

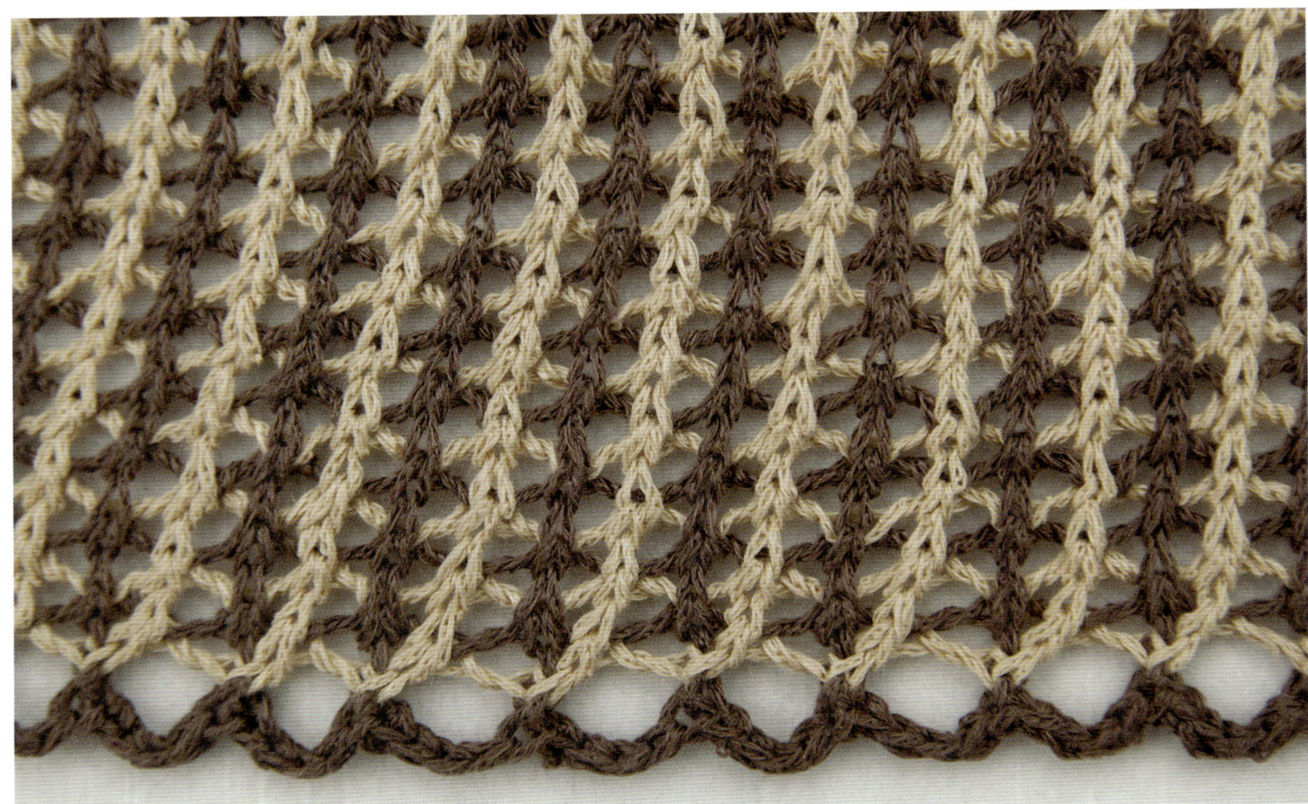

Work Chart B a total of 6 times. [224 sts]

Work Rows 1 and 2 one additional time. [226 sts]

Final Round: Remove beginning of round marker, slip last stitch from the RH needle to LH needle, replace marker. *YO twice, sl1-k2tog-psso; rep from * to 2 sts before marker, YO twice, ssk, YO twice, k1, YO twice, k2tog, YO twice, *ssk-pssf-sl, YO twice; rep from * to 2 sts before marker, ssk. [232 sts]

Using the faux picot bind-off method (see Cast-On/Bind-Off, page 109), BO all sts.

FINISHING

Weave in ends. Fold cowl along the increase and back seams so that it is a triangular shape and block lace open, pulling the edging out. If you have crease lines where piece was blocked flat, refold so that they are flattened out, steam, and pat lightly to remove creases. Trim ends.

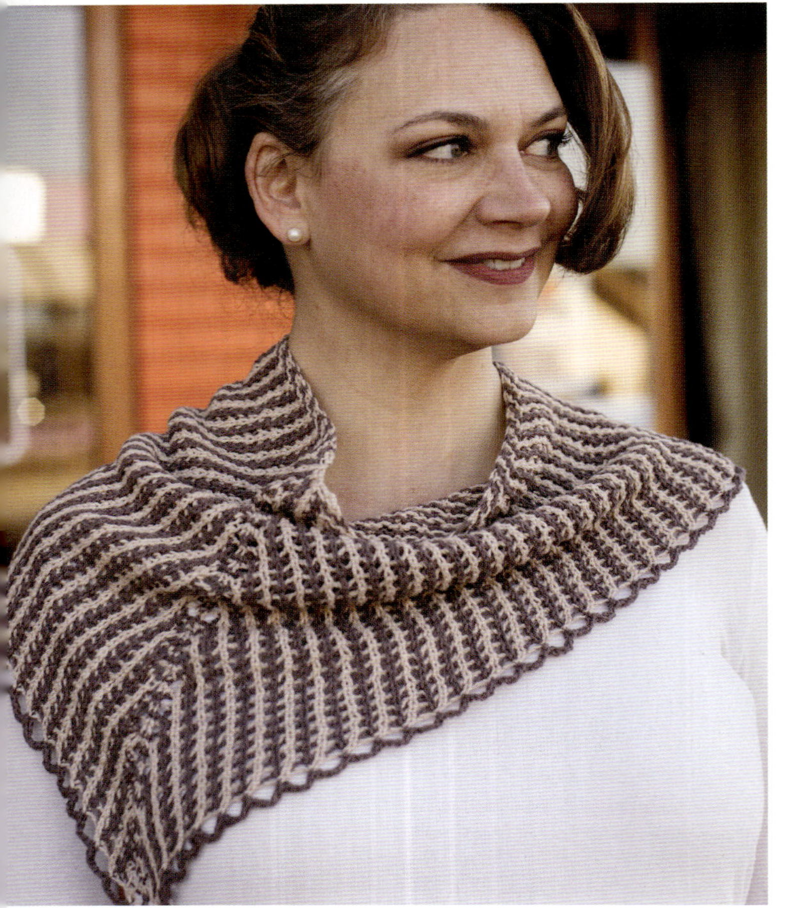

Willow Bloom

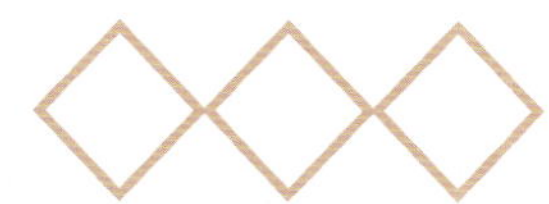

The fuzzy yarn in this pattern posed a challenge. As discussed in the front of the book, it is a visually noisy yarn. Attempting any intricate colorwork pattern with this would have been futile. Instead I chose to capitalize on the traits of the yarn to fill in and create a dense background for the traveling willow blooms. I have included a swatch of the same pattern with the color positions swapped so that you can see what a significant change your color choices can make in the end product. I love them both, but in the end I decided on the blue dominant palette for my mitts. You can make your own decision.

Finished Measurements: 7.25"/18.5 cm hand circumference, 7.25"/18.5 cm long

Sizes: One size

Yarn

  Weight: Sport

  Knit Picks Andean Treasure; 100% baby alpaca; 110 yd/101 m per 1.76 oz/50 g

  Color A: Sapphire Heather (1 skein)

  Color B: Finnley Heather (1 skein)

Needles: US size 6/4 mm, preferred needles for working small circumference (see Knitting in the Round, page 105)

Notions: Stitch marker

Gauge in Stockinette over 4"/10 cm: 20 sts and 24 rows (see A Note on Gauge, page 12)

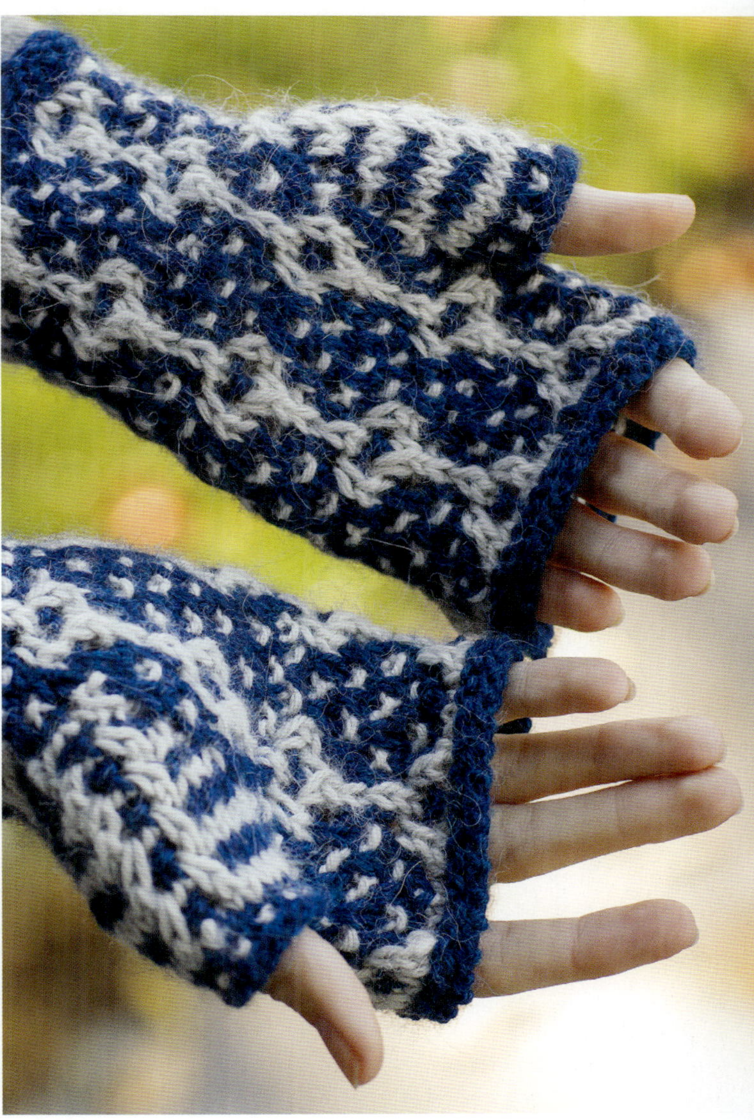

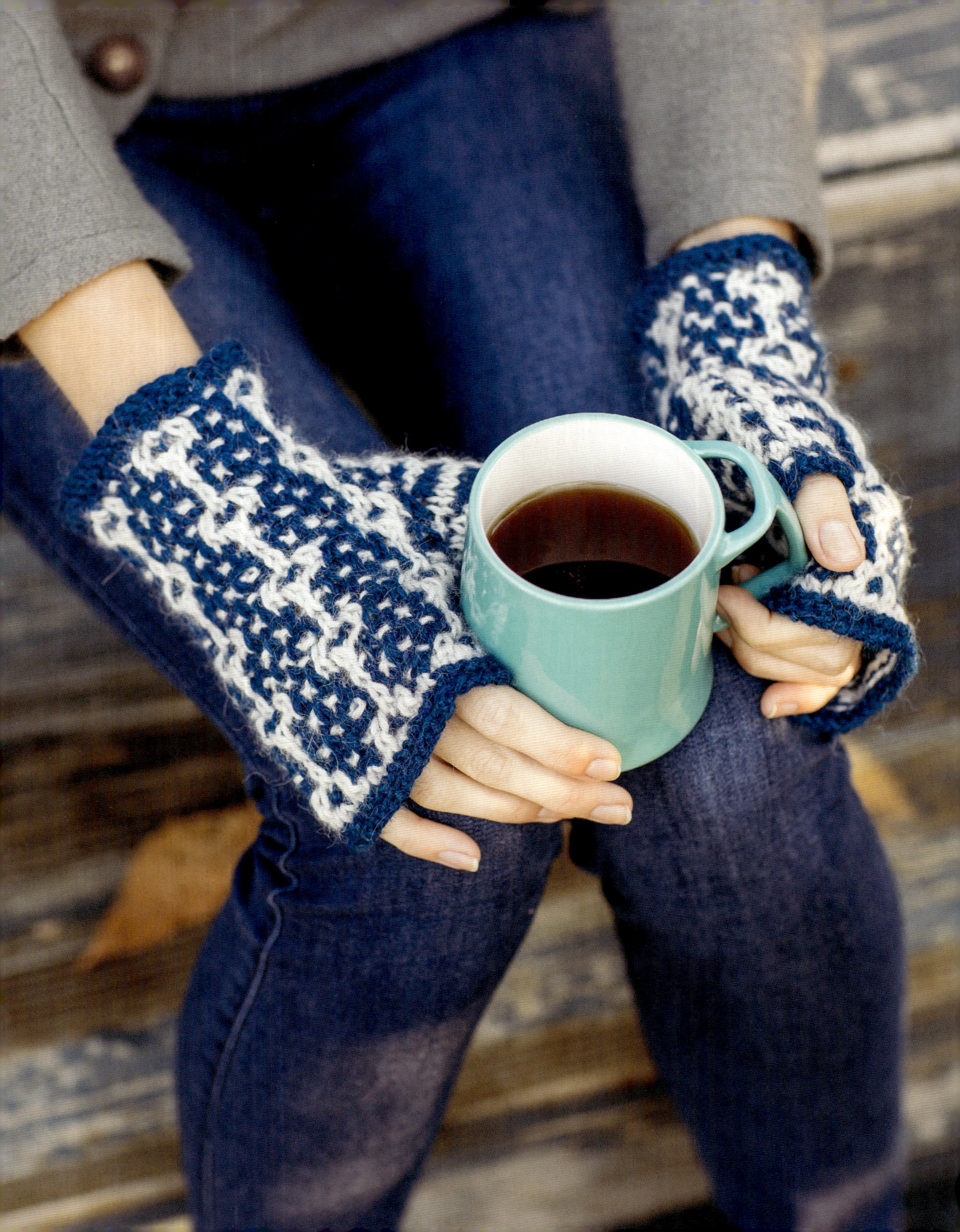

Instructions

Using Color A and cable cast-on method (see Cast-On/Bind-Off, page 105), CO 40 sts.

Knit one row.

Place marker to indicate beginning of round and join to work in the round, being careful not to twist sts.

Round 1: Purl.
Round 2: Knit.
Round 3: P2, (k3, p5) four times, k3, p3.

BODY

Join in Color B.

Work Chart A once, repeating each round 5 times around, then work Rounds 1–8 once more.

GUSSET

Work Gusset chart as follows.
Next Round: Work first 7 sts of chart, place markers (pm) to frame thumb increases as shown and complete chart, repeating indicated section 4 times. [42 sts]

Complete Gusset chart. [54 sts]

HAND

Next Round: With B, (sl1, k1) three times, sl1, transfer 15 gusset sts to waste yarn, using backwards loop method (see Cast-On/Bind-Off, page 105), CO 1 st, [(sl1, k1) four times] four times. [40 sts]

Work Chart A Rounds 14–16, then Rounds 1–16, and then Rounds 1–4, repeating each round 5 times around.

END

Round 1: Remove end of round marker, slip first st to RH needle, replace marker, with B, *YO, k2tog, YO, k1, YO, ssk, YO, sl1-k2tog-psso; rep from * to end of round.
Round 2: Knit.
Round 3: With A, knit.
Round 4: Purl.
Round 5: Knit.

Using the expandable lace bind-off, knit variant method (see Cast-On/Bind-Off, page 109), BO all sts.

THUMB

Transfer held sts to needle. [15 sts]

With B, pick up and knit three sts in thumb gap, place marker to indicate beginning of round. [18 sts]

Round 1: With B, k5, k2tog, YO, k1, YO, ssk, knit to end of round.

Chart A

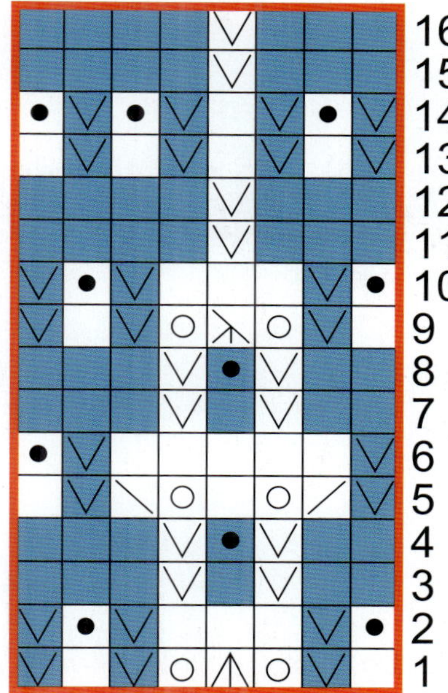

Repeat x 5

	k		Color A
•	p		Color B
V	sl	—	Repeat
O	YO		
/	k2tog		
\	ssk		
/\	CDD		
⋉	sl1-k2tog-psso		

Gusset Chart

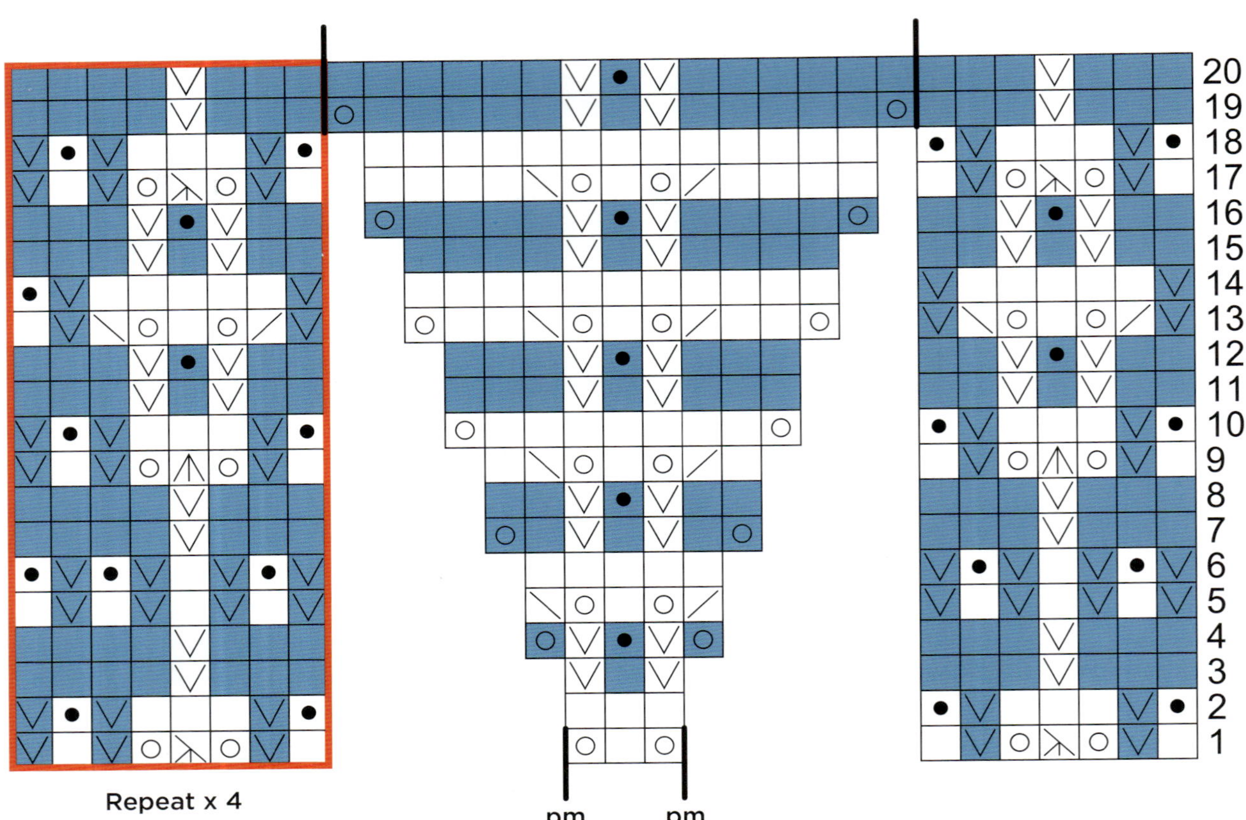

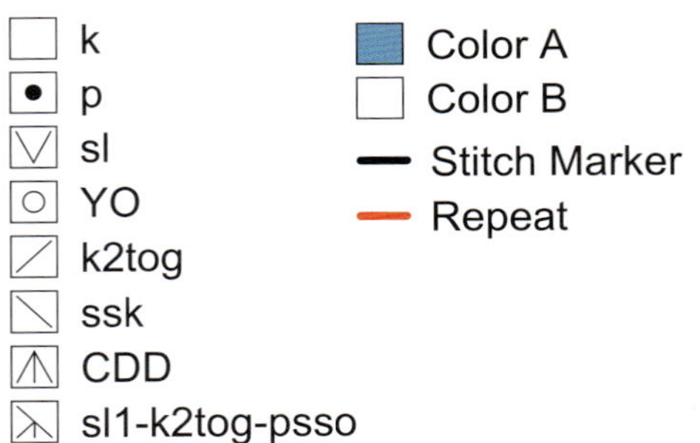

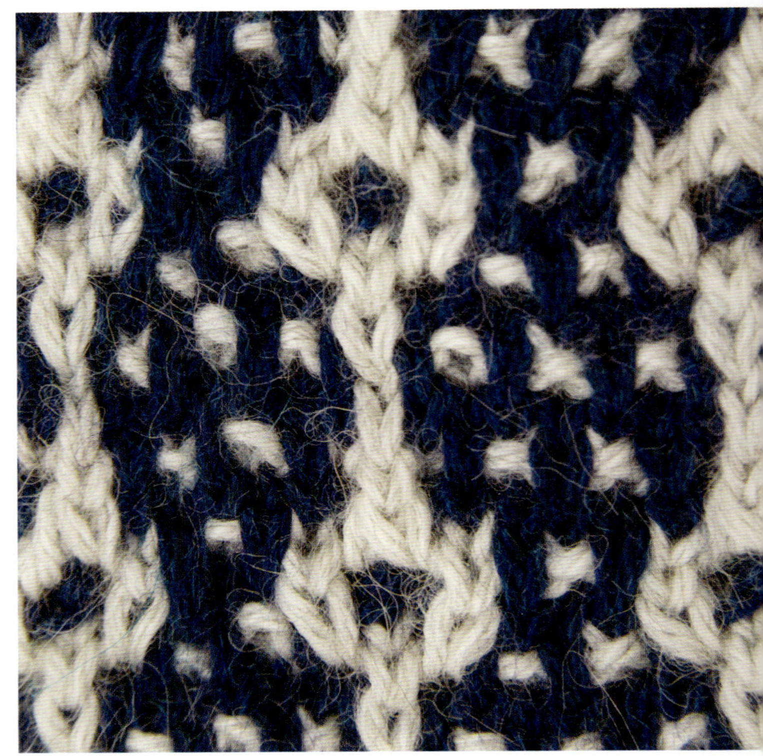

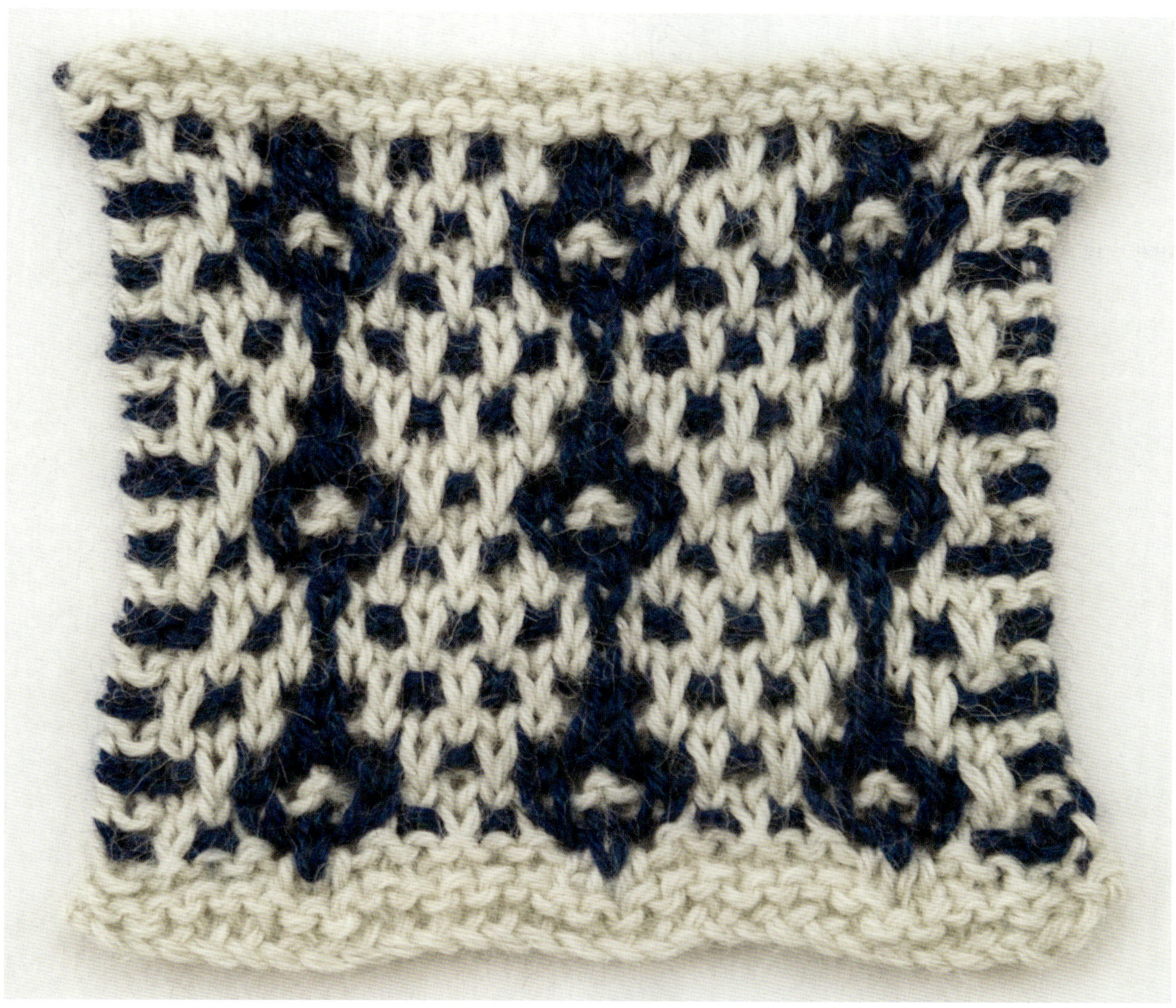

A swatch of the same pattern with the color positions reversed

Round 2: Knit.

Rounds 3 and 4: With A, knit.

Round 5: With B, *k1, sl1; rep from * to end of round.

Round 6: *P1, sl1; rep from * to end of round.

Round 7: With A, knit.

Using the expandable lace bind-off, knit variant method (see Cast-On/Bind-Off, page 109), BO all sts.

Make second mitt same as first.

FINISHING

Weave in ends using yarn tails to neaten up any holes at the thumb joins. Block gently. If you have crease lines where piece was blocked flat, refold so that they are flattened out, steam, and pat lightly to remove creases. Trim ends.

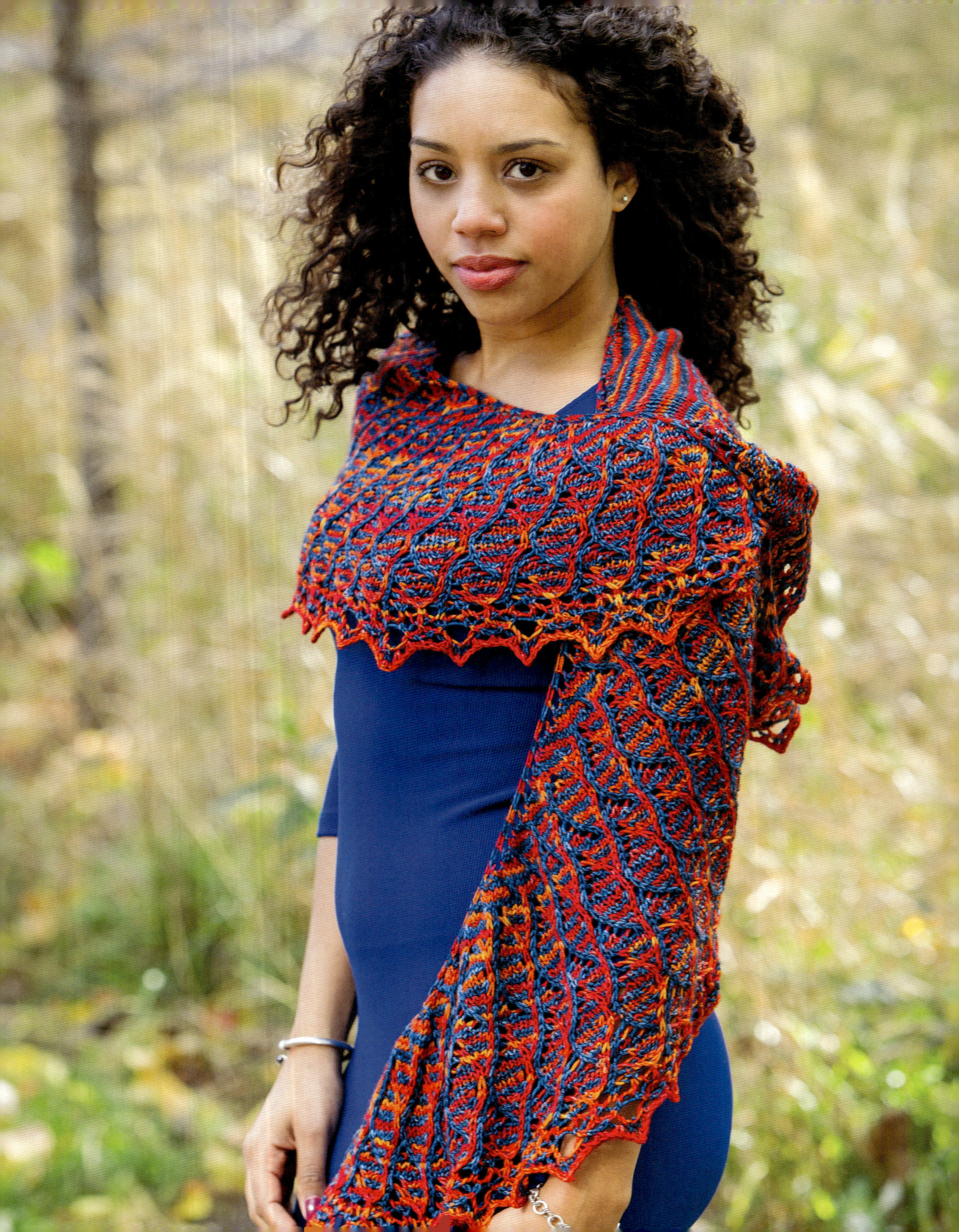

Fractured Helix

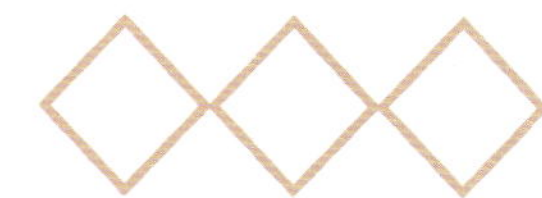

When you take increases and their matching decreases and separate them by multiple stitches, these intervening stitches move in very interesting ways, which creates a fun canvas to play with the slipped stitches. This shawl is a heavily modified version of a lace stitch called Flame Chevron. As you can see, adding mosaic to this lace has transformed it into something utterly unlike chevrons. And something utterly beautiful.

Finished Measurements: 16"/40.5 cm long, 49"/124.5 cm wingspan

Sizes: One size

Yarn

   Weight: Sport

   Dragonfly Fiber Damsel; 100% merino wool; 335 yd/306 m per 4 oz/115 g

   Color A: Kelpie (1 skein)

   Color B: Walking on the Sun (1 skein)

Needles: US size 7/4.5 mm

Gauge in Stockinette over 4"/10 cm: 20 sts and 26 rows (see A Note on Gauge, page 12)

Special Stitches

YO2: in this pattern, YO2 is not a double increase; on the following row, drop one of the loops and knit into the other.

kYOk: knit, yarn over, knit; knit into the next stitch but do not remove the stitch from the LH needle, YO, knit into the same stitch a second time. [2 stitches increased]

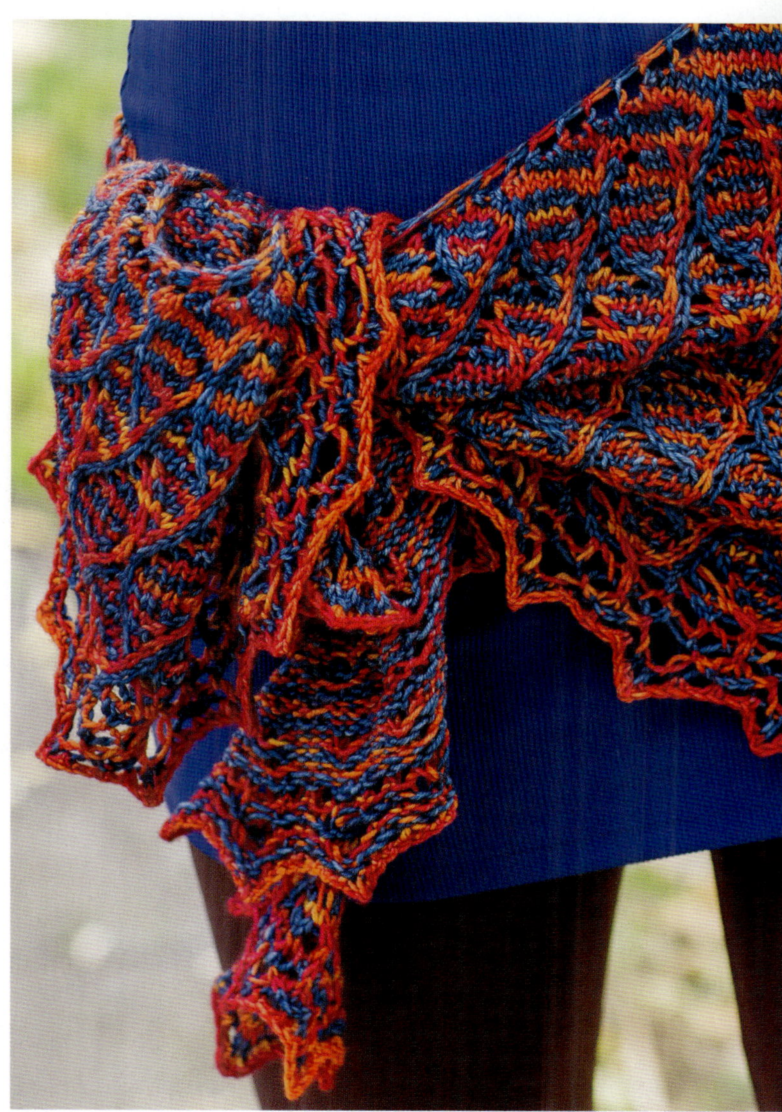

Instructions

Using Color B and long tail cast-on method (see Cast-On/Bind-Off, page 107), CO 5 sts.

SET UP
Row 1 (RS): K5.
Row 2 (WS): K2, YO, k1, YO, k2. [7 sts]

Join in Color A.

Row 3: With A, k2, kYOk, k1, kYOk, k2. [11 sts]
Row 4: Sl1-wyif, k1, YO, k1, p5, k1, YO, k1, sl1-wyif. [13 sts]

STRIPED SECTION
Row 1 (RS): With B, k2, kYOk, knit to last 3 sts, kYOk, k2. [4 sts increased]
Row 2 (WS): Sl1-wyif, k1, YO, k1, purl to last 3 sts, k1, YO, k1, sl1-wyif. [2 sts increased]
Row 3: With A, k2, kYOk, knit to last 3 sts, kYOk, k2. [4 sts increased]
Row 4: Sl1-wyif, k1, YO, k1, purl to last 3 sts, k1, YO, k1, sl1-wyif. [2 sts increased]

Repeat Rows 1–4 four additional times, then work Rows 1 and 2 once more. [79 sts]

Next Row (RS): With A, k2, kYOk, k3, k2tog, knit to last 8 sts, ssk, k3, kYOk, k2. [81 sts]
Next Row (WS): Sl1-wyif, k1, YO, k1, purl to last 3 sts, k1, YO, k1, sl1-wyif. [83 sts]

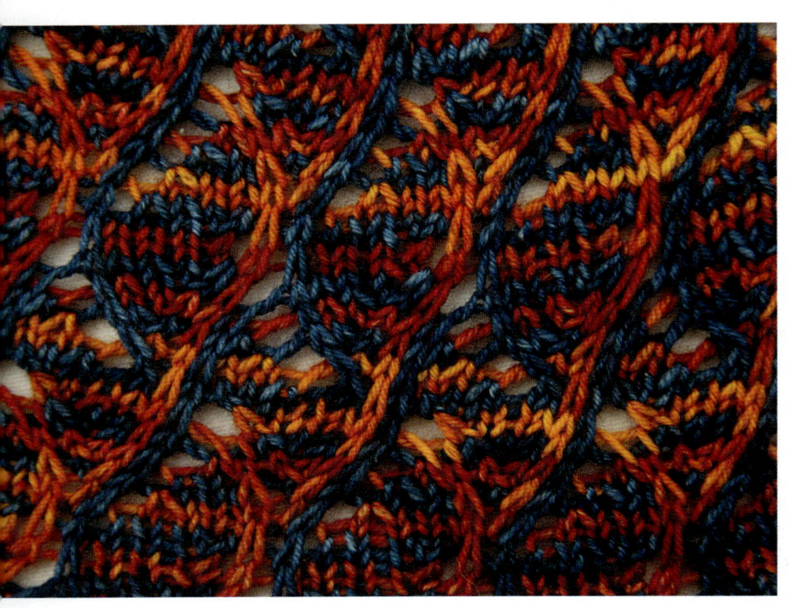

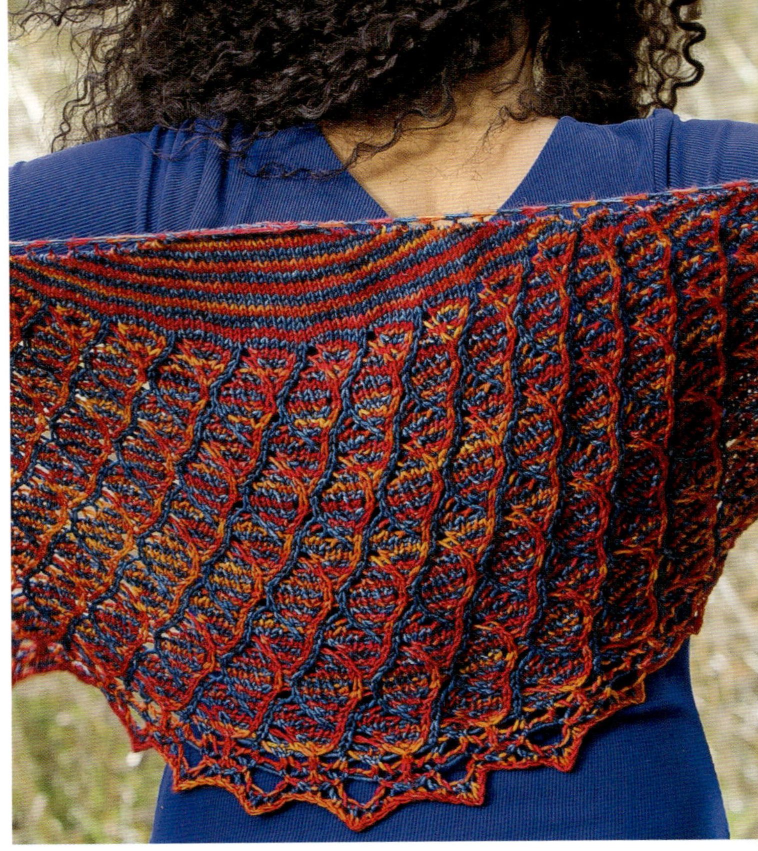

BODY
(Work Charts A, B, and then C) four times. Then work Chart A once more. [381 sts]

Stitch Count Table for Body				
Repeat Number	1	2	3	4
Stitch Count	153	223	293	363

Work Chart D once. [411 sts]

Next Row (RS): With B, k2, kYOk, k2, [YO, sl1-k2tog-psso, YO, (k1, YO) 3 times, k1] 57 times, YO, sl1-k2tog-psso, YO, k1, kYOk, k2. [586 sts]

With WS facing, and using expandable lace bind-off, purl variant (see Cast-On/Bind-Off, page 109), BO all sts.

FINISHING
Weave in ends. Block aggressively, curving the top edge up and around to allow to lie flat. Trim ends.

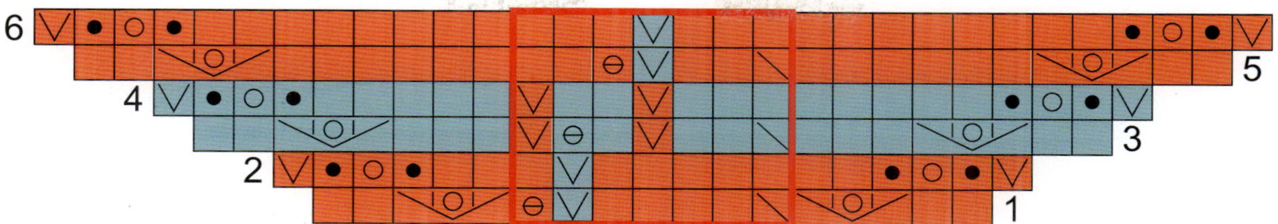

Chart A
6
5
4
3
2
1
Repeat

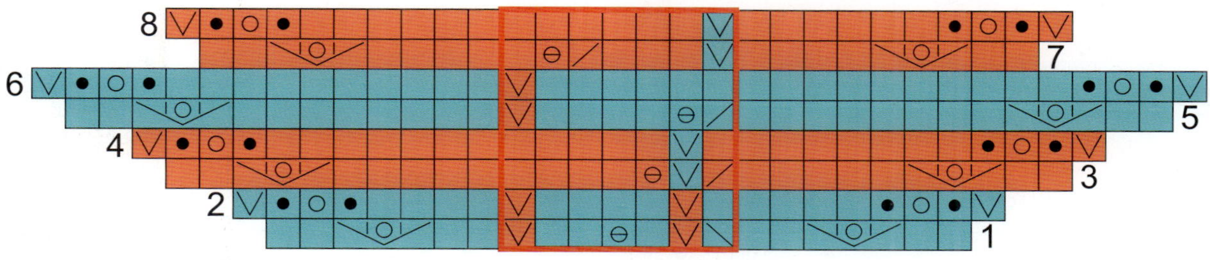

Chart B
8
7
6
5
4
3
2
1
Repeat

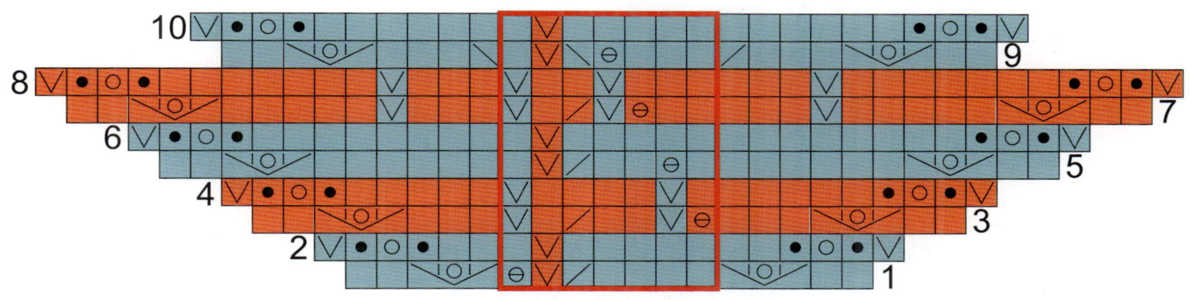

Chart C
10
9
8
7
6
5
4
3
2
1
Repeat

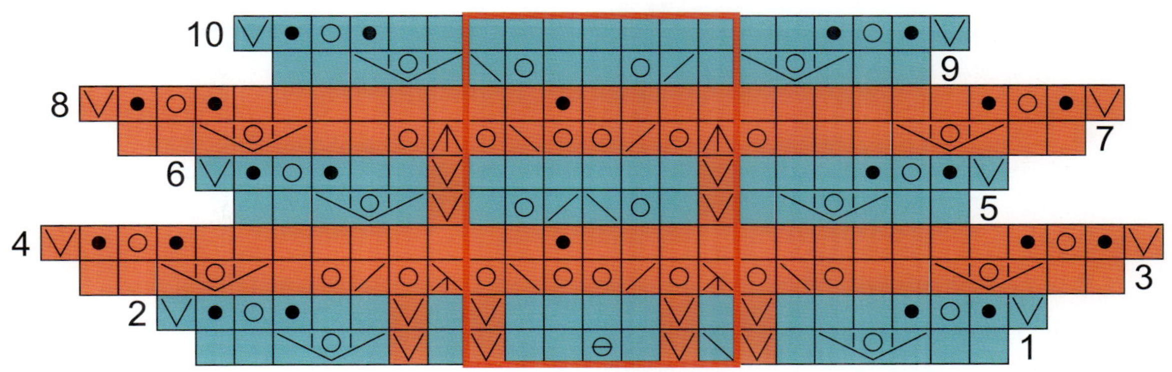

Chart D
10
9
8
7
6
5
4
3
2
1
Repeat

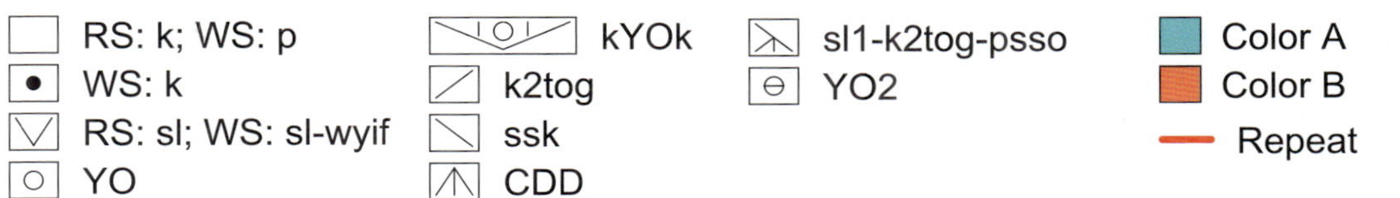

RS: k; WS: p
WS: k
RS: sl; WS: sl-wyif
YO
kYOk
k2tog
ssk
CDD
sl1-k2tog-psso
YO2
Color A
Color B
Repeat

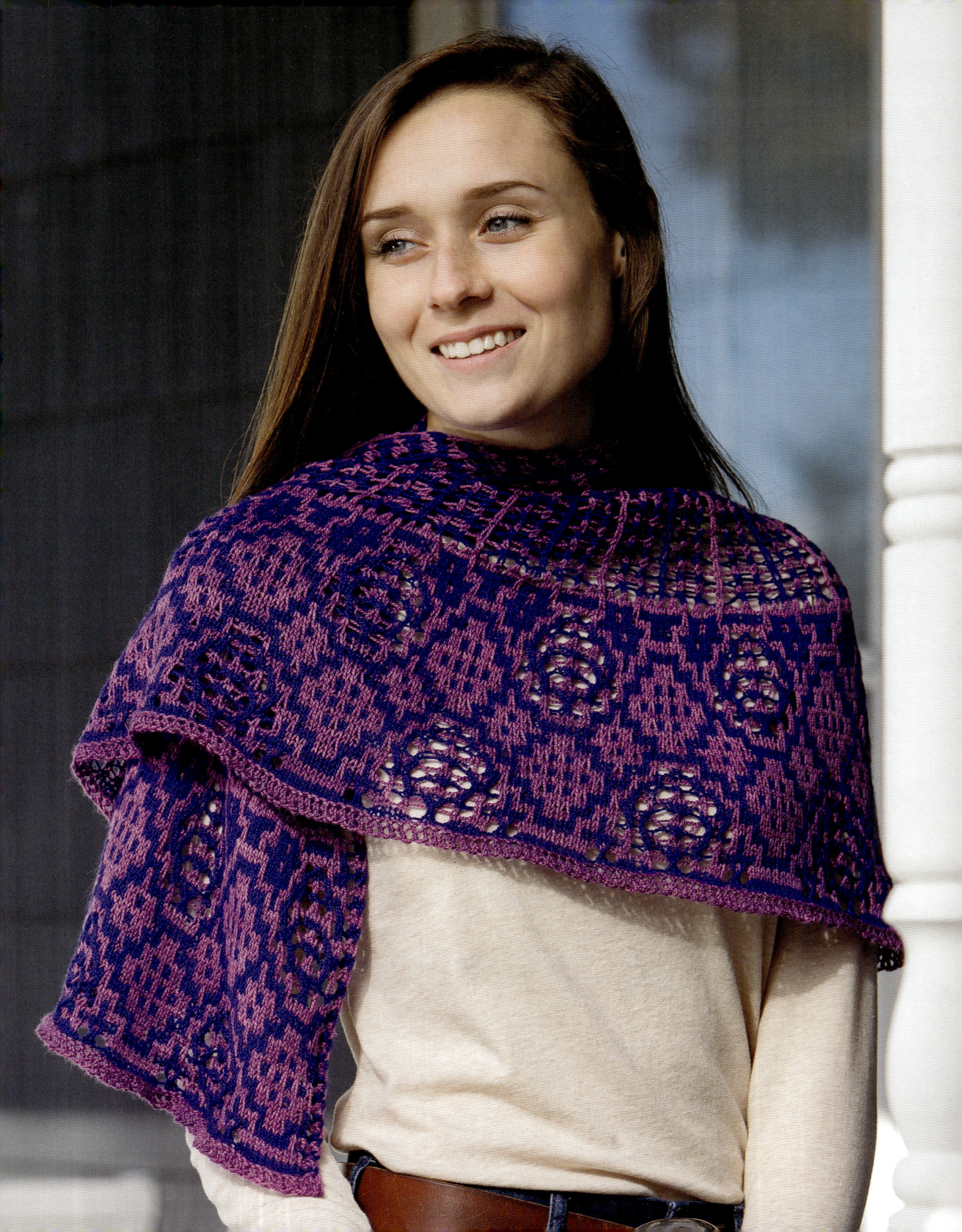

Knitting in the Round

There was a time when the only way to knit in the round was by using double-pointed needles (DPNs). It is a fine way of knitting in the round and many knitters are devoted DPN users. But over the years innovations for knitting in the round have proliferated so that a knitter is spoiled for choice when it comes to options.

Circular needles are readily available and they can be used in many different ways. The knitter can match the circumference of the needle to the circumference of the project and simply knit away. There is also a widely used technique where the knitter uses two circular needles at a time. And a third option is to use an extra-long cable for the "magic loop" method. Personally, I am a devotee of the magic loop method and all of the in-the-round projects in this book were knit in this manner.

In this book, I have chosen not to specify an in-the-round technique. Each knitter should do what is most comfortable and produces an enjoyable knitting experience for them. For the patterns where the circumference of the piece decreases (such as the top of hats or those pesky thumbs), if you find it easier to switch from one method to another or pull out your DPNs, please do!

Cast-On/Bind-Off

There are many ways to begin and end your project. For each project in this book, I have chosen and at times developed the appropriate technique to meet the needs of the project. In the following pages, you will find step-by-step instructions for executing the methods used in this book. For a few of the particularly tricky steps I have included photographs for clarification.

BACKWARDS LOOP CAST-ON

With needle in right hand, hold working yarn in left hand under tension.

1. Lay left thumb on top of working yarn, drop thumb behind yarn and then bring up under yarn to form a loop.
2. Insert RH needle knitwise into front leg of loop and transfer to RH needle.
3. Tighten loop on RH needle by pulling on working yarn.

Repeat steps 1–3 until you have cast on desired number of sts.

CABLE CAST-ON

Set up: Make slip knot, leaving a long tail for weaving in later; place slip knot on LH needle.

1. Insert RH needle into st on LH needle knitwise, wrap working yarn around RH needle and pull through new st.
2. Place new st on LH needle without twisting.
3. Insert RH needle between the last two sts on LH needle from front to back, wrap working yarn around RH needle and pull through new st.
4. Place new st on LH needle without twisting.

Repeat steps 3 and 4 until you have cast on desired number of sts.

CIRCULAR CAST-ON

Set up: Create a loop with your yarn with the working yarn up, the tail down, and the loop to the left of the crossing point as shown.

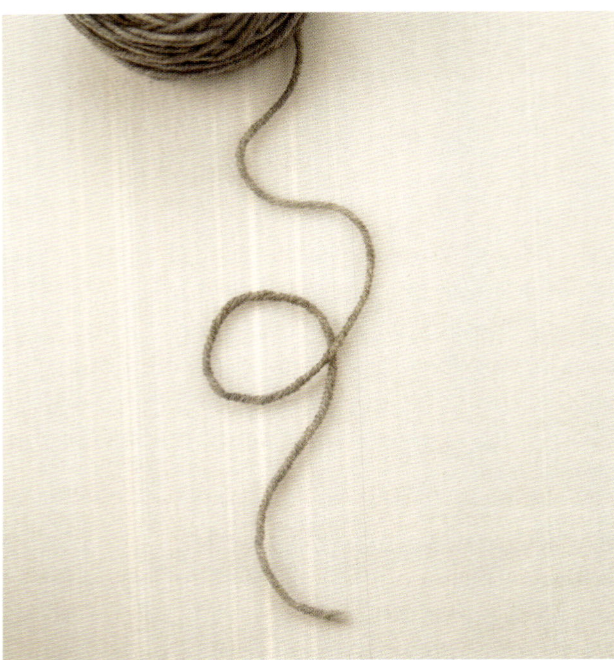

The working yarn will lay on top of the tail end. Pinch the crossing point between your thumb and fourth finger, tensioning the working yarn with your index and middle fingers.

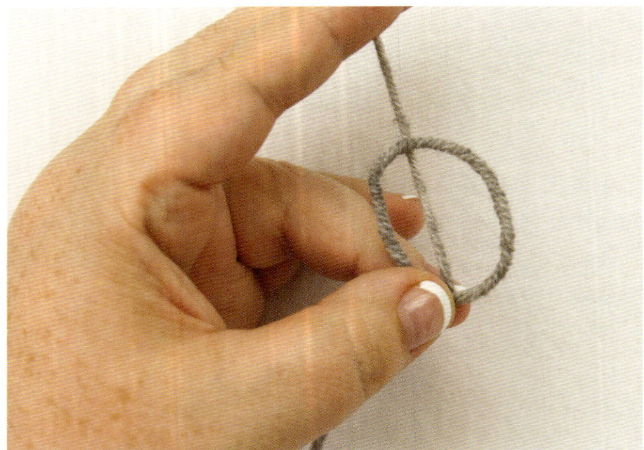

1. Insert needle into the loop and behind the working yarn from right to left, pull working yarn through the loop (1 st formed).

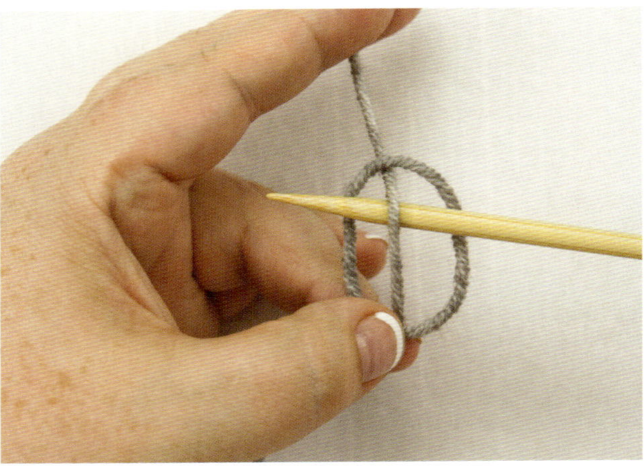

2. Without going through the loop, put the needle behind the working yarn from right to left (second st formed with YO).

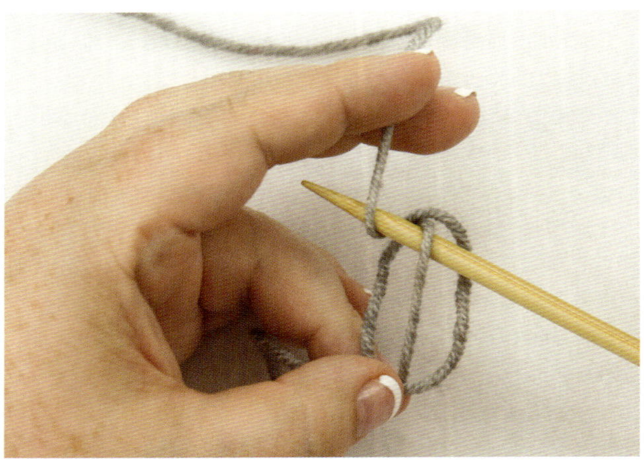

Repeat steps 1 and 2 until you have cast on
desired number of sts.

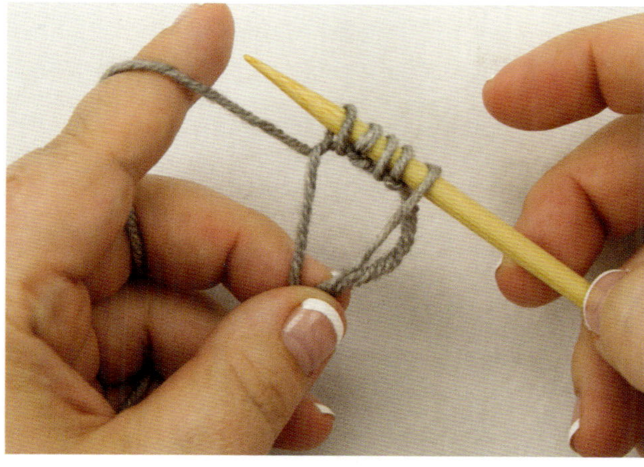

Note: If casting on an even number of sts,
the last st will be a YO and can be added just
before starting your first round. Position sts for
preferred method of knitting in the round, and
after you have completed a few rows pull on yarn
tail to cinch closed the hole.

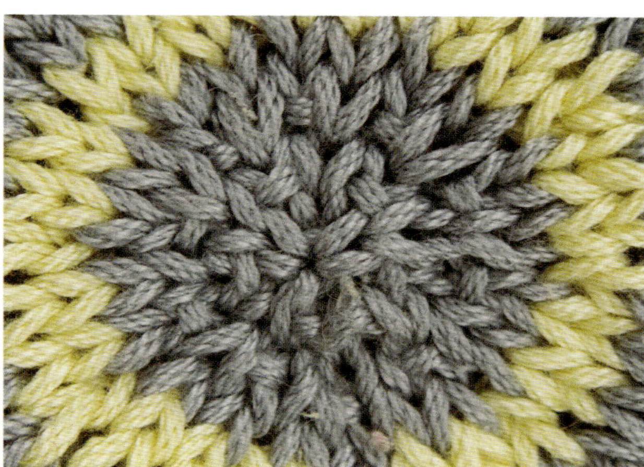

KNITTED CAST-ON

Set up: Make slip knot, leaving a long tail for
weaving in later; place slip knot on LH needle.

1. Insert RH needle into st on LH needle knit-
wise, wrap working yarn around RH needle and
pull through new st,

2. Place new st on LH needle without twisting.

Repeat steps 1 and 2 until you have cast on
desired number of sts.

LONG TAIL CAST-ON

Set up: Make slip knot, leaving enough extra
yarn in tail for casting on desired number of
sts. Place slip knot on your RH needle and
keep it from slipping off with your index finger.
Hold yarn in your left hand with working yarn
running over your index finger and tail yarn
running over your thumb.

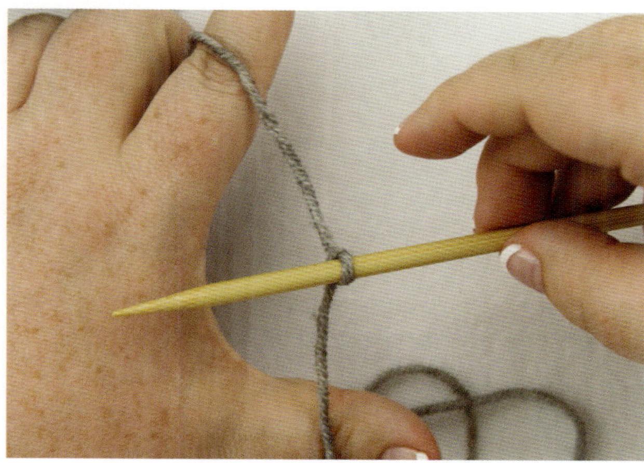

Hold both ends in the palm of your hand,
grasping them with remaining three fingers; it
will look similar to holding a slingshot.

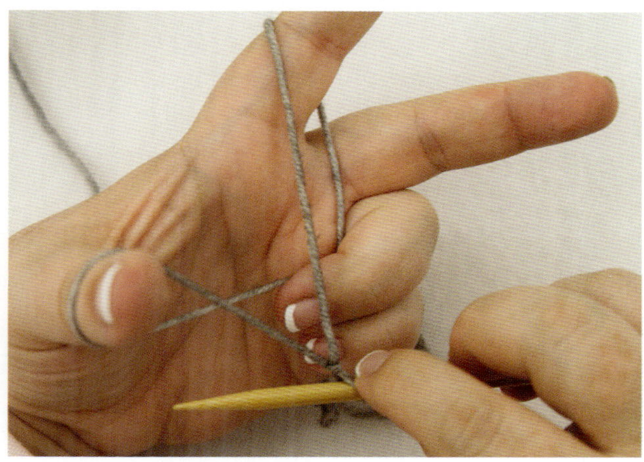

1. Bring needle down beneath the leftmost strand held around the thumb and up between the two strands looping the thumb.

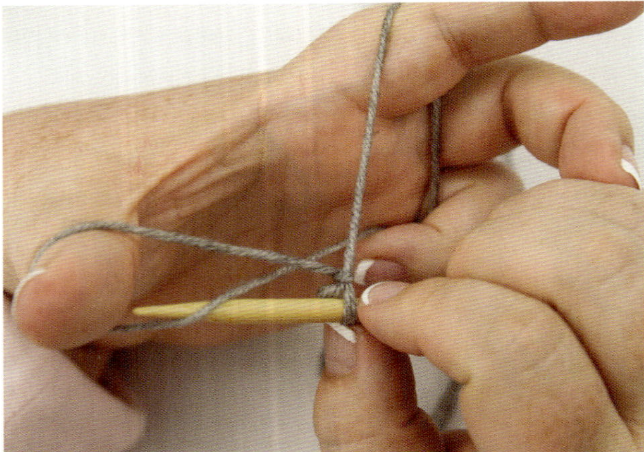

2. Take the needle over the rightmost strand around the thumb, over and behind the leftmost strand of yarn around your index finger; bring the tip of the needle down between the two strands looping your index finger.

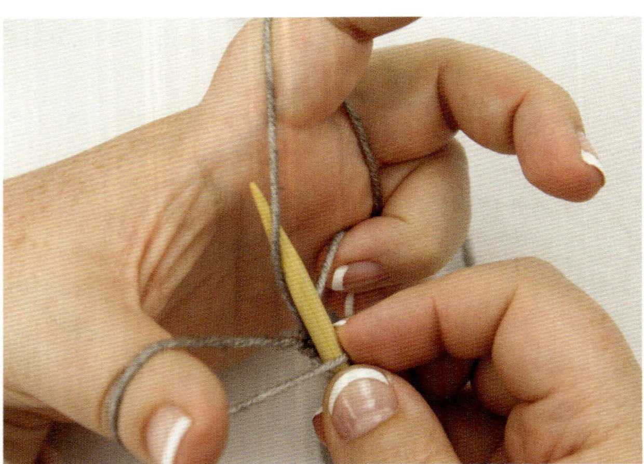

3. Pull this leftmost strand on your index finger through the loop you've made on your thumb, taking it back through the path you just made. Remove your thumb from the tail loop of yarn, lifting it up and over the needle.

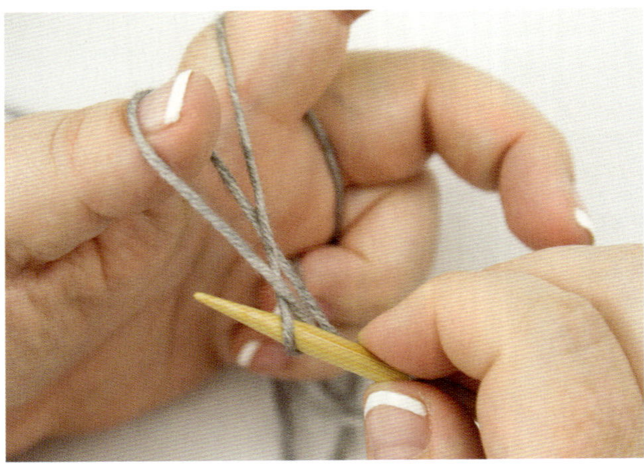

4. Move your thumb back under the loose tail of yarn to tighten the st and return to the starting slingshot position.

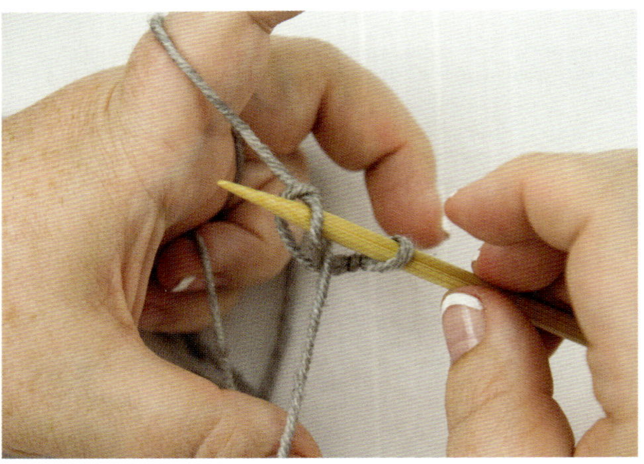

Repeat steps 1–4 until you have cast on desired number of sts.

LONG TAIL CAST-ON, TWO STRAND VARIANT

Work as for the long tail cast-on but instead of estimating the tail length use two strands of yarn, like the inside and outside of a center pull ball. Holding both strands of yarn as if they are one strand, make a slip knot leaving tails for weaving in later. When placed on the needle it will look like two sts but should be considered one. Run the yarn you intend to be your working yarn over your index finger and use the second strand as your tail yarn. Once you have cast on the desired number of sts, cut the second strand leaving a tail to weave in later.

2 X 2 RIBBING BIND-OFF

Set up: K2, lift rightmost stitch on RH needle up, over, and off the tip of the needle.

1. Move yarn to front.

2 and 3. Return new st to LH needle and p2tog.

4. Move yarn to back.

5 and 6. K1, lift rightmost stitch on RH needle up, over, and off the tip of the needle.

Repeat steps 1–6 until all sts are bound off.

EXPANDABLE LACE BIND-OFF, KNIT VARIANT

Set up: Slip first st.

1. K1.

2. Insert LH needle through front legs of sts on RH needle and k2tog-tbl.

Repeat steps 1 and 2 until all sts are bound off.

EXPANDABLE LACE BIND-OFF, PURL VARIANT

Set up: Slip first st.

1. P1.

2. Insert LH needle through back loops of 2 sts on RH needle and p2tog.

Repeat steps 1 and 2 until all sts are bound off.

EXPANDABLE LACE BIND-OFF, KNIT/PURL VARIANT

Set up: K2, insert LH needle through front legs of sts on RH needle, and k2tog-tbl.

1 and 2. P1, insert LH needle through front legs of sts on RH needle, and k2tog-tbl.

3 and 4. K1, insert LH needle through front legs of sts on RH needle, and k2tog-tbl.

Repeat steps 1–4 until all sts are bound off.

FAUX PICOT BIND-OFF

Set up: Working into the first double YO, k1, p1, insert LH needle through front loops of 2 sts on RH needle, and k2tog-tbl. Do not allow YO to fall off of LH needle.

1–4. K1 into double YO but do not allow YO to fall off of LH needle, insert LH needle through front loops of 2 sts on RH needle, and k2tog-tbl. You will have a total of four bind-offs into the double yarn over.

5. K1.

6. Insert LH needle through front loops of 2 sts on RH needle and k2tog-tbl.

Repeat steps 1–6 until all sts are bound off. When weaving in ends, use end to neaten join.

KNIT/PURL BIND-OFF

Set up: K1.

1. P1, lift rightmost stitch on RH needle up, over, and off the tip of the needle.

2. K1, lift rightmost stitch on RH needle up, over, and off the tip of the needle.

Repeat steps 1 and 2 until all sts are bound off.

KNIT/PURL STRETCHY BIND-OFF

Set up: K2.

1. Bring yarn to front.

2. Insert LH needle through back loops of 2 sts on RH needle and p2tog.

3. Move yarn to back.

4. K1.

Repeat steps 1–4 until all sts are bound off.

KNIT/PURL STRETCHY BIND-OFF, IN PATTERN VARIANT

Set up: K1, p1, lift rightmost stitch on RH needle up, over, and off the tip of the needle.

Bind off in pattern as follows.

If the next stitch is a purl:
1. Move the yarn to front.
2. Slip st on RH needle to LH needle and p2tog.

If the next stitch is a knit:

1. K1.
2. Lift rightmost stitch on RH needle up, over, and off the tip of the needle.

End row as a knit st.

VERY STRETCHY LACE BIND-OFF

Set up: K1.
1. YO, k1. [3 sts on RH needle]
2. Insert the LH needle through the front legs of the first two sts on the RH needle and k2tog-tbl. [2 sts on RH needle]
3. Lift the rightmost stitch on the RH needle up, over, and off the tip of the needle. [1 st on RH needle]

Repeat steps 1–3 until all sts are bound off.

Joining Techniques

KITCHENER STITCH

Hold needles with live sts parallel to each other with points aiming to the right and the working yarn coming off the back needle.

Set up: Insert yarn needle purl-wise into the first st on the front needle and then insert yarn needle knit-wise into the first st on the back needle and pull through yarn. Both sts remain on the needles.

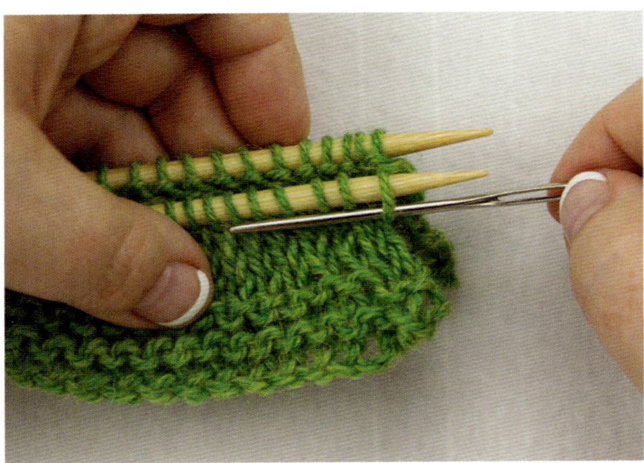

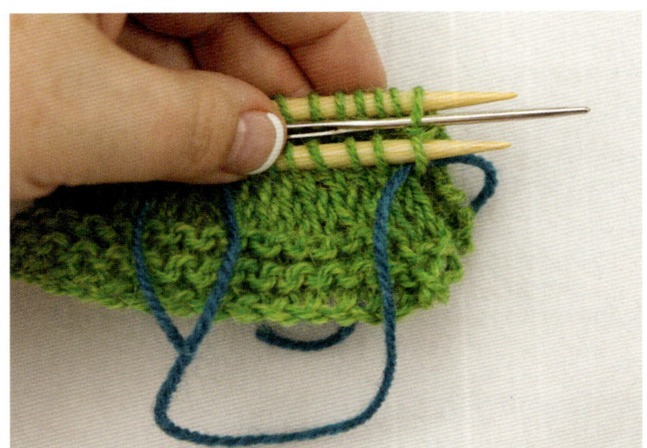

1. Insert yarn needle knit-wise into the first st on the front needle and pull the yarn though, dropping st from knitting needle.

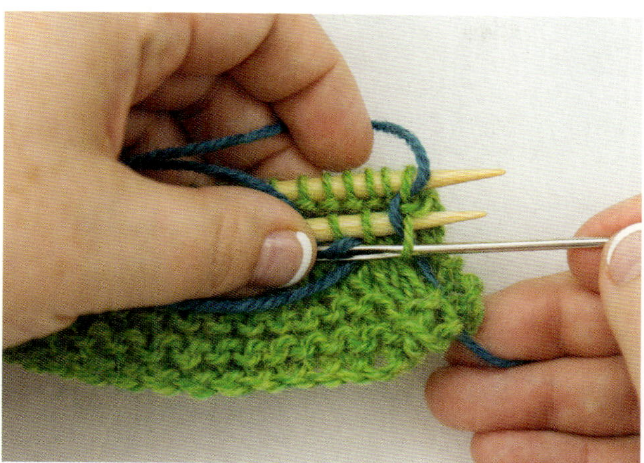

2. Insert yarn needle purl-wise into the next st on the front needle and pull the yarn through, st remains on the needle.

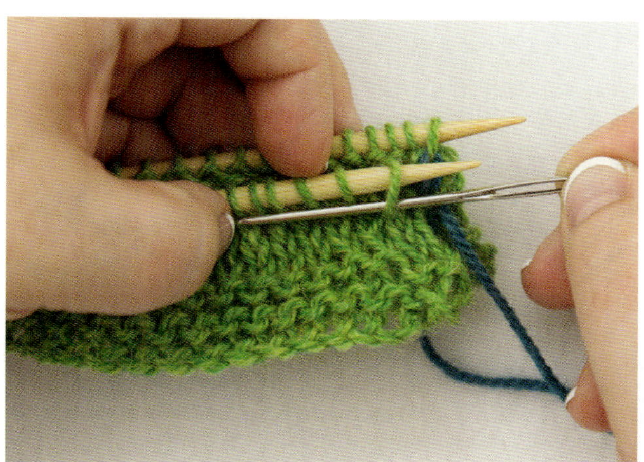

3. Insert yarn needle purl-wise into the first st on the back needle and pull the yarn through, dropping st from knitting needle.

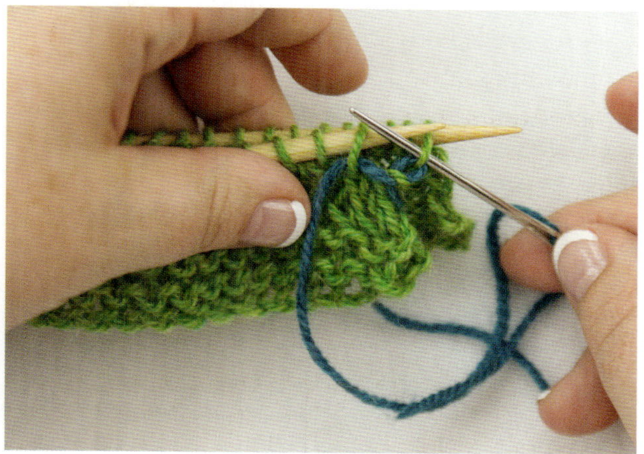

4. Insert yarn needle knit-wise into the next st on the back needle and pull the yarn through, st remains on the needle.

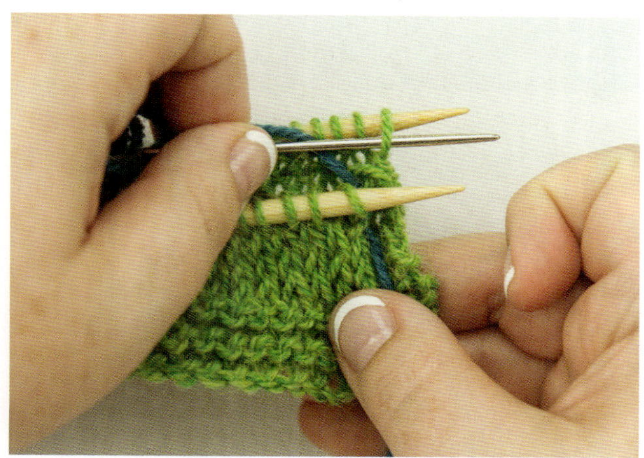

Repeat steps 1–4, tightening yarn as needed as you progress, until you have reached the final two sts then work step 1 followed by step 3.

HORIZONTAL MATTRESS STITCH (FOR JOINING CAST-ON OR BOUND-OFF EDGES)

Set up: Line up edges to be joined. Use your yarn needle with yarn threaded through for the following steps.

1. Insert the needle from right to left behind the V formed at the base of first st on the bottom edge; pull the yarn through the st. On the first st only, leave a tail to weave in later.

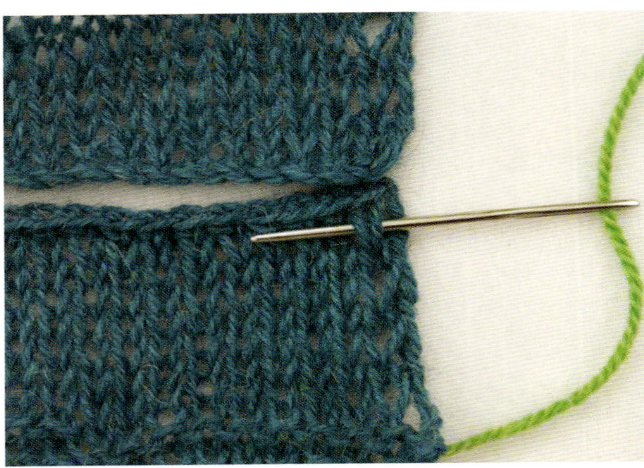

2. Insert yarn needle from right to left behind the V formed by first st on the top edge, making sure your yarn passes in front of the edges of the fabric not behind, pull through yarn.

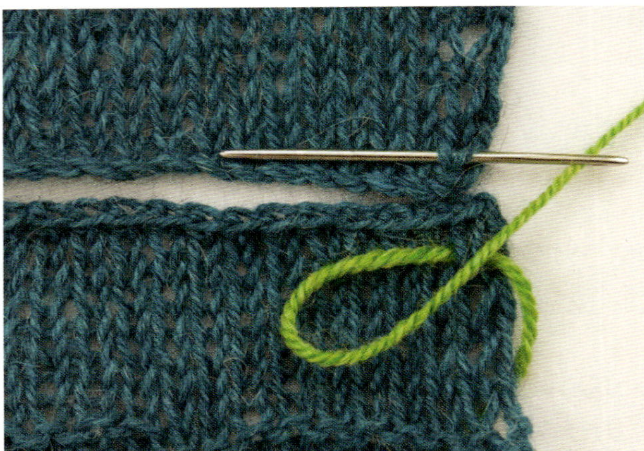

Repeat steps 1 and 2, tightening yarn as needed as you progress, until all sts have been joined to their corresponding st on the other edge.

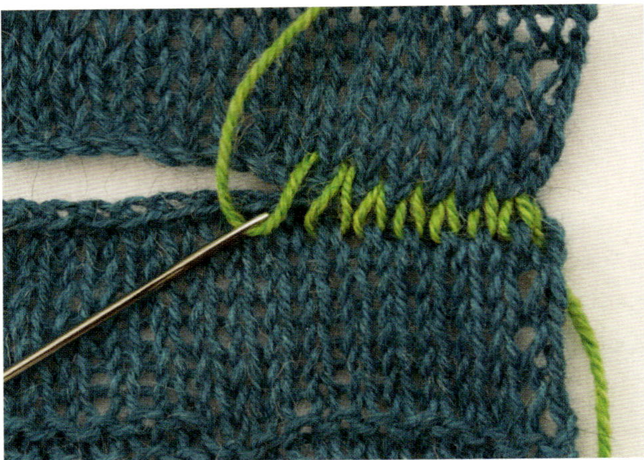

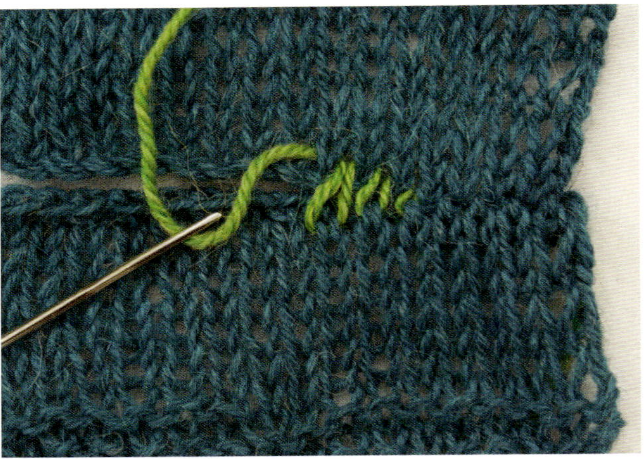

BO	bind off as instructed in each pattern.
CDD	central double decrease; slip two stitches as if to k2tog, knit next stitch and pass both slipped stitches over together.
CO	cast on as instructed in each pattern.
k	knit; insert RH needle from left to right through front loop of stitch, wrap yarn around RH needle and pull through stitch.
k2tog	knit two together; insert RH needle knit-wise through the next two stitches on the LH needle and knit them as if they were one stitch. One stitch decreased.
k2tog-tbl	knit two together through the back loop; insert RH needle from right to left through the back loop of the next two stitches on the LH needle and knit them as if they were one stitch. One stitch decreased.
kfb	knit front back; knit into the front of the next stitch but do not remove the stitch from the LH needle, then knit into the back loop of the same stitch. One stitch increased.
kfYO2b	knit front, double yarn over, knit back; knit into the front leg of the next stitch but do not remove the stitch from the LH needle, wrap the working yarn around the RH needle twice and then knit into the back loop of the same stitch. Three stitches increased.
kfYOb	knit front, yarn over, knit back; knit into the front leg of the next stitch but do not remove the stitch from the LH needle, wrap the working yarn around the RH needle once and then knit into the back loop of the same stitch. Two stitches increased.
k-tbl	knit through the back loop; insert RH needle from right to left through the back loop of the next stitch on the needle and knit. This twists the stitch.
kYOk	knit, yarn over, knit; knit into the next stitch but do not remove the stitch from the LH needle, YO, knit into the same stitch a second time. Two stitches increased.
LH	left hand.
M1L	make one left; pick up the strand of yarn that runs between the two stitches, inserting LH needle from front to back, and then knit through the back loop of created stitch. One stitch increased.

M1R	make one right; pick up the strand of yarn that runs between the two stitches, inserting LH needle from back to front, and then knit through the front loop of created stitch. One stitch increased.
p	purl; move yarn to front of needles, insert RH needle from right to left through front loop of stitch, wrap yarn around needle and pull through stitch.
p2tog	purl two together; insert RH needle purl-wise through the next two stitches on the LH needle and purl them as if they were one stitch. One stitch decreased.
pm	place marker.
rep	repeat. Instructions following an * or within ( ) or [ ] are to be repeated the number of times indicated.
RH	right hand.
skp	slip, knit, pass slipped stitch over; slip one stitch knit-wise, knit next stitch, insert LH needle into slipped stitch and pass it forward over end stitch and drop slipped stitch off of needle. One stitch decreased.
sl	slip; slip stitch purl-wise with yarn held to wrong side of knitting.
sl1-k2tog-psso	slip one - knit two together - pass slipped stitch over; slip one stitch knit-wise, knit two together, insert LH needle into slipped stitch and pass it forward over end stitch and drop slipped stitch off of needle. Two stitches decreased.
sl-wyif	slip with yarn in front; slip stitch purl-wise with yarn held in front of the stitch being slipped.
sm	slip marker.
ssk	slip, slip, knit; slip two stitches knit-wise separately, return slipped stitches to LH needle and k2tog through the back loop. One stitch decreased.
ssk-pssf-sl	slip, slip, knit - pass slipped stitch forward - slip; ssk then return new stitch to LH needle, pass the next stitch forward over the new stitch and drop off the front of the needle, slip stitch purl-wise back to RH needle. Two stitches decreased.
ssp	slip, slip, purl; slip two stitches knit-wise separately, move yarn forward, return to LH needle and p2tog. One stitch decreased.
st(s)	stitch(es).
YO	yarn over; wrap yarn entirely around RH needle to create new stitch. One stitch increased.
YO2	yarn over twice; this is a non-standard stitch instruction. For the purposes of mosaic lace, this is not an increase. Wrap yarn entirely around RH needle twice to create two new stitches. On the wrong side row, drop the first loop and work into the resulting elongated stitch.

Baah! Yarn
760.917.4151
baahyarn.com

Berroco, Inc.
401.769.1212
www.berroco.com

Dragonfly Fibers
301.312.6883
www.dragonflyfibers.com

Gale's Art
404.457.4015
www.galesart.com

Knit Picks
1.800.574.1323
www.knitpicks.com

Malabrigo
US: 786.427.1048
Europe: +44 20 3514 1551
www.malabrigoyarn.com

MissBabs Hand-Dyed Yarns & Fibers
427.727.0670
www.misbabs.com

Patons
1.888.368.8401
www.yarnspirations.com

Phydeaux
530.533.3144
www.phydeaux-designs.com

Plymouth Yarn®
215.788.0459
www.plymouthyarn.com

Tahki Stacy Charles
718.326.4433
tahkistacycharles.com

The Fibre Company/Kelbourne Woolens
US: 267.766.5480
UK: +44 (0) 7749 466 37
www.thefibreco.com

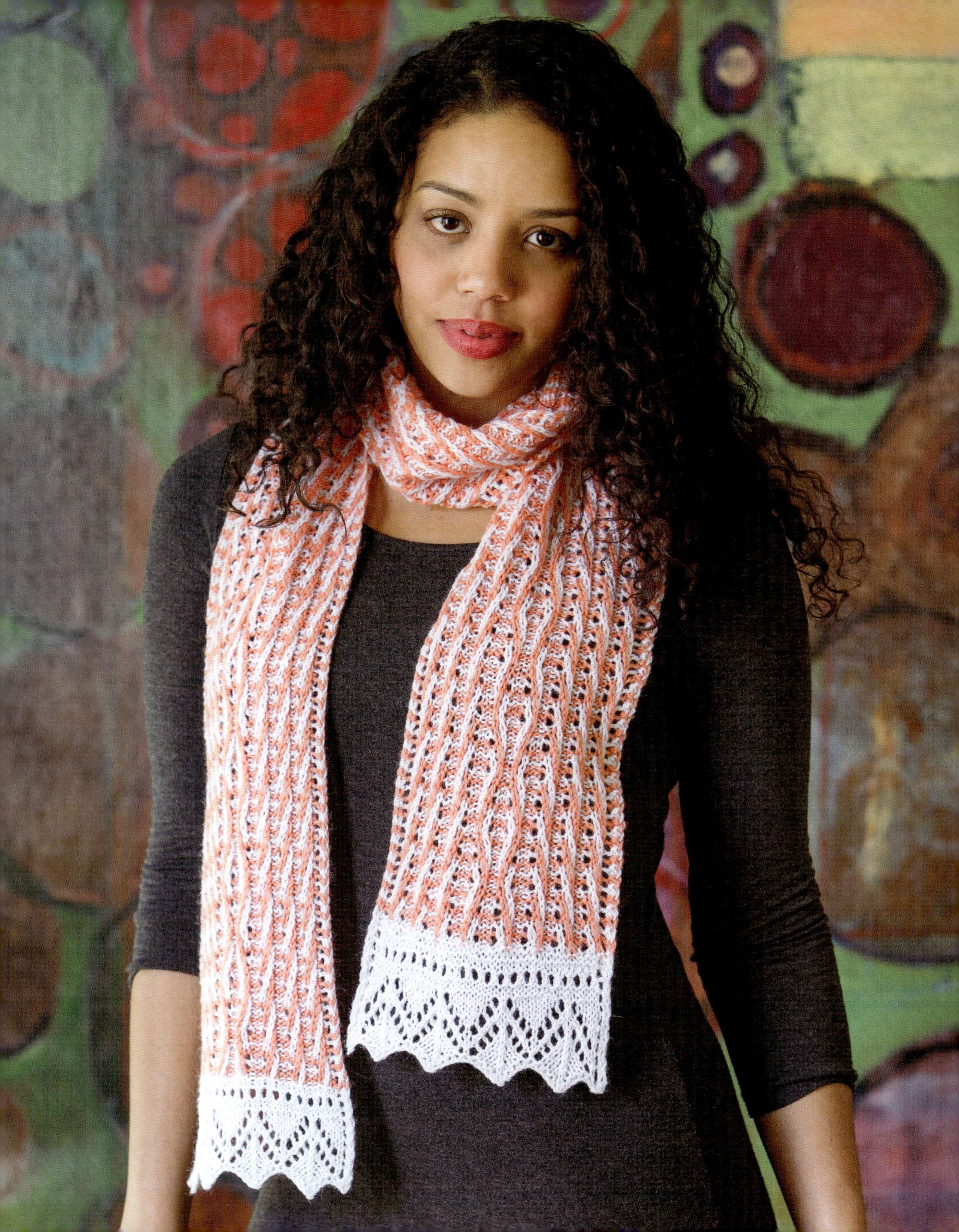

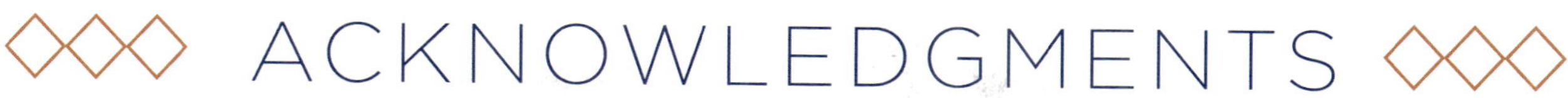

ACKNOWLEDGMENTS

I t may be my name on the cover, but it took the hands and minds of many people to make this book a reality and I would like to take a moment to acknowledge them.

Technical editors are indispensable in ensuring that the patterns are accurate and free of errors. My thanks to both Heather Zoppetti and Tana Pageler for their services in this area.

It took a lot of knitting to make all of the samples in this book come to life and I thank Lois Mitchell for being my extra pair of capable hands.

I may or may not have an inordinate fondness for commas and run on sentences. The thanks for keeping this proclivity in check goes to several eagle-eyed proofreaders, namely Heather Zoppetti, Trish Marickovitch, and Betty Salpekar.

The beautiful models who made my accessories come to life are: Chelsea Drummond, Emily Drummond, Rosemary Fernandez, Valerie Joern, Edward Maurer, Stephanie Owen, and Sonja Szubski.

Thank you to Pam Hoenig for making me believe that I could write this book in the first place.

And finally, this book would not exist if it were not for the unfailing support of my loving family. Thank you Roger and Elliott for putting up with endless knitting and a distracted Mom for the duration of this project. I love you both.

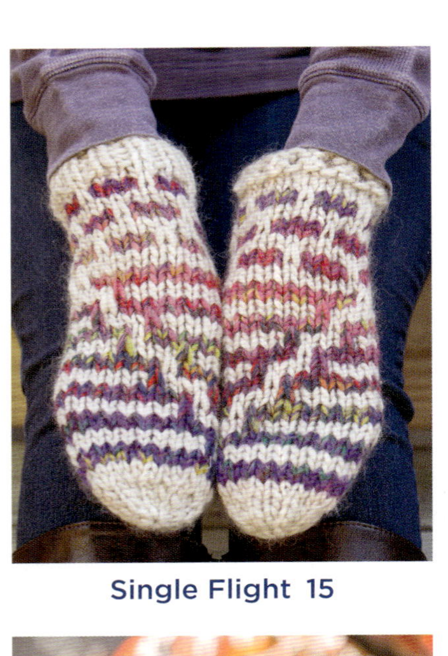

Single Flight 15

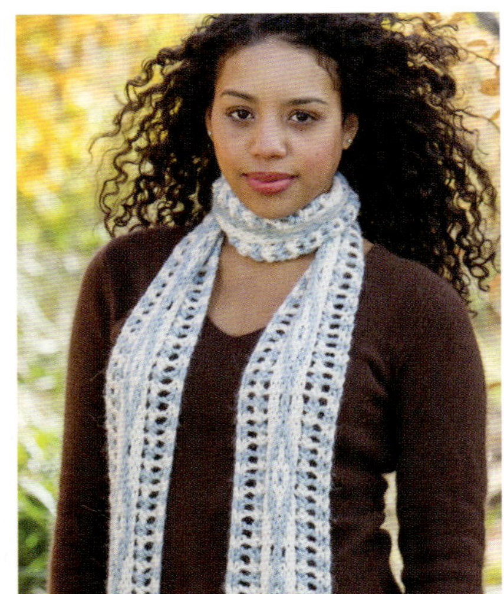

Lozengy Scarf 19

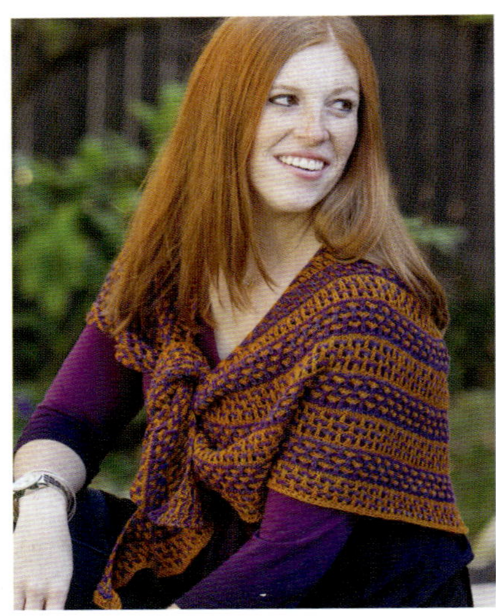

Love Child 23

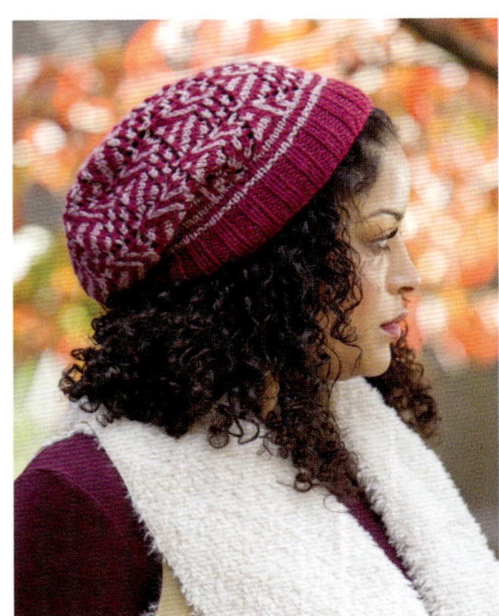

Sailing Diamonds 27

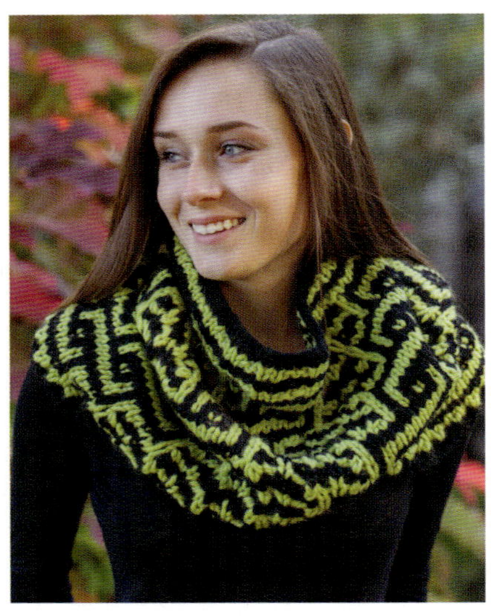

Your Princess Is in Another Castle 31

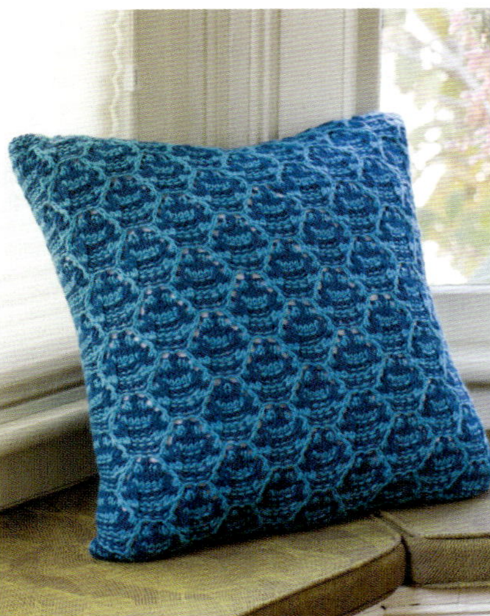

Cush Job 35

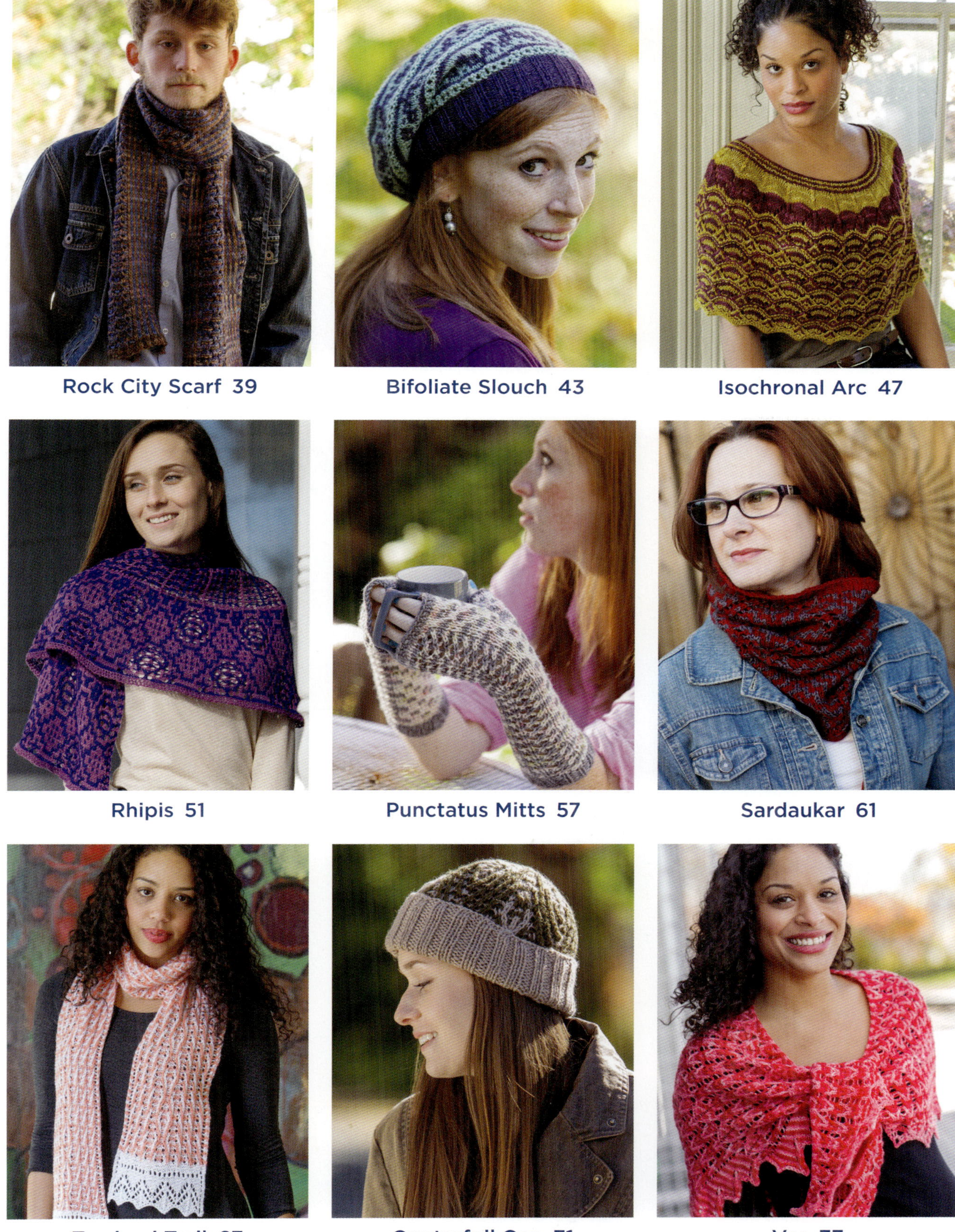

Rock City Scarf 39

Bifoliate Slouch 43

Isochronal Arc 47

Rhipis 51

Punctatus Mitts 57

Sardaukar 61

Tamiami Trail 67

Quatrefoil Cap 71

Ves 77

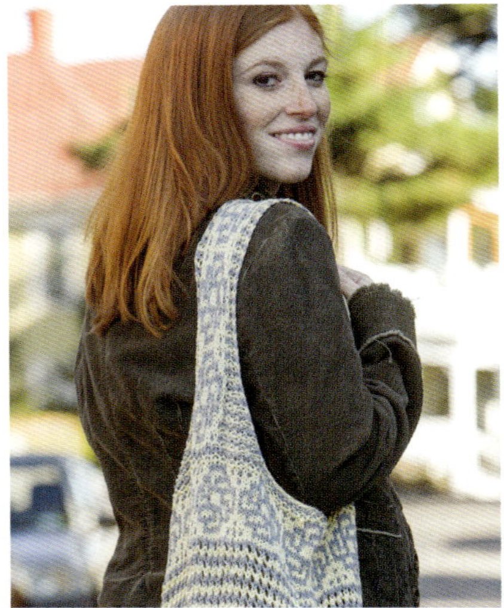

Pinwheel Market Bag 81

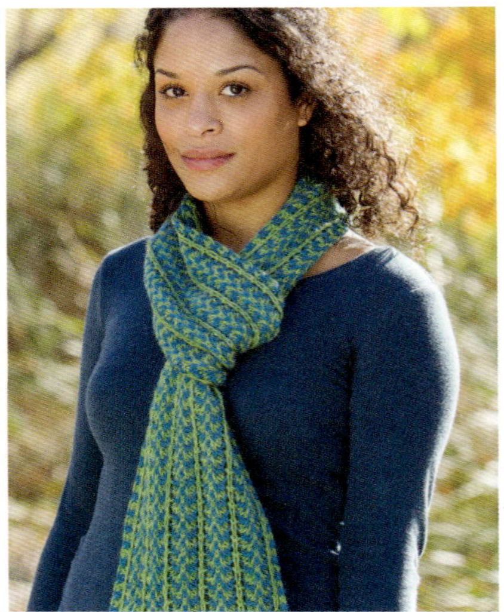

Clupeidae 87

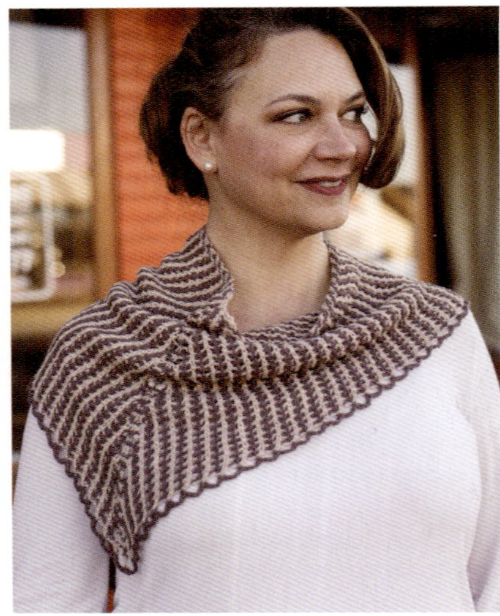

Lacy Pinstripe Cowlette 91

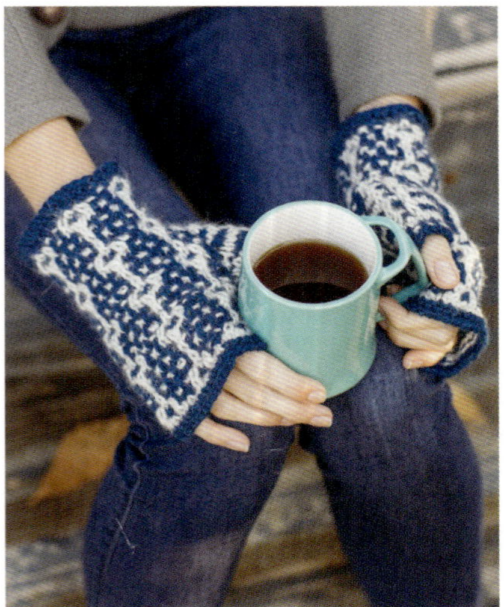

Willow Bloom 95

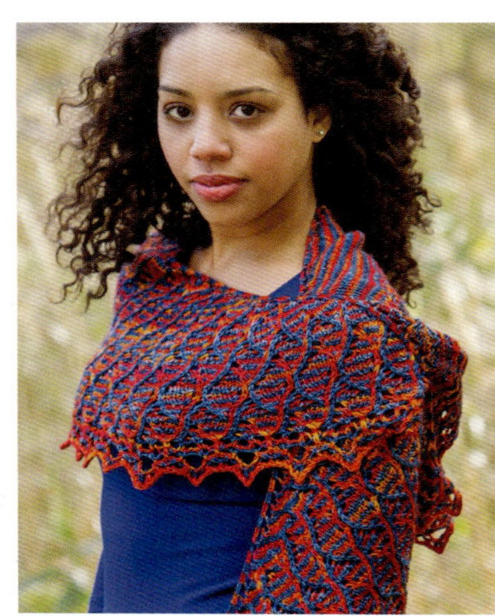

Fractured Helix 101